Bless Your Heart

A DEVOTIONAL FOR SOUTHERNERS

WITH DAILY OLD-TIMEY SAYINGS

BY ELISABETH ALTAMIRANO-SMITH

SOUTHERN PORCH AND PEN

Dedicated to my husband, Domingo.

Thank you for your loving support, always and in everything. I love you.

Southern Porch and Pen Publishing

Edited by Joyanna Love

Library of Congress Cataloging-in-Publication Data

ISBN 979-8-218-25545-9

Altamirano-Smith. Bless Your Heart: A Devotional for Southerners with Daily Old-Timey Sayings

For more information or inquiries, contact southernporchandpen@gmail.com.

Preface

1 Peter 3:15 says, "But in your hearts revere Christ as Lord. Always be prepared to give an answer to everyone who asks you to give the reason for the hope that you have. But do this with gentleness and respect."

For many years, I worked as a church secretary to Reverend Rob West, (who is too humble in ever wanting to be referred to as "Reverend"). Every year, he encouraged everyone in the congregation to write a devotion; a testament of their Christian life. As secretary, I would put the devotions into booklet form and distribute them throughout the county. On more than one occasion, I heard "Bro. Rob" encourage writers to write from personal experience instead of writing a sermon because people can identify easier with life experiences. In my own remembrance of those written, the devotions that are most memorable are the ones where the author opened their life to the reader because the devotion was relatable. So, I have made a collection of my life stories and how our lives are directly related to living a close relationship with God in hopes that something from my life might lead readers to their own closer relationship with God.

While Christianity is not specific to just Southerners, there is a unique heritage and teaching points within the South. My grandmother was repetitive in teaching all her grandchildren about our family heritage. Those teachings came many times in the form of old-fashioned sayings and folk stories (idioms). Our inheritance of those old sayings is part of who we are and can be applied to our Christian witness for future generations.

We are all called to share the Christian message with the world regardless of background. No matter where you find yourself in life, God needs you to use your talents and personality to reach someone (you might be the only person that can reach them) spiritually.

I hope you enjoy these short stories and collection of old-timey sayings, but more importantly, I hope that they touch your heart, mind, and soul and bring you closer to God.

Additionally, please feel free to use the back pages of this book for your prayer requests.

May you be blessed,

Elisabeth Altamirano-Smith

JANUARY 1

"If you lie down with dogs, you get fleas."

"Cleanse me with hyssop, and I will be clean; wash me, and I will be whiter than snow." Psalm 51:7

One of my favorite things about living in the South is the never-ending "sayings" and expressions that all Southerners live by. My grandmother had a hundred of them that were passed down, through generations and undoubtedly came from our great ancestors. A few of my favorites are "if you lie down with dogs, you get fleas" and "if you play with dirt, you get it on you." Even those old timey expressions remind us that our past will always be part of us. However, the New Year is a time for a new you and self-discovery. If you have felt weighed down by the past and old sin, now is the best time to shake it off. After all, "broken crayons can still color."

It is no secret that the entire Bible is made up of imperfect people. All those people went on to play major roles for thousands of years in what is known as the "greatest story ever told." If you are already having negative thoughts and doubts about your future success, know that every story's success is about consistently trying again (See Exodus 7-12 where Moses has to visit Pharaoh EIGHT times and ask him repeatedly to free the Jews.) It takes boldness and audacity to keep trying over and over. If you don't quite feel "froggy" enough to begin again, ask God for the strength. He will have you feeling "finer than frog hair split four ways."

Prayer:

Thank you, God for a new year and a new opportunity. Be with me this year as I start afresh. Cleanse me from all negative thoughts and feelings associated with my past. Empower me to be the best version of myself this year and to glorify Your kingdom in doing so. In Jesus' name. Amen.

"Put your best foot forward"

"Remember not the former things, nor consider the things of old. Behold, I am doing a new thing; now it springs forth, do you not perceive it?" Isaiah 43:18-19

The New Year brings mixed emotion for many. For some, last year was full of hurt and loss. Others had joyous events and made life-long, happy memories. Regardless of how you deemed last year, most everyone always welcomes in the New Year. What will it hold? Will it be the best year of my life?

A fresh new beginning has started for us, and we all want it to be better than ever before. In our lives, God gives us a new opportunity every day so that we can make a fresh start. We are constantly comparing our success to others and our past. We all feel an enormous pressure put on us by society in some form to marry the right person, be successful, be healthier, be attractive, be more productive, factor in reflective meditation time, organize our home, etc. Our failures dictate to us the areas that we need to work on for our "New Year's resolutions."

Forget all of the brokenness. God has something better than what you have seen before. He is God. He can move the mountains. In Isaiah, He is promising something wonderful for us. Pour out your praise for Him now, at the beginning of the year and thank Him for it.

Prayer:

Oh Father, help us in our new beginnings. You know where we come from and where we want to go. Hear our prayer and fulfill us to Your will and destiny for our lives. I commit my life to You this year. In Jesus' name. Amen.

JANUARY 3

"It is all grist to the mill."

"But the LORD said to Samuel, "Do not consider his appearance or his height, for I have rejected him. The LORD does not look at the things people look at. People look at the outward appearance, but the LORD looks at the heart." I Samuel 16:8

The prophecy of I Samuel 16 declared that young, small David was to become the next great king of his time. He was chosen above all of his brothers. At the time, it appeared that young David was inadequate by comparison, but God knew better and looked deeper.

What have you judged that was inadequate? Have you considered how you perceive all of the people in your daily life (the grocery clerk, your mail carrier, how fast you are served in a restaurant, how the person is driving in front of you)? We are demanding adequacy all of the time, and that seems only right. After all, we don't want to live in an inadequate world. However, consider that this moment, the person or circumstance was created by God. God has created this. Can you look at the heart of the person and still judge them?

God asks for us to look at the heart. Everything God has made is useful and has purpose. Constant prayer for the Spirit to be your guide will help you understand the usefulness God intended you to see. Only then will you be able to decipher if it is your will or the will of God when interacting with others.

Prayer:

Holy Spirit, help me in all decisions to choose the right path. Give me discernment in knowing what God's will is. In life's difficult moments when encountering people that I do not think are doing an adequate job, help me in that moment respond as a Christian. Help me respond with love. In Jesus' name. Amen.

"The last drop makes the cup run over."

"When he saw the crowds, he had compassion on them, because they were harassed and helpless, like sheep without a shepherd." Matthew 9:36

Imagine the times you have seen a group of people harassed and helpless. Where did you see them? What were they doing? How would you describe their appearance?

The times that I have witnessed people that were harassed and helpless, I would describe them as having some or all of these characteristics: tired, disliked, worried, without resources, silenced, hurting (physically and emotionally) poor, dirty.

Our world is full of the harassed and helpless. Take a look on the internet, TV, magazine, and community. Jesus saw these people, and chose to be with them, without doubt listening to and loving them (even having dinner with them). He said, "They are like sheep, without a shepherd."

Jesus is not specific as to which group of people it is in Matthew 9:36. It is not known if they were from a certain town that had been under hardship or what was the cause of stress was; only that they were harassed and helpless. As Christians, have we listened to, loved and told the harassed that Jesus loves them?

Prayer:

Help us open our hearts, God, that everyone may know Your abundant love is available to all. As Your workers here on this Earth, help us spread that love and message to the oppressed. Create in us a hunger and thirst to seek these people out and learn how to truly be compassionate. Teach us, Lord. In the name of our loving Savior to all. Amen.

"What can't be cured must be endured."

"Wait on the Lord: be of good courage, and let thy heart be strengthened: yea wait on the Lord." Psalm 27:14

Having a problem arise in your life that you don't have any control over feels like carrying a cross at times. Loss of a job, health issues, and relationship problems are just a few that can keep us awake at night.

What we lack control over gives us anxiety and stress. We are left bargaining with God and pleading with Him to "please grant us this prayer". When difficult times arise, the need to repair a bad situation feels like a broken levy. In our humanness, we see the severity of the "cracked levy" and the water seeping out and know the problem will soon become a dangerous flood if we do not fix it. Our resources during this time are patience and faith.

The entire Bible is based on patience and faith, sometimes in crisis. (See the stories of the Israelites waiting to find the Promised Land, Sarah and Elisabeth for a child, and even Jesus before His arrest). It is human to feel desperation during desperate times but in all of these testaments, God concludes with a great victory for His children. This victory starts with giving the crisis to God. Even if you are going through the pain of endurance, you do not have to endure it alone.

Prayer:

God, help me to have peace that You are in control. Give me the strength to let my issue leave my grasp, so that You can weave and make something beautiful from it. You have made everything in this day and supplied everything I need up until this moment of my life. Help me have patience and the faith to know that You will keep providing and that Your plan is great, and goes further than I can see. In Jesus' name. Amen.

"Two heads are better than one."

"The star they had seen rose and went ahead of them until it stopped over the place where the child was. When they saw the star, they were overjoyed. On coming to the house, they saw the child with his mother Mary, and they bowed down and worshiped him." Matthew 2:9b-11

During "Epiphany" or "Three Kings Day" we remember those three magi that set out to find an extraordinary sign that would change the future. A change marked in astrology at the time could only mean that a new age was dawning. Even though we might not encounter a bright star in the sky, we nonetheless experience new chapters in our life. Western culture marks New Year's Eve as a modern window of change for our life.

To face tomorrow (good or bad) it is wise to reflect on "The Wise Men." How must they have felt to be wandering lands unknown during tumultuous times, searching for something unknown? Tomorrow is not always promised to be a positive life experience. Yet the Magi had faith and hope that they would prevail. It must have seemed strange to the Magi that the "ruler from Judah who will shepherd God's people," a prophecy long foretold, was not found in the palace with Herod or even a nice home, but in an animal hut. Tomorrow's outcome might be in an unpredicted setting and one that you would not have selected for your life. Even though life's circumstance is ever-changing, we can find comfort in knowing that God is with us and we are not facing it alone.

Prayer:

Thank you, God for the birth of Jesus, our Savior, and a reminder that in this new age there is time to start again, that we might always live with You in life eternal. In Jesus' name. Amen.

"He's the real McCoy!"

"Jesus looked at them and said, 'With man this is impossible, but with God all things are possible." Mark 10:27

People are designed to try to micro-manage everything on earth. From the beginning, God put Adam in control over the animals and to be a good steward to them. We have slowly evolved into trying to manage everything: the animals, help direct other people, help heal other people through medicine and technology, travel across the world and space to learn more and obtain new resources. It really should come as no surprise that we quickly become overwhelmed and maxed out.

Humans can achieve a great deal, but it is important to remember when overloaded and stressed, that we are not God. It is equally important to ask for God's help during those moments. God is the "real McCoy." He can see and knows all. The issues that are most stressful to us are the ones that seem impossible, but with God all things are possible. God used Moses to stretch out his staff to open the sea. God used Joshua to bring down the walls and city of Jericho. God used Ananias to turn the assassin Saul's heart to stop killing Christians. Whatever your battle is, allow God to use you – no matter how impossible it seems.

Prayer:

God, use me in a powerful way to turn the "impossible" into "possible." Even if I feel that I am in the middle of a storm, You are the real McCoy and creator. You alone have the power to change and direct the future. Protect me and guide me to be Your vessel. Take away my fears and replace it with Your strength. You are the Alpha and the Omega. In Jesus' name. Amen.

"There is no shame in not knowing; the shame lies in not finding out."

"Jesus said, 'Peace be with you! As the Father has sent me, I am sending you.' And with that he breathed on them and said, 'Receive the Holy Spirit. If you forgive anyone's sins, their sins are forgiven; if you do not forgive them, they are not forgiven.'" John 20:23

I took a long family vacation this week and drove our family hundreds of miles across state lines. During the hours of being in the car, it is a long time to think, and it crossed my mind that we pass all sorts of people when we drive on the road. The town I live in is small, and I always imagine it full of nice people that don't sin much. I can't imagine that there are "bad people" in my town, but on the highways, it opens my mind there are "bad people" certainly driving alongside of me, and probably also living in my town. Killers, rapists, pedophiles, users, abusers, kidnappers, but why stop there? People that are hungry to destroy your happiness, scream curse words and tell you that you are nothing, adulterers, greed, pride, anger, deceit, lying, and don't forget all of the white sheep that are ready to kill the black sheep.

Jesus said, "Peace be with you! As the Father has sent me, I am sending you." He breathed on them and said, "Receive the Holy Spirit. If you forgive anyone's sins, their sins are forgiven; if you do not forgive them, they are not forgiven."

In my human simplicity it is hard for me to imagine that God forgives people so easily. Some of these sins hurt me just imagining them, but I don't have to imagine God struggling to forgive them. He says it in the Bible, without hesitation.

What is your sin? Do you have something shameful that only you and God know about? When you apologize you have met the grace of the Lord. He has pardoned you instantly. What are the sins of others that have hurt you? Are you wishing something bad for them? Remember that without hesitation God has pardoned you and welcomed you with "Peace be with you! Receive the Holy Spirit". These are difficult words to say to an enemy, but it is what God wants from you. Pray for God to help you take the first steps and make it easier for you.

Prayer:

Dear Heavenly Father God, thank You for forgiving me for all of my sins. In Your love and perfection You show us how to love more. I ask for help with forgiving someone, *(person's name)*. It is difficult for me to forgive them. You know my heart and what happened, but I know that You love them also. Help me to forgive them. Put softness in my heart for their situation. Help me when I see this person to speak "Peace be with you. Receive the Holy Spirit."

You are great and powerful, God. I know that You will be with me. Help me reflect your love. In Jesus' name. Amen.

"Time and tide wait for no man."

"For we are God's handiwork, created in Christ Jesus to do good works, which God prepared in advance for us to do." Ephesians 2:10

Anytime there is a huge job coming, I always jump in ahead of my deadline to work on the project. This is not true of everyone. In my life, I have had many learning opportunities that God clearly wanted me to understand that some people are two weeks ahead of their deadline and some people are two weeks late. There is not an "in between" deadline person. Working with these different deadline types, I also learned that I cannot control the "late" deadline personality and force them to turn in their work. Somehow numbers and paperwork don't seem like they will make or break the world within a day to some. What if turning the project in late would make or break the world?

God has entrusted us with a task; a unique gift inside of each of us, and it is a real, call-to-action responsibility for us to get to work on it. Some of us may have started working on our tasks many years ago and just gave up on it, forgot it, and are relaxing on the side lines waiting for the timer to sound. It is important to remember that someone, somewhere may be depending on you to do what God has called you to complete. Your spiritual gifts will change your life, your family, friends, community, and world. The best time to begin working on God's project is now because it allows you to reach more people during your lifetime.

Prayer:

Almighty God, Help us put away the distractions to keep our eye on Your plans. Help us identify within ourselves our own spiritual gifts and use them. In Jesus' name. Amen.

JANUARY 10

"United we stand, divided we fall"

"And we know that all things work together for good to them that love God, to them who are the called according to his purpose." Romans 8:28

Some favorite childhood memories are sitting with my grandmother while she quilted. I would bring her whatever she needed while interviewing her about her childhood. I loved that time with her, and love the memories I have of her stories. There was a closet that all family members had left their clothes behind at some point in time. She would go through the closet, take out long forgotten shirts from 20 years ago, cut them up and apply them to her quilt. I remember thinking that some of the shirts were ugly and that the quilt would look better if she would leave that fabric out. In the end, by the time she spread the pieces out with other prints, they were not even noticeable and made the quilt prettier, because now the quilt had contrast and design.

In the years since then, she has passed away. I love all of the "ugly" prints now because they are great symbols to me of how in time, God can change some people that are difficult to like. God adds them to His greater plan, and in the end we all work together beautifully with contrast and design.

We all know someone ugly in spirit. Many things make us dislike a person all of which can't be named here. Whatever makes them "ugly" to you, know that God is the quilt maker. He sees everything. Ultimately, He will decide what belongs.

Prayer:

Heavenly Quilt Maker, Help me trust in Your plan and design. Give me peace even when I don't always understand Your plan. May we all work together for the good and glorify the Kingdom with our contrasts in harmony. Thank You for Your creation and skillful eye. In Jesus' name. Amen

"Wonders will never cease."

"We wait in hope for the Lord; He is our help and our shield. In him our hearts rejoice, for we trust in His Holy name. May your unfailing love be with us, Lord, even as we put our hope in you." Psalm 33:20-22

My, how our prayers change as we grow older! When I was young, I used to pray for a certain boy to like me, and that I would pass my test at school, even though I had not even spoken to said boy or picked up a book to study! I had expectations for certain things to happen and ultimately prayed for *my* will to be done. Looking back those prayers seem silly and adolescent to me, but I find myself praying adult versions of them. As adults, we pray for a certain job, healing of a sickness, or for acceptance from peers. When do the details of our prayers become adolescent to God? Do we suddenly seem mature to God in our mere 20 year growth on earth? To someone as omnipotent as God, we probably always sound adolescent, but does that keep God from wanting to hear what is on our heart and mind? When a five year old runs to you with a message and is excited to talk to you, do you shut them out? In the same way, God wants to hear every prayer. Nothing is too great. Nothing is too small. Anyone that has given so much attention to detail in creating us certainly cares about every detail.

Prayer:

Lord, You are our hope. You know what is on my heart and mind. I need You. I place my trust in You and rejoice in Jesus' name. Amen.

JANUARY 12

"Youth is wasted on the young."

"Fear not, for I have redeemed you; I have summoned you by name; you are mine." Isaiah 43:1

Most of my childhood was spent growing up on our family farm. We did not have the largest farm in our neighborhood. Our neighbor had about a thousand hogs. They also had four daughters that I grew up with and consider my closest childhood friends. Being friends with them meant that I got a first class seat to seeing baby farm animals, and I loved it.

When the school bus would drive down our street in the afternoon, every child in the bus would hold their nose and ask how could we "stand living in that smell." It felt shameful, but at the same time these neighbors were made of gold. Even at the age of eight, I realized their value and integrity.

A few years later, I came to realize that many people make fun of Southerners and their accents. There is a common stereotype that people who live in the South are poor, ignorant, and imbred. The only truth of this simple joke seems to be that poverty does exist here, but it exists everywhere. It is easy to forget in this conundrum of ignorance and name-calling that God created in the South: every Oak tree, Magnolia Tree, every golden sunset cast in wide open spaces, and banana pudding.

The things that separate us and divide us are also what make us unique. You are a creation of God, beautifully and wonderfully made.

Prayer:

Dear Father, thank You for the peace and countryside You made that flourishes in the South. Help us to see that we are unique to the world, a rare variety that has special gifts and talents. In Jesus' name. Amen.

"It ain't over, till it's over!"

"Then Jesus said to him, 'Get up! Pick up your mat and walk.'" John 5:8

In the United States' short-lived history (in comparison to other countries), Southern states have a long history of turmoil. For the most part, when I hear about the South's ugly past, (Trail of Tears, Civil War, and Civil Rights), they are all topics that make me (and many of us) feel uncomfortable. Any time there is any proverbial battle wound, it will leave a scar forever. No matter what comes after, the scar will always remain. That is a truth that every Southern will attest to.

History can never be undone once it has happened but the future can offer hope and change. If anything can be said for history books it is that our history is not finished yet. God is working in our lives every day, every minute in the people we meet, our responses and our dreams. Our story is not complete yet. I think about some of my favorite childhood stories like Sleeping Beauty. What would have happened if the princess never left the protection of the cottage in the forest, or the prince never sought to save her? The story always continues to evolve and gets better, as does ours with hope in the Lord.

Prayer:

Dear Father, Help us see the faults we are carrying with us into the future. Help us learn from the past and create a new, better future for ourselves and community. Help us see the victory in today, *Your* victory and claim it! In Jesus' name. Amen.

"Many hands make light work."

"Go into all of the world and help spread the Gospel." Mark 16:15

Like most good Southerners, I love to mosy down to the beach during the summertime. It is probably the closest I will come to feeling like a cat lying in the sunshine; warm sand that soaks in my bones, and birds that swirl around me, laughing in the wind.

I recently saw a video on social media of someone drowning at the beach. Remarkably, the crowded beach comes together within seconds and forms a human chain that measures out a few hundred yards. Once the human chain is formed, they are able to reach out to the person in trouble and save them. It is a remarkable example of what people can accomplish when working together.

Likewise, when Christians work together it is usually such a rare remarkable act of love and unity that the entire world cannot help but to take notice. Ever heard the expression, "Many hands make light work?" Put that expression into Christian action by forming a human chain of Christian friends to reach out to others and help them. Get together with your friends to discuss what difference your group can make and complete that action together.

Prayer:

Dear Father God, thank You for the remarkable network of Christian friends that live in the world. Thank You for giving us someone to share our feelings, dreams, and hope for the world with. Bless our friends and allow us to bless our enemies as we share the love that You give us. Help us utilize our Christian friendship so that we can reach all of the world. In Jesus' name. Amen.

"The apple doesn't fall from the tree."

"Then Jesus told his disciples, "If anyone would come after me, let him deny himself and take up his cross and follow me." Matthew 16:24

It is no secret that children mimic adult behavior. During my cousin's 2nd grade Christmas performance, he sang "Bad to the Bone" instead of the Christmas carol the music director taught him. His father loved the performance, but his mother sank down into her seat. We all learn behaviors from the people we live with, look up to, and admire. At a separate Christmas performance, I witnessed a 3 year old take out a handkerchief out of the top of her shirt, blow her nose, and then place it back into the top of her dress.

Likewise, adults all learn behaviors as they grow. As adults, we tend to pick up on the way the world judges and mistreats others.

Jesus loves everyone, not just the popular crowd. He taught people about a better way of life and then claimed them if they were willing to change. He did not discriminate and picked the "unlikely" and "unloved." Adults lose that ability somewhere during their maturity and it is a characteristic of the Lord; likely lost in worldliness. Do you love others like Jesus?

Prayer:

Dear Heavenly Father, Forgive us for sometimes skipping over people we find undesirable. Help us extend a hand of friendship. Open our eyes to people that are different than we are, so that we may befriend them, and fulfill God's love here on Earth. In Jesus' name. Amen.

JANUARY 16

"It takes one to know one."

"Come to me, all who labor and are heavy laden, and I will give you rest. Take my yoke upon you, and learn from me, for I am gentle and lowly in heart, and you will find rest for your souls. For my yoke is easy, and my burden is light." Matthew 11:28-30

My friend, Christi and I "are cut from the same cloth.". Rarely in life do you find a person that completely "gets you" without even having to speak. Our common interests are traveling, food, all animals (but dogs mostly), high society living, and kindness. She has been my go-to friend in trips, hosting tea parties just for fun, and offering advice when I needed it most. I'm not sure who I would be today without knowing her.

We all usually have a "go-to" person who makes life more tolerable. Life gets hard sometimes and without a go-to person it feels like we may not make it. In the midst of those difficult times without a shoulder to cry on, there is a "go-to God." He knows all of your interests, hobbies and cares. He was the Creator of them. No one knows pain and suffering like Jesus, who was betrayed by friends, mocked, beaten, spit on and crucified. When we hear "it takes one to know one," Jesus knows you and has experienced crisis himself. He can make whatever you are suffering through tolerable and give you strength to get through difficult times.

Prayer:

Dear God, Only You really know all that I am going through. I ask You to give me the strength to get through each day. Help me. Blanket me with Your peace. I ask You to be my "go-to God." Protect and restore me. In Jesus' name. Amen

"Slowly and surely wins the race."

"I waited patiently for the Lord; he inclined to me and heard my cry." Psalm 40:1

When I was in junior high school, I remember thinking how ridiculous some of the aerobics were in gym class. At 12-years old and being an energetic tomboy, it was hilarious to raise my arms over my head, lean to the right and count to 10 while listening 80's pop music. The exercises seemed elementary, and I was not sure that I was achieving anything.

Years later after I became an adult, a popular exercise came out that really put me through "the grind." It was the kind of exercise that promises that you will lose thirty pounds in a month. After a week, I felt like I needed a walker to move around. My knees hurt from the impact and abuse of putting my body through the ringer. It finally occurred to me that my junior high teacher was giving our body a warm-up before class. Although it was not something I looked forward to, my body needed it.

Life is the very same way. Whatever your dreams and prayers are for the future, you probably are not able to automatically jump to that goal. There is a warm-up period. People usually do not instantly meet the right person to spend their life with. People are not born with college degrees. There is a process and events that must first take place in life to help you "warm-up." In time, God will eventually get you to where you need to be if you seek His counsel.

Prayer:

Dear Father, thank You for the warm-up periods in our life. Help us be patient in trusting Your plan. Help us look for the good moments along the way until we get to where we need to be and meet Your vision. In Jesus' name. Amen.

"All is for the best in the best of all possible worlds." – Gottfried Wilhelm Leibniz

"But ask the animals, and they will teach you, or the birds in the sky, and they will tell you; or speak to the earth, and it will teach you, or let the fish in the sea inform you. Which of all these does not know that the hand of the LORD has done this? In his hand is the life of every creature and the breath of all mankind." Job 12:7-10

Everyone has insecurities whether they like to admit it or not. In my single days and reuniting with an ex-boyfriend I had not seen for a few years, I had packed on some extra weight and was worried how "fat" I would look. While I was excited to see him, after a while, my excitement turned to anxiety over my extra weight.

While I was out shopping one day, I came across a bottle of skin crème in a beauty store that promised to "reduce the appearance of cellulose." The majority of the bottle was in Russian lettering, so who knows what the rest of the bottle warned, but the promise of making me look thinner made any warning unimportant.

On the evening of our date, I rubbed half of the bottle all over my body. I rubbed it on my neck, on my arms, my legs, everywhere that was visible with fat. I was ready to be transformed! As I got to the restaurant to see him, I could feel the crème starting to tingle, and I thought "oh good! It's starting to work!" By the end of dinner, I felt like I had forty electrical units on. My body felt like it was literally on fire! I had to quickly leave to go home and take a shower, unapologetically! Nothing about the dinner was enjoyable because I kept thinking I might have to call an ambulance!

What part of yourself do you not like? Every person has something physical or part of their personality they would like to change. There are many models and celebrities on television who starve themselves in order to look thinner, but body image issues aren't a new concept. Since the beginning of humankind, people have tried to change the way others perceive them. Queen Elizabeth I put shoulder pads in her dresses to look more dominant and "in-charge." In ancient Japan, women blacked out the enamel on their teeth to make their skin seem fairer. Ancient Chinese women deformed the bones in their feet so that they would seem more petite.

God made each and every culture, each and every body type, and all personalities. He was the Designer. People rave over fashion and designer labels, but nothing is more designer than you. Have you ever heard a Chanel dress sing? Each person is an example of God's ability, and He thought you were perfect.

Prayer:

Dear Heavenly Father, God thank You for the difference in each of us. Help us to love ourselves the way You see us; the way You created us. Help us to embrace all of who we are so that we can shine and let others see the light reflecting that belongs to You. Help us also affirm others with their unique abilities and qualities. We love you! In Jesus' name. Amen.

"There is only one captain of a ship."

"For the Spirit God gave us does not make us timid, but gives us power, love and self-discipline."

2 Timothy 1:7

When someone is verbally attacking you it feels horrible. The person that is delving out hate and inconsideration might be a person you are in a relationship with: husband, daughter, co-worker, friend, pastor, etc. It hurts much worse when you know the person versus a random stranger because you have invested love. When the other person speaks words of hate and frustration sometimes the best response is no response. In what might appear as being "timid," may actually equate to great "self-discipline." When Jesus was on trial and being questioned, He was reserved and minimized His responses because He knew He could not win in their accusations (Luke 22:67). Even though there were many accusations and denials in Luke 22, all of Jesus' actions and words were of love.

Having to share the same space with anyone that is in opposition to you can be difficult but can be a blessing. God already knows that person and has been intentional in allowing them to know you. You can equip and prepare your heart when being around them. Preparing your heart and being patient is not always easy, but it is possible with the power of God. What follows might be the start of a new relationship and the opportunity to learn something from them, or them learning from you and leading them to Christ.

Prayer:

Help us Father, during our trials and tribulations. Help us have the right words to say but also to know when not to say anything. Be with us. Strengthen us. Guide us. In Jesus' name. Amen.

"Practice what you preach!"

"If any of you lacks wisdom, let him ask God, who gives generously to all without reproach, and it will be given him." James 1:5

It is difficult to stop doing a bad habit that you have done for an extended period of time. I've seen people put money in a "Swear Jar", wear rubber bands on their wrist to punish their bad temper and use chewing gum to stop smoking. It can be just as difficult to encourage someone else to leave their bad habits behind.

The decisions we make for our daily life matter. Jesus' image would not have lasted thousands of years and He certainly would not be remembered as a kind, generous, loving, forgiving and patient Lord if He did not set a pure example.

When dealing with someone that is living a "bad habit" lifestyle the best line of defense is to approach them with humility (realizing you are just a person as well). Next, reach out to your Christian mentors for wise counsel on how to successfully reach the person spiritually. Finally and most importantly – pray! God offers answers to those who seek His counsel (James 1:5).

It is important when approaching others about their lifestyle to examine your own life. If you have a mustard stain on your shirt, it might not be wise to tell someone to stop eating mustard.

Prayer:

Dear Father, thank You for giving us a cleaner way of life, free from the oppression of the world. Help me clean my own life so that I may set an example to others. Humble me so that I do not sound like a Pharisee. Allow love to shine through my face so that the person can truly see that I care about them. In Jesus' name. Amen.

"To each his own."

"Are not two sparrows sold for a penny? Not one of them will fall to the ground apart from your Father. Even the hairs of your head are all numbered. Fear not, therefore; you are of more value than many sparrows." Matthew 10:29-31

My senior year in high school, I bought a new Beatles T-shirt to wear back to school. Even though it was the 1990's I loved the Beatles (and still do!) One day, during science class, a well-liked kid in my class also walked in wearing the same Beatles shirt! For some reason, its okay to dress as "twinsies" when it is your best friend but horrifying when anyone else does it. His friends came to me and said, "he had the shirt first, you can't wear yours," but I loved the shirt. It was brand new, and I didn't cave. We settled on a Beatle quiz showdown, with them asking the two of us little known Beatle trivia. I'm pretty sure that he won, but I always thought afterward, "surely, there is enough Beatles to go around!"

Fortunately, there is enough Jesus to go around. Sometimes as a new Christian or someone that hasn't been living a "Churchy" life, it is easy to feel like you might not pass the Jesus trivia showdown with others. "I don't know that much about the Bible," "I can't pray well. Ask someone else that is good at it," and "I don't know scripture" are all really common feelings that people have. The great news is that whether you know a little bit about Jesus or you are a scholar –there is enough Jesus to go around.

Prayer:

Dear Father God, thank You for loving me no matter my background or how much I know about You. More importantly, I love you and know you love me. Strengthen me when I am out in the world and feel intimidated and not good enough like some of the other people I see. In Jesus' name. Amen.

"Expect the unexpected."

"Now to him who is able to do immeasurably more than all we ask or imagine, according to his power that is at work within us. To him be glory in the church and in Christ Jesus throughout all generations, for ever and ever!" Ephesians 3:20-21

Growing up with my parents was interesting, but especially my dad. His favorite passtime was pigeon racing. He was constantly documenting and reading pigeon literature to be the next great pigeon expert. He would also mix different products and foods to try to train them to win the annual regional pigeon race. He was an enthusiast to say the least!

Any time someone finds a passion and interest it sounds a little "over the top." Many times, people choose a career in the field they're passionate about. My mother could talk about real estate for days. Both of those interests (pigeons and real estate) were enjoyed in part because they connected my father and mother to other people that shared their interests.

One of the amazing powers of church are the Christian relationships. In all networks, whether pigeons or Christians, you are going to have some "bad apples" that make it less enjoyable sometimes. However, it is such a great feeling to be around other enthusiasts that share your interests, prayers, and can celebrate life with you. If a church's "bad apples" are keeping you away – persevere (to another church if need be!)

Prayer:

God, thank You for the gift of church and other Christians. Help us forgive the few that offend us so that we can fully enjoy the togetherness with other enthusiants. In Jesus' name. Amen.

"Turn your face toward the sun and the shadows fall behind you."

"Whoever is generous to the poor lends to the Lord, and he will repay him for his deed." Proverbs 19:17

One of my favorite writers, Mark Twain, once said, "kindness is the language which the deaf can hear and the blind can see." I think back to all the kindnesses that people have shown me in my life, (there have been so many). Perhaps one of the kindest experiences I have witnessed was in Venezuela. While waiting to catch a plane, I remarked to the woman sitting beside me that I liked her earrings. She instantly took them off and gave them to me. One of the people in my group that was traveling with me explained that it was common culturally in Venezuela to gift someone what they complimented you on. I tried giving the earrings back to her, but realized she would not accept them. Not knowing what to do, I took off my favorite ring and gave it to her. Since then, I have thought about her frequently. We were both unable to speak the other's language, yet we communicated just fine. She was kind and simple. We both knew that we would never see each other again. There was nothing to financially gain as I was a punk-rock teenager in blue jeans, and she was a prim 50-year-old woman. Her kindness, even though lasting for only a few minutes, made an impact of my life. Kindness is more than just giving people money and "stuff." It is a physical action that we deliberately make or ignore every day, in every hour. Kindness is a way of life and was part of Jesus' trademark.

Prayer:

Dear Heavenly Father, forgive us for not loving Your people. We pass by the spiritually hungry every day and get angry with them. Forgive me. Let the love and kindness we show, glorify You. In Jesus' name. Amen.

"A rising tide lifts all boats."

"Carry each other's burdens, and in this way you will fulfill the law of Christ." Galatians 6:2

Have you ever had a secret to your life, so deep and so painful that you never told anyone? Perhaps it is something that you are ashamed of and you felt the community would judge you unfairly for. It is a weighted burden that your past is stained by, so you threw a rug over it and went on with your future. Most people have something in their past that they would like to forget, so they don't mention it.

One of my favorite lines in *Gone With The Wind* is when Scarlett says, "I can't think about that right now. If I do, I'll go crazy. I'll think about that tomorrow." Of course, she does not bring many things back up in the story-line. She just keeps going about her life and making the best out of it that she can. Life is full of pain, twists, turns, and failures. Even talking about things can seem like added unnecessary, self-inflicted trauma.

It is important to pray for everyone: enemies and friends because we all have a battle that we are fighting. Many times even friends hold in secrets that have hurt them in the past. All of those secrets weigh a person down and keep them from living their happiest life. God instills hope and offers a fresh future for everyone. It is important to pray for everyone; that we may all be liberated from sin and death and the way the devil lies to us.

Prayer:

Dear Lord, thank You for giving us hope for the future. Help me share God's message of hope, love, and forgiveness with people in my life when they need to hear it most. In Jesus' name. Amen.

"There is a time for everything."- Ecclesiastes, The Holy Bible

"Jesus wept." John 11: 35

People tend to forget the humanness that Jesus lived. He is frequently seen in a super-Holy stance with a white robe that seems unobtainable to most people, especially the "real sinners." Jesus' life was full of real-life experiences including having to run for his life as an immigrant into another country for safety (on a donkey), being beaten, spat on, name-called, and mobs of people conspiring against Him.

Hurt is widespread here on Earth. Our loved ones sometimes commit suicide. Children are murdered. Many injustices happen and there is not an end in sight to the ugliness that people unleash on one another.

"Jesus wept" is another reminder in scripture of how human Jesus was and that He can relate to the troubles modern people face. His time is not all spent listening to choirs of angels singing and walking on streets of gold, but acknowledging the hurt of this world and the ways it affects us.

Remember that Jesus wept. He knows the world is full of hurt. He was human enough to feel it Himself. Whatever hurt you are experiencing or going through, Jesus has also endured that same feeling of pain and agony. Share your pain and feelings with Him.

Prayer:

God, only You know the pain each of us is going through and the things that we worry about. Blanket us with Your love and protection as we draw near to You. In Jesus' name. Amen.

"Cowards die many times before their death."

"He said to his disciples, 'Why are you so afraid? Do you still have no faith?' They were terrified and asked each other, 'Who is this? Even the wind and the waves obey him!'" Mark 4:40-41

I have always jumped head first into adventure. I love to travel and love people. Even if I do not see "eye to eye" with someone, I still appreciate their opinion. However, we all have something we are afraid of. Even though it seems cliché, I have a fear of heights. The only times in life I thought I was going to lose my mind was when I was somewhat elevated and thought I was about to fall. I remember once during a visit to the Vulcan statue in Birmingham, Alabama my father tried to "cure" me by jumping up and down beside me to prove that the see-through floor was secure. Needless to say, it resulted in me crawling over to the stairwell and taking the stairs down. (The elevator was also see-through.) I am also horrified of going up in my attic because the way down is 20 feet in the air. My poor husband tried to take my hand and guide me once, but it felt like being pulled to my death. I eventually came down after I had made a royal scene!

Everyone has a fear. Moses didn't speak well and was afraid of telling royalty what they were going to do. God asked Jonah to go one direction, he went the other way. The disciples who were aware of Jesus' abilities were even afraid of being in a storm with Jesus in their boat.

The truth is that no matter what our scenario and fear is, Jesus is in our boat too. Even though, we might not physically have a boat in our situation, He loves us and is always with us. "Everything is possible for one who believes." Matthew 9:23

Prayer:

Dear Heavenly Father, Thank You for giving us peace and hope in Your presence. Help us to remember that the circumstance of our fear is not important because You are greater. Everything is possible for the one who believes. We love You. In Jesus' name. Amen.

"She has a bee in her bonnet."

"What, then, shall we say in response to these things? If God is for us, who can be against us? He who did not spare his own Son, but gave him up for us all—how will he not also, along with him, graciously give us all things? Who will bring any charge against those whom God has chosen? It is God who justifies." Romans 8:31-33

Even when I was a child, I have loved swimming at night. During my last night swim, I relaxed and floated to a reclining position; nothing to be heard except the sound of my own breathing. Suddenly–WHOOSH! I felt something fly past my face. I opened my eyes and tried to come to a standing position to defend myself. I looked up to see that I was being dive-bombed by a bat! Practically drowning myself, I ran in slow-motion through water. Once calm and "safe," I considered what had just happened. The bat must have heard my breathing on the pool's surface and thought I was a bug. That was ENOUGH for me–I never swam outside at night again!

It's strange how certain events in our life can turn our "favorite things" into things we avoid. When people have bad encounters at a church, it can keep them from going to church for years. It is safe to say that the world is endlessly imperfect. Life will continue to have occassional events that are difficult moments to get over. However, life is a collection of good moments with the bad. It's all part of living. The best thing to remember is that God is always in the background and cheering us on.

Prayer:

God, thank You for the variety that we get with each new day. Even in our scarriest and worst moments, allow us to learn from those experiences. Help us to connect to new people that may be experiencing something similar. In Jesus' name. Amen.

"One kind word can warm three winter months."

"Ask, and it will be given to you; seek, and you will find; knock, and it will be opened to you." Matthew 7:7

"Let us therefore come boldly unto the throne of grace, that we may obtain mercy, and find grace to help in time of need. " Hebrews 4:16

There have been several times in my life that I felt hopeless and didn't know if I could make it through the day. My father dying, being rejected in a relationship, and leaving my home church are just a few examples. There are times that you will go through where no one seems to have the knowledge or ability to heal your soul– only time and God can do that. Waiting on your soul to heal hurts. Besides for hurt, you might feel abandonment, anger, and a mix of other emotions that feels overwelming.

I once heard a wise pastor say that when he feels in the midst of a horrible situation and there is not enough time to really invest in prayer to ask God for what you want, just send God a quick prayer of, "Help!" An example of this is if you are about to engage with someone that you know doesn't like you. "Help" is a quick way for God to send the Holy Spirit to help you.

Whether your trials in life are seemingly long-term or acute, ask God for "Help." You might not have the words or strength to articulate a prayer during a difficult time. Faith is trusting that no matter what is in the future, God is already there.

Prayer:

God, help me. You know my need and I ask for Your help, protection, guidance, and mercy. In Jesus' name. Amen.

"Do not wash your dirty linen in public."

"Let your light so shine before men, that they may see your good works and glorify your Father in heaven." Matthew 5:16

My friend, Judy passed away recently. She was 85 years young. For most of her life, she worked in a multi-cultural city at a steel company. She worked alongside many nationalities and enjoyed learning about their cultural differences, especially their recipes. She saw and loved all people as equals.

The main thing that comes to mind about Ms. Judy was her kindness. I once saw a home décor sign that said "Act in such a way that you are living proof that there is a loving God." She was that person.

Hopefully, we have all met someone like Ms. Judy. If she had sin in her life it wasn't apparent. She was an excellent spokesperson for God. I would (and will) gladly follow her anywhere because it was pleasant to be in her company.

On Earth, God has given us the opportunity to live a life that reflects God's immaculate love, acceptance, grace, and forgiveness. He has essentially given us a lump of clay and asked us to form something beautiful with it. It is up to us to form and shape our life. If we see something about it that we don't like and don't seem to have control over it – pray. God will hear your request.

Prayer:

Dear Father, You are the Master Potter and beautiful. You have placed us all here to reflect your love. Help me wih my self-control and the way I interact with other people. Let them feel Your love radiate through my life, so that they are confident of Your existence. In Jesus' name. Amen.

"Do not rock the boat."

"He arose, and rebuked the wind, and said unto the sea, 'Peace, be still.' And the wind ceased, and there was a great calm." Mark 4:39

One of my favorite pass-times as a child was helping my father tend to our honeybees. There were several important rules always to be remembered, such as "don't make any quick movements." Each time we robbed the bees, I usually got stung once or twice, and it was pivotal for a 10-year old to understand that breaking the rules would likely warrant more stings.

Even though it gets to be 100 degrees in the South, it was necessary for protection to wear long sleeves, my hat, and veil draped over my collar which was secured by wrapping the drawstring around my waist. It wasn't an outfit quickly taken off.

I'll never forget one summer we were out by the hives with thousands of bees flying everywhere (which gives off a beautiful humming sound I can still hear when I think of it), and suddenly I began to feel bees crawling around inside my pants and underwear! My first instinct was to swat at them, but I would surely get stung in doing so, and it would attract other bees to me. I calmly told my father that I could feel them inside my pants, asking him what to do. He said I could take the risk of having a few sting me or I could walk far away from the hives and take my clothes off to release them. I did the later.

We all have had moments in our life that feel like bees crawling around on our underwear. Freaking out and "losing our cool" will only end in getting stung. If the situation is out of your control, try to get to safety, give your problem to Jesus, and trust in Him.

Prayer:

God, You know our hearts and what we consider dangerous and scary. Watch over us. Calm us during the storm and remind us that the wind and waves obey You. In Jesus' name. Amen.

JANUARY 31

"First impressions are the most lasting."

"Your God is present among you, a strong Warrior there to save you. Happy to have you back, he'll calm you with his love and delight you with his songs." Zephaniah 3:17

As a mother with a newborn, I am frequently waking up every two hours throughout the night. It. Can. Be. Exhausting! I am the only one at his aide in the middle of the night. I usually spend an hour tending to his needs, then we go back to sleep for two hours to wait for the next cry. Even though I am sleep deprived during the day and night and am developing circles under my eyes, I always love to feel the warm comfort of him laying on my chest as I pat his back. The ten pounds of baby weight is a celestial hug, and it is the warmest, most loving hug that I've ever known. Whatever the issue is in your life, God yearns to hold you in His arms and pat your back. He yearns for that celestial hug and connection with you.

What is the reason you are crying every two hours? It is not likely that it is from having a wet diaper or because of hunger, but it doesn't matter. Are you going through a divorce? Have you been diagnosed with a terminal illness? Have you lost your job and don't know how you will make ends meet? God is the divine parent that cradles us, feeds us, and nurtures us. Even after I have tended to my baby and have set him back in his bassinet, I still watch him out of concern. I make sure he is breathing well and going to be okay. Likewise, God is not only with you but watching you.

Prayer:

Loving Father, You know what is on my heart and why I cry. You are with me even when I can't see it. Protect me and help me. Give me strength and comfort to get through the night. I will 'fear no evil, for I know You are with me.' In Jesus' name. Amen.

"What cannot be cured must be endured."(revisited)

"Have I not commanded you? Be strong and courageous. Do not be afraid; do not be discouraged, for the LORD your God will be with you wherever you go." Joshua 1:9

When I was a child our house burned down and we lived in a hotel room for about three months. That December, I had my most memorable Christmas. Mother bought a 2-foot Christmas tree and put it on the TV console. Also on the console was a porcelain doll. It was a wonderful Christmas and even though there was not a Christmas feast, I had everything I could want: my parents, a roof over our heads, and something to eat.

During those months, I began to read the Gideon's Bible in the night stand. My parents were good people but Christian culture was not something I was raised with. It was my first time reading the Bible and to pass the time I committed to memorizing the Lord's Prayer. Eventually, time came when we moved out of the hotel. Our new neighbors asked my parents once a week if they could take me to church. After a year my father said "Let's ask her and let her decide," which was followed by my resounding "yes!" It was my first experience in church and filled my very tired and poor nine-year-old life with music, ancient scripture, friends, and even greater, the opportunity to talk to God.

God is always there in every experience, but it is not always evident at the time. Seek and trust in Him in every season.

Prayer:

Dear Father God, Thank You for always being constant in our life. Even when we are not aware of Your presence, comfort us and give us peace. Help us to see our daily joys and triumphs. In Jesus' name. Amen.

"It will all be the same in a hundred years hence."

"Jesus answered, 'I am the way and the truth and the life. No one comes to the Father except through me." John 14:6

Growing up, I loved listening to my parents' genre of music from the 1960s and '70s. I know more about that era of musicians than I do my own. Wide-legged bell bottoms and "hip huggers" were popularized (again) in the late 1990s. One of my favorite dance clubs in the 1990s was called "Bell Bottoms" in downtown Birmingham and the dance floor centered around a 1960s Volkswagen "Bug" car. My parents liked the music from their time, but they also would sometimes listen to *their* parents' music from the 1940s like The Platters, Andrews Sisters, Big-Band music and old mountain folk songs. Generations always try to repeat what was popular in the generation before them.

A life that is always retold and always trending over 2,000 years later is the account of Jesus Christ. Over centuries, everything popular has eventually phased out, but the story of Jesus is still relevant.

When I was younger, I always wondered why 80 and 90-year-olds still went to church. It seemed to me that they had probably already achieved a certain level of Christianity and understood the doctrine. Later, I realized that they continue to go to Bible studies because the story of Christ is a bottomless well of knowledge and still relevant for all levels and age groups. Jesus is timeless and the ultimate example to follow.

Prayer:

Dear Father God, how brilliant and amazing You are to still be Number One above everything after all this time. Help me see what is important in life and that worldly possessions don't really matter. In Jesus' name. Amen.

"He takes the cake!"

"For we do not wrestle against flesh and blood, but against the rulers, against the authorities, against the cosmic powers over this present darkness, against the spiritual forces of evil in the heavenly places. Therefore take up the whole armor of God, that you may be able to withstand in the evil day, and having done all, to stand firm." Ephesians 6:12-14

Have you ever been tormented by a nightmare or painful memories? When I was expecting the birth of my son, several times I woke up from an awful nightmare in which he was involved. Whatever horrible thing you can imagine involving a baby, it is likely that I dreamed it.

Nightmares or reliving bad events gives us an awful feeling, mainly because we have no control of the outcome. We feel powerless. However, God gave us a powerful weapon against it – the power of our voice! When I wake up, I pray aloud for God's protection over my household, and speak directly to the Devil and tell him that God is King – so "BE GONE! In Jesus' name!"

To some, that might sound a bit extreme, but God's power *is* extreme. Even Jesus spoke out against demons and told them to get lost. If you take an honest look around our world you can see all of the sin that plagues the world. God is still around to help for those that cry out to Him.

Prayer:

Dear Father, I ask You to protect my family and my house. Wash my surroundings in Your holiness. I rebuke any evil that lurks there. Satan, You have no power here so be gone! In the mighty name of Jesus, Amen.

"The work praises the man."

"How sweet are your words to my taste, sweeter than honey to my mouth!" Psalm 119:103

When my family goes out to eat Italian, I love when the server brings the cheese grinder, hovers it over my hot plate and says, "Say when." It is a simple pleasure that I love not only because I love cheese and seeing the grinder operate, but I also love that ten seconds of importance when I feel like extra attention is given to my pasta and that the employees actually care about my experience. They could easily put the cheese on my table for me to dispense myself, but it wouldn't have the same affect. I would hate if the other people at my table were to respond on my behalf, "stop giving her cheese" or "don't give her any." It would rob me from the experience.

Others around us can rob us of our Christian experience if we allow them. Worship is the most meaningful experience that we need to fully bask in. Public worship is a freedom that not every country allows. It is one of the most life-changing, personal moments given. However, in a secular world you should expect to be called "fanatical" or a "Bible-thumper." People make fun of and degrade what they don't understand. Don't let anything or anyone limit your time with God. We all have different experiences and no one knows what you have been through to praise the way you do.

Prayer:

Lord, I exalt Thee and lift Your name high! You are the reason I am here and have given purpose to my life. Let me look for more time that I can spend with You, thanking you, telling others about You and learning more about You. You complete me and I am grateful. In Jesus' name. Amen.

"Silence is golden."

"Be quick to listen and slow to speak." James 1:19

Has anyone ever called you a yellow-bellied liver? If they have it probably stuck with you. I heard someone use that phrase 30 years ago and thought it was so incredibly ridiculous I can't forget it! Even for those who have not been called that specific phrase, we all have been called some name or had negativities spewed at us at some point in our life. Perhaps you have been cast as a bad person because of your political party, or perhaps you were the caster, quick to call the person with a different viewpoint an "idiot."

Name calling is not a new vice. It comes from unrighteous anger and losing control. During Jesus' time there were plenty of people with different viewpoints, not all popular ones. Some people were grouped as "Samaritans," considered "untouchables" with leprosy or nearly stoned as being an "adultress."

Each person's viewpoint and placement in life is different. We were not all meant to be the same. Jesus did not travel around calling people "Samaritan," "Dirty" or "Adultress," He claimed them and asked them to join His team and live a new, better life with Him. He knew that calling them anything negative would have created distance instead of building a bridge.

Prayer:

Dear Father God, close our mouth when we feel unrighteous anger coming on. We ask for Your help in communicating with our opposition. Help us break bread with them and join the same table instead of creating walls and warfare. May the world see that Your love is unique above all others. In Jesus' name. Amen.

"What's good for the goose, is good for the gander."

"You desire but do not have, so you kill. You covet but you cannot get what you want, so you quarrel and fight. You do not have because you do not ask God. When you ask, you do not receive, because you ask with wrong motives, that you may spend what you get on your pleasures." James 4:2-3

If you had siblings growing up, you might have found yourself wondering why your sibling got special privileges that you didn't get. One Christmas, my aunt gave my sister a beautiful porcelain doll with a peach dress. She gave me a cloth-faced baby doll with yarn for hair. Even though it was age appropriate, I wanted her porcelain doll. My poor mother, seeing that I was in distress went out and bought a porcelain doll for me. As a four-year old, I eventually broke her fingers off leaving a sharp glass edge and she was thrown away.

In adulthood, we also see things that others have that we desire. It does not seem fair when others are seemingly living "the good life" and no one notices us, especially God. Our mindset is "how can God bless them, when I should be the recipient of such a blessing?!" Only God can decide what we are due in life. If we are envious and take it for ourselves, such as I did getting a porcelain doll, it might come to hurt us just as the sharp dangerous edges that broke off. Only God can see and know what blessings might potentially hurt us.

Prayer:

God, thank You for Your endless blessings. Thank You for always supplying us with what we need. We trust in you to bless us and know what is best for our lives. Bless these people that You have gifted these things to. In Jesus' name. Amen.

"You look like death warmed over."

"This is my commandment: Love each other in the same way I have loved you." John 15:12

Most of the dogs that I have had in my life had a strong loyalty and obedience to me. If we went to the park or a strange location, I could let them out of the car for a stroll and call them to come back to me when I was leaving. I am not sure what made the difference, but my mother's dog, "Pepper" was quite opposite. Pepper came to my mother later in his life. She saw him on television on the morning news and drove across the state because she felt "connected to him." Most of the dogs that I've had were good ole country dogs. They lived on a farm, and it showed. We are not sure where Pepper came from but suspect it was high society. He was a fluffy Schnauzer mix and had the personality of David Tutera. On an outing one day, I took all of the dogs (Pep included, as we lovingly dubbed him) for a drive in the country. They all loved having their hair blow in the wind. After a while, I stopped in a very rural area, so the dogs could use the bathroom. There weren't any houses around, and it was just us. When it was time to go, I called for them, and they all ran to jump in my car. Allie, Dan, but no Pepper. Pepper was about 100 feet away and had a crazy look in his eye. There was no way he was coming. I called, pleaded, and then angrily told him to get in, all to which he ignored and ran around the forest and road. I finally got the idea to act like I was leaving him to scare him into jumping in the car. I drove off and as I looked in my rearview mirror, I could see him chasing us as hard as he could. I stopped and said, "okay, now in you go!" but he gave me the same crazy look and started running around the trees again. So, I drove a ways to "really" scare him... which led to him chasing us ... which led to again, him refusing to get into the car. A car passed by and looked at me thinking that I was dumping my dog as Pepper was chasing us for dear life! After about 30 minutes, I called my mother and gave her a description of where we were so she could come help and try to collect her crazy dog. When she got to the spot in the road that we were waiting, Pepper ran right to her and jumped into her arms! She looked at Pep and said, "Oh, you look pitiful and hot! Do you need some water!?" I thought to myself, "We all need water for dealing with him!"

We all know a "Pepper" in our daily life. We all encounter "crazies" every day at work, in our family, and at the grocery store. Sometimes people say the wrong thing, don't present themselves very well or have crazy actions and you don't understand what happened to the person for them to be so socially unacceptable. Who knows what happened to Pep in his lifetime for him to act like that. I imagine someone used to call him and then spank him, and he never got over it. I can't say that I blame him. The good news is that God has created us all. Even when we meet people that are different than us, you can be assured that God made them and loves them. God also commands that you love everyone, even the crazies, those that you categorize as being "very different than you" and those that seem undesirable. Jesus is often pictured with His arms stretched wide, caught in action right before He hugs and embrace you. Jesus said to love "as I have loved you." That means going the length for those you consider less than you.

Prayer:

Dear Heavenly Father, thank you for loving us without end. Help us love and embrace those around us that seem crazy, have a bad attitude or quirky actions that we don't think of as normal. We know that you love them. Help us to know them better and understand why and who they are so we can connect in a more meaningful way. In Jesus' name. Amen.

"Worrying never did anyone any good."

"I can do everything through him who gives me strength." Philippians 4:13

Call it my creative heart or my crazy side, but as a child, I frequently would play games to get myself through less than ideal situations. A few examples are when I was forced to rake leaves in the yard or wash the porch, I would pretend I was Cinderella. When I would hear a car nearing our house, I would stop to give a lamenting look so the passerby would think I was a real-life Cinderella princess trapped in tower. During summer months and walking across a parking lot, I also frequently considered myself one of Moses' wandering Jews crossing the desert for 40 years. As an adult, I continue to play such games but on a lesser scale. These are examples of silliness but there are serious things that we all go through that have us all feeling tired like a Cinderella or exhausted like the Israelites. People around the world use many different coping mechanisms. Some are restorative, like prayer, and exercise while others are harmful like drugs.

For those that use restorative measures, God always gets them to a safe place. Placing one foot in front of the other will take you to tomorrow, no matter how painful. Popular culture has everyone saying "I'm fine" and posting selfies but the reason Cinderella and the Israelites resonates with everyone is because they aren't "fine." Jesus went through His own trial and knows what it feels like to be down. When you find yourself crying, cry out for Jesus and He will carry you.

Prayer:

God, thank You for sending us Your son, Jesus. During our toughest times in life when we think we can't go any further You pick us up and carry us. God we love You. We lay our problems at Your feet and need the comfort of Your love and rest. Give us strength to get through today. In Jesus' name. Amen.

"There is an exception to every rule."

"Trust in the LORD with all your heart and lean not on your own understanding." Proverbs 3:5

Once when applying for a job position, I asked an older cousin of mine (who also worked for the company) if I might use her as a reference. When I met her for lunch to ask, I was surprised when she responded with, "no, I don't think that would help you any." Later that afternoon and weeks after, I couldn't help but feel annoyed with her refusal to help me. However, after about a month, I heard from the company and was hired.

The position that I was hired for was partly to listen to and brainstorm with the manager and his problems. After working there for several months, I learned that his arch-nemesis was my Cousin Mary! Cousin Mary knew that the entire time but never said anything. I guess she felt it would have discredited her somehow.

Leaning not on your own understanding is a difficult thing to do. Whatever is on your heart and bugging you, know that trusting in the Lord is the answer. You might not ever get to see the big picture of why a situation is working out like it is. Sometimes the situation might even seem unjust. It might take 20 years to see the big picture or God might be using your actions as a chess piece to help another person. Every difficult scenario could possibly be a "Cousin Mary" in God's big plan.

P.S. God also eventually worked out Cousin Mary and my manager's conflicts. God is good!

Prayer:

Dear Heavenly Father, Give us peace that You are the Grandmaster in this world. With every action and non-action, in things we enjoy and things that have hurt us – You will work things together in Your masterplan. In Jesus' name. Amen.

"Beggars cannot be choosers."

"In all your ways acknowledge him, and he will make your paths straight." Proverbs 3:6

On more occasions than I would like to remember, I can think of several times where I cried out for the Lord and was desperate for him to change a situation that I did not like. I remember when my father had been diagnosed with cancer and came to live his remaining days at my house, and asking God (pleading with God) to go ahead and take my father to Heaven. His pain and agony was a horrible thing to listen to and feel helpless about. The old expression "beggars can't be choosers" equates to the person not having a choice– that you are stuck in a bad situation and what you receive is out of your control. Even though not always felt, God's presence was always there with me. I did have a choice of choosing peace and deliverance because I chose God. God had equipped me at the age of 24 to know how to properly care for my dad; turning him every couple of hours, making his bed with him in it, etc.). God gave our family the strength to get through each day. On the day he passed, we played music in his room and sang. We chose God's peace and love to comfort us.

While death is a very different experience for everyone, God is there to comfort us. However, God is someone you choose to invite. Even though you might be in a dire situation, you can choose the peace that passes all understanding.

Prayer:

God, thank You that even in our most difficult moments we can chose a different ending. Thank You for giving us the hope of eternal life. In Jesus' name. Amen.

"Charity starts at home."

"Do not conform any longer to the pattern of this world, but be transformed by the renewing of your mind. Then you will be able to test and approve what God's will is—his good, pleasing and perfect will." Romans 12:2

One of my favorite songs to sing at karaoke is "Harper Valley PTA." It was a popular song in the 1960s about a mother that the PTA didn't think was setting a good example to her young daughter. "So Ms. Johnson wore her mini-skirt" to school to tell the members about their own sins.

As a Christian, we have all heard on more than one occasion that we are self-righteous, judgmental, and don't account for our own sins. Someone told me one time that "in anger true words are spoken." There is truth to that expression. Many Christians are quick to judge (especially on social media) when we think people need a wake-up call about the sin that is surrounding our community. We don't care about the feelings that we hurt because we don't have to see their face as we call them "abominations to the Lord."

Instead of giving the account of others' sin when you see it, start delving it to yourself at home. Everyone has sin that they need to work on. It is not a warm, fuzzy feeling when examining yourself and how you treat others, but it should "start at home" in the same way that "charity starts at home." Whether it is being self-righteous, over-eating, over-spending, or judging others, we all have areas that we need to work on to bring us closer to God.

Prayer:

God, I lay my sins at Your feet and thank You for the freedom to start fresh with each day. I ask You to be with me and help me in a culture of finger-pointing. Help us love like You loved and help spread Your message of love. In Jesus' name. Amen.

"Failing to plan is planning to fail."

"Come now, you who say, 'Today or tomorrow we will go into such and such a town and spend a year there and trade and make a profit'— yet you do not know what tomorrow will bring. What is your life? For you are a mist that appears for a little time and then vanishes. Instead, you ought to say, 'If the Lord wills, we will live and do this or that.'" James 4:13-15

My husband and I restored our 1895 home, built by great-great-grandfather. For the first two weeks of working there, I hauled off trash and broken furniture. At that time, it was just me working on the house, so moving a ratty sofa by yourself is not for the faint of heart! The house was still in need of: pulling up nails in the floor, wiring, plumbing, and much more! Life can really add up and feel overwhelming sometimes. The key to finishing the enormity of the house was planning what areas needed help first. Having a to-do list helped me be more productive.

Even though to-do lists are usually thought of when working, there is not a reason a to-do list can't be applied to your Christian life. Have you thought about having Christian goals or do you settle for just living with the title as "Christian?" What are things you want/need to bring you closer to God (reading the Bible, praying, etc.) Are there unique ways you want to witness to the world through volunteering? If you know your spiritual gift, are you sharing it? Making a plan for your Christian life can only elevate your relationship with God. Make a plan to plan!

Prayer:

God, thank You for the never-ending ways we can celebrate and encounter You! Help me identify what areas I can grow with You and include them in my daily life. In Jesus' name. Amen.

"Fine feathers make fine birds."

"My dear brothers, take note of this: Everyone should be quick to listen, slow to speak and slow to become angry, for man's anger does not bring about the righteous life that God desires." James 1:19-20

One of my favorite teachers in school, Ms. Robinson always kept herself in immaculate condition. Even though she was teaching 100 ten-year olds each year, her short hair was always permed, combed, and sprayed to perfection. She also always wore a knee-length pencil skirt and heels. Even though 30 years has passed since my time in her classroom, she continued to look the same; always poised, calm, and eloquent. During her time teaching, I am sure that the thousands of students that had her class noticed her poise and example. When I was in my 20s and attended her church, I started paying extra attention to the way she voiced important issues and her responses when getting mad (which were subtle). She was classy, gentle and gave every job her best effort. She was athletic and cut her own lawn. She was a Good Samaritan, served Meals on Wheels well into her 90s, never spoke ill about anyone and certainly never put anyone down. I haven't lived up to her level of goodness but would call her a moral mentor. Hopefully, we all have known a "Ms. Robinson" in our life – someone that we want to live up to, never disappoint, and who makes the world a better place to live in. In addition to knowing these moral mentors, we need to be them. Knowing them has already blessed us because we see that exceptional living is possible. The only thing that is keeping us from being these saints is our own willpower and obedience to God. The areas that we need to work on are equivalent to sin and separate us from God.

Prayer:

God, help us with the areas that separate us from You. Let us be quick to listen and slow to anger. Close our mouth when temptation comes. Help us be the difference in this world. In Jesus' name. Amen.

"The only way to understand a woman is to love her."

"Love is patient and kind; love does not envy or boast; it is not arrogant or rude. It does not insist on its own way; it is not irritable or resentful; it does not rejoice at wrongdoing, but rejoices with the truth." I Corinthians 13:4-8a

Love is a 365-day job. I know I can be difficult to love sometimes. I like to fact check during conversations. I also like certain household items, like a writing pen or toe-nail clippers to maintain their location. While I like to think I am close to perfect, I frequently lose my car keys. One night, my husband had to retrace my steps back to a parking lot where I thought I might have dropped them. The look on his face was indescribable.

He can "be a pill" too though. He likes to clutter workshop items on the porch. He tries to save every glass bottle. (He tries to save everything, for that matter!) He also clears his throat during dinner (every night).

While a list of our imperfections sounds like hatred and a battle-cry, it is in fact, a testament of our love. Love is not always easy. Love is forgiving and patient. It is knowing when to go for a walk and knowing when to forgive small grievances (and big ones, too.) God loves us whole-heartedly, even with all of our quirks. God always forgives us from our many sins and wants the same for our relationships. It is the biggest part of loving someone.

Prayer:

Father, You are the perfect image of love. Thank You for defining what love should be. Help us show that to others. Help us to respond to actions in love and forgive the way You do. In Jesus' name. Amen.

"Don't bite off more than you can chew."

"But seek first the kingdom of God and his righteousness, and all these things will be added to you. Therefore, do not be anxious about tomorrow, for tomorrow will be anxious for itself. Sufficient for the day is its own trouble." Matthew 6:33-34

Like all southern grandmothers, my Grandma Hazel was a wonderful cook! Her potato salad was second to none, and it was everyone's favorite on holidays. She took several cloves of garlic, smashed them, and let that strong pungency marinade into the mixture overnight. I came to learn this secret by getting a mouth full of garlic and biting down on it. What I thought was about to be my first taste of heavenly potato salad was an awful, burning stinky mess inside my mouth instead! When I made a face and spit it out she said, "oh no, I forgot to take the garlic out." Needless to say that was a memorable occasion that led me to check the salad from then on.

Taking on a full plate of anything in life has it's ups and downs. When there is so much going on, it is hard to dissect the entire plate. It is no wonder that busy lives frequently experience "biting down" on what feels like emotional garlic pods. The events we are filling our lives with can all be wonderful things: school, work, social clubs, church choir, volunteering, but God requires us to devote and dedicate meaningful time apart from the world so we can understand His message and magnitude.

Prayer:

Dear Lord, thank You for the many creative outlets and events You allow us to decorate our lives with. Help us clearly see what must be done and help us be better stewards of time. In Jesus' name. Amen.

"Give light and people will find their own way."

"Now to him who is able to establish you in accordance with my gospel, the message I proclaim about Jesus Christ, in keeping with the revelation of the mystery hidden for long ages past, but now revealed and made known through the prophetic writings by the command of the eternal God, so that all the Gentiles might come to the obedience that comes from faith— to the only wise God be glory forever through Jesus Christ! Amen." Romans 16:25-27

Usually anytime I get any kind of new gadget I like to read the instruction manual. It saves time later when I need its services in the moment.

God gives us a wonderful instruction manual with the Bible. Just like when my vacuum cleaner needs to switch functions, and I flip the toggle from floor to hose, knowing the Bible thoroughly has its benefits as well. When something comes along that we need quick spiritual relief from, knowing exactly where in the Bible the answer is gives quick relief.

God gave us life instructions, hopefully not in vain. Families have been separated, enslaved, and tortured, all while the same book sits on our bookshelf, many times, collecting dust.

Prayer:

Lord, forgive me for not always devoting myself to You. May I pour my time and prayer into understanding Your Word, so that when uncertain times come, I am prepared. In Jesus' name. Amen.

"Work smarter, not harder."

"Even though the fig trees have no blossoms, and there are no grapes on the vines; even though the olive crop fails, and the fields lie empty and barren; even though the flocks die in the fields, and the cattle barns are empty, yet I will rejoice in the Lord! I will be joyful in the God of my salvation!" Habakkuk 3:17-18

I remember one spring when I was about six, my father built a workshop beside our house. He was a handy man that could build just about anything, and when he needed an extra hand he frequently used his work as a teaching point for me and my sister. We both sometimes lamented during the lessons as construction was not our forte. When he poured the concrete floor, he called my teenage sister out to help him shovel the concrete and smooth it over. Being a teenager in the 80's with big hair, big earrings, and clothes, she did not welcome the experience. She started to voice her opposition (in the best way you could voice opposition with my father) and said that the concrete was ruining her shoes. My father went inside the house and brought out two long sandwich bags and told her to slip the sandwich bags over her shoes. She began to cry, "why am I having to do this?"

I am sure my sister and I would both still hate the idea of forced construction work, but our childhood experiences made us stronger, and more resilient adults.

People frequently feel abandoned by God in difficult times. "why is this happening to me?" and "why is God punishing me?" are frequent questions when people are enduring trials. In the Bible, Jesus told us that we will have tough times, but also reminds us that He will always be with us. In many Biblical accounts, the person that is going through something difficult continues to praise God and is eventually blessed for it. The Bible reminds us that no matter what the situation is, praising God is the appropriate response.

"Always be joyful. Never stop praying. Whatever happens, give thanks, because it is God's will in Christ Jesus that you do this." 1 Thessalonians 5:16-18

"By reciting psalms, hymns, and spiritual songs for your own good. Sing and make music to the Lord with your hearts. Always thank God the Father for everything in the name of our Lord Jesus Christ." Ephesians 5:19-20

Prayer:

Father, You know what I am dealing with. You are the Creator. You are everything good! I will continuously look to You and praise You. Amen.

FEBRUARY 18

"Patience is a virtue."

"Let us not become weary in doing good, for at the proper time we will reap a harvest if we do not give up." Galatians 6:9

Have you ever tried to rush baking a cake? How did that work out for you? Perhaps you were able to smooth it over with a beautiful icing or the first bite tasted perfect, but eventually your fork worked down to the center of the cake and you tasted the not-so-great gumminess of dough. If baking is not your favorite pass-time, as a Southerner surely eating is, and you have tasted a failed cake or piece of cornbread that doesn't quite "take the cake."

We have all heard that "patience is a virtue" and that "love is patient." Patience is something that God requires from us. It is our choice to be patient but "jumping the gun" on something you want for your life will end up tasting like gummy cake.

Jonah from the Bible tried changing the course of God's plans. He did not have the patience or foresight to trust God. His plan landed him being caught in a sea storm and tossed by the ship's crew into the mouth of a whale. Some skeptics have argued the validity of the story through the years, but if you consider some of the "gummy cake" circumstances that your life has possibly experienced, you already know it is possible.

Trusting God's will for your life is not easy. Patience is ultimately having faith that God will make things right and understanding that He is already in control.

Prayer:

Teach me to be patient with myself, life, and others. Teach me to trust Your sense of timing. I surrender to Your timing and will, God. In Jesus' name. Amen.

"Be careful what you pray for."

"Rejoice always, pray without ceasing, give thanks in all circumstances; for this is the will of God in Christ Jesus for you." 1 Thessalonians 5:16-17

It can be difficult to know what to pray for and downright painful for some people when they are asked to pray aloud in public. For several years, I felt embarrassed for some church members to hear me pray aloud. They were seasoned Christians that had been going to church for 70 years, I felt that surely my young voice had nothing to offer them. In time, I realized that my prayer wasn't for them and became more confident when praying for a group. While my prayers are still soft spoken and humble, I want them to be, as I am praying to God, Almighty.

I began gaining confidence when I heard an acronym associated with praying: ACTS (Adoration, Confession, Thanksgiving, Supplication) which guides you through every part of the prayer.

One of the known top fears is public speaking. Praying aloud in a group setting goes hand in hand with that phobia, especially when you are praying heartfelt vulnerable thoughts and feelings that others can hear.

On more than one occasion, I have heard to "not pray for patience because God will put you in jail/jury duty" to learn how to deal with undesirable situations. God is not a mean God and does not delve out cruel punishments to make us better, especially through our devotion to Him. Similarly, I have also heard people say, "be careful what you pray for" to categorize God into someone that is seeking pleasure in our discomfort.

In Acts 17:24-28, Paul writes, "The God who made the world and everything in it is the Lord of heaven and earth and does not live in temples built by hands. And he is not served by human hands as if he needed anything, because he himself gives all men life and breath and everything else. From one man he made every nation of men that they should inhabit the whole earth; and he determined the times set for them and the exact places where they should live. God did this so that men would seek him and perhaps reach out to him and find him, though he is not far from each one of us. For in him we live and move and have our being."

By this account, God is described as someone with endless resources who loves people. When speaking to Him remember that you are speaking to the face of love that loves you whole-heartedly. Speak freely and with ease.

Prayer:

Dear Heavenly Father, it can be difficult at times to know how to communicate with You. Sometimes, I don't have the words or know how to adequately ask for all that I need. Send me signs of Your love and promises that I might gain confidence with our relationship. May I trust You in all things instead of my own sense of what is right for my life. Tear down my fears and insecurities of what others might think of my prayers to You. Help me convey my heart adequately in a way that pleases You. In Jesus' name. Amen.

"Bless your heart!"

"Bear with each other and forgive one another if any of you has a grievance against someone. Forgive as the Lord forgave you." Colossians 3:13

Southerners have a big heart. "Bless Your Heart" is not just another slogan. It is deeply rooted in the way that southerners respond to everyday life. Only in the South (at least nowhere else that I have witnessed) will people listen to your broken heart, make you a pie, pray for you, bring you groceries and give you a ride when you are down on your luck. This big-hearted generosity helps inspire country singers to sing about the genuine culture of their motherland, their loved ones (present and past) and the goodness of what they experience in our community. If someone in the community doesn't seem to fit the bill, we Southerners even have a long list of forgivenesses that we use for the person's shortcomings. "He has been going through a lot lately." "She didn't have good examples growing up and doesn't know any better." And so on.

How is it with this enormous love, that we still have a problem forgiving our enemies? Using the word "enemy" reminds you that you don't like the person. I encourage you not to use it and replace it with "best friend" instead. Love that person like your best friend. What lengths would you go to if your best friend needed you? The only way to find a friend is to be one.

Prayer:
Dear Heavenly Father, thank You for making us a loving people. Thank You for the goodness and grace that grows here. God, help us love everyone like our best friend. Inspire us to invite our new "friends" to events; that we may fully get to know them and love them the way that You do. In Jesus' name. Amen.

"Knock on wood."

"Behold, I stand at the door, and knock: if any man hear My voice, and open the door, I will come in to him, and will sup with him, and he with Me." Revelation 3:20

One of my favorite popular images of Christ is an image commonly found on church windows: Jesus knocking at the door. The image is meant to inspire the gentleness of Jesus knocking on your heart's door. Accepting Jesus is choice; otherwise the image would depict Jesus kicking the door down. Ever know anyone that was so eager to persuade your opinion that they came kicking all of your doors down with name-calling and insults, too? You probably do not remember them with fondness and are not eager to join their social circle. Likewise, people are not interested in joining any organization of yours if you kick their doors down. Encouragement and grace are few in the world. Things like murder and war are formed where Christian love is lacking. No where in the Bible does Jesus force feed us anything. Christian love, gentleness, and humility are what woos us and woos the rest of the world.

You can "catch more flies with honey than with vinegar." Gentleness and knowing how to speak with people is an art, one that we are not all born with. However, whatever you are spiritually lacking in life, you can ask God for and He will bless you with it. Ask Him for the ability to talk to people and win them to the kingdom and He will oblige.

Prayer:

Dear Father God, help us be reminded of Your wooing and love when encountering others. Thank You for knocking gently when You yearn for a relationship with us. Weaken our arms when knocking at other's doors. In Jesus' name. Amen.

"A cat may look at a king."

"Do not keep talking so proudly or let your mouth speak such arrogance, for the LORD is a God who knows, and by him deeds are weighed."
I Samuel 2:3

Several years ago, my pastor asked me to collect hand-written devotions from church members and print a booklet to distribute throughout our community. Of all the congregants, I tried to select people from all walks of life that readers would enjoy hearing from. Among the fifty people that I asked to write, I was surprised to learn that several of them were illiterate. Despite learning this, I happily took their devotion down by hand as they told it to me. Equally important as the words they were telling me, was the strong silent message that they were just as important to God, as I am, or anyone else.

Society tends to look down on certain castes of people or professions if they are not impressive enough, but in this mix of middle-upper class business people, literacy was an issue. I never disclosed who they are because it is not important. God holds them as equals to all others and their testimony is just as important as anyone else's. Even if that person doesn't realize it yet, God has them in a season of learning. With that person's freewill, God will use them for His kingdom..

Prayer:

Dear God, thank You for the many different people You put in our lives. Even though some seem unworthy to us or are difficult to deal with, we know that You have made them, love them, and will use them in a powerful way. Help us to love and respect all in the same way that You love and accept us. In Jesus' name. Amen.

"Careless talk costs lives."

"Be kind and compassionate to one another, forgiving each other, just as in Christ God forgave you." Ephesians 4:32

Being married can be a wonderful blessing. Through all of my husband's perfections, good looks, talents, as well as possessing the full embodiment of spiritual gifts: patience and kindness (which was needed most in order to tolerate living with me) it should not surprise me (or any couple) that your mate is not perfect. Yet, usually once a week I am surprised that he has not cleaned his tools up yet or volunteered to wash dishes. In the peak of my frustration, sometimes I even have the thought (for a brief moment) to throw the tools away or perhaps, that eating permanently on paper plates would grab his attention. It is easy to become frustrated and respond in a negative way. However, God reminds us that none of us are perfect and that grace should be given.

Even Jesus experienced disappointment with His disciples. In Matthew 26, while waiting to be arrested which He knew would lead to His death, Jesus said to His disciples, "My soul is overwhelmed with sorrow to the point of death. Stay here and keep watch with me." Shortly, thereafter His disciples fell asleep. How sad, scared and disappointed, Jesus must have felt. Yet, He still felt an abundant love in order to later die for them.

On which topics do you feel most annoyed with people? Grace is needed there the most. Look for God's help where you are lacking.

Prayer:

God, what perfected grace and love You have given us! Forgive us as we forgive others. We love You and want to be the reflection of Your Son. In Jesus' name. Amen.

"Even from a foe a man may learn wisdom."

"Therefore, accept one another, just as Christ also accepted us to the glory of God." Romans 15:7

Growing up, my mother was always working. I spent a large amount of time sitting at her office waiting for her to finish. I felt unwanted and bored and was practically forbidden from talking to her co-workers and "bothering them." Sometimes she even asked me to sit under her desk "unseen," when important customers came in. Only later in my adult life did I realize the weight that my mother was carrying.

In most families, the mother is either the bread winner or the homemaker. In my family, my mother was both. She was stretched thin. Looking back, she was a rock-star that somehow managed to excel in everything she touched. Only after years of considering all of these things did I realize that she was on my side the whole time. Her quick responses and limited time with me was just a reflex of her carrying the world on her shoulders.

It is important to remember that God equips others differently than He does you. Even though you might have a bad encounter with someone or feel unwanted, others are on their own unique journey. There is not really a way to "walk a mile in his shoes," because God gave them an entirely different shaped foot. Sometimes we only witness part of other's lives, and not the entire scenario. Because we can never fully know the entire story, grace is required for every encounter and every person.

Prayer:

God, even though we may not always agree with others, help calm our emotions when we feel let down by others. In Jesus' name. Amen.

"Fine words butter no parsnips."

"Therefore, having put away falsehood, let each one of you speak the truth with his neighbor, for we are members one of another." Ephesians 4:25

When I was about five, I gave our family dog a haircut. My father came home and saw the dog, and asked me if I cut the dog's hair, which of course, I responded with a resounding "no." Being a wise man he calmly said, "Okay. Well, I will have to see if I can find out what happened to him." About an hour later, he asked me to take a walk in the woods with him. During our hike, he explained that a certain kind of poisonous tree can hurt dogs, make their hair fall out and then they die. Being an avid nature lover, I didn't question him.

We eventually came to a tree, and he said, "Well this is unfortunately the poisonous tree. So, I guess I will take our dog to the vet's office for him to die." I immediately started crying and confessed that the dog hadn't been anywhere around the tree. That it was ME!

I know now that no such tree exists and even though I was punished that day the memory makes me smile at how wise and loving my father was in trying to teach me a good lesson. Similarly, our Heavenly Father has many good lessons to teach us. Sometimes life gives us painful lessons but nonetheless, they make us wiser and will eventually be used to advance us to the next phase of our life. What difficult times have you been through? Ask God for help in understanding and how you can use that to help others for the glory of God's kingdom.

Prayer:

Father, Use the trials in my life to equip me for the future and as a spiritual warrior for someone who needs me. All of the goodness and glory is Yours. In Jesus' name. Amen.

"Curiosity killed the cat (but satisfaction brought him back)."

"Enter by the narrow gate. For the gate is wide and the way is easy that leads to destruction, and those who enter by it are many. For the gate is narrow and the way is hard that leads to life, and those who find it are few." Matthew 7:13-14

As a child, I loved watching a popular science show that came on every Saturday morning. If I had the supplies, I always tried to replicate the lab experiment. During one episode, the host shared that sticking a magnet to your T.V. screen would create a rainbow effect because of the electrons and magnetic field. For whatever reason, the only magnet that we had at our house in the early 1990s was brick-sized. I rushed to get it! I waved it across our wooden Zenith and sure enough, bands of color filled the screen in a beautiful display that followed wherever the magnet was! What the host never mentioned is that only small refrigerator magnets should be used. Thus, there was a large yellow blob left on the screen and I had damaged our only T.V.

Curiosity can be an awful thing. Besides for "killing the cat" and destroying your T.V. it can ruin lives and destroy your happiness. It is important to know where the line is and when to stop. Curiosity can also lead to good. We have explored other planets, and have modern medicine and technology — all because of someone's curiosity. The important difference is always seeking to know God and be closer to Him in every curious venture.

Prayer:

God, help us know the difference in healthy and dangerous curiosity. Let us continuously seek Your face in every action we take. In Jesus' name. Amen.

"There's no rest for the wicked."

"Dearly beloved, avenge not yourselves, but rather give place unto wrath: for it is written, Vengeance is mine saith the Lord." Romans 12:19

Has there ever been anyone you clashed with? We all have someone we struggle to get along with. Maybe your conflict is on a deep, historic level that has been going on for years and you have a long list of grievances with that person.

Growing up, my sister and I "fought like cats and dogs!" There is 12 years difference in our ages. I can remember her drawing an invisible line in the back seat of the car and telling me not to touch "her" side which of course led to me placing my finger over the line. Once during a disagreement, I remember quickly lying on the ground to yell out for my parents' help because "she pushed me!"

These stories don't sound that original when speaking with other people. My friends have their own traumatic stories their siblings put them through. Ah, childhood!

One would think that these stories are limited to childhood, but the truth is I have a group of people that I still would enjoy banishing to another planet. Any type of vengeance is just adding more conflict to conflict. God declaring vengeance is His, is because He is the only one that truly knows how to stop it and the only way it will ever be resolved.

Prayer:

Dear God, take our anger and annoyance with other people away. I am placing my conflict with that person at Your feet. You not only see the person, but made them. Fill me with peace, love, and encouragement to do better. In Jesus' name. Amen.

"Sleep tight! Don't let the bed bugs bite!"

"Then I heard every creature in heaven and on earth and under the earth and on the sea, and all that is in them, saying: 'To him who sits on the throne and to the Lamb be praise and honor and glory and power, for ever and ever!'" Revelation 5:13

As a child, I loved spending the afternoons at the old barn near our home. My Daddy kept his pet pigeons there, our cows hung out there waiting for someone to notice that they were hungry and there was a nearby farmhouse to explore.

One day, I found inverted ant hills in the dirt that were under the barn. My father told me that little creatures live inside them called "antlions." Of course, I was fascinated and being the tomboy I was, instantly dug one up to examine it. I learned that this quiet, harmless insect that would normally go unnoticed was actually beneficial and ate ants and any other bug that fell into its well.

It would be nice for God to plant antlions in our life to weed out bothersome things, and He does! God has gifted us life-helpers in the creation of the Bible, church, prayer and other people. If your life feels like a bedbug infestation, try looking for his life-helpers. Life-helpers are quiet and can also go unnoticed but can make a world of difference!

Prayer:

Dear Heavenly Father, the marvel of Your creations are endless! Thank You for antlions and for life-helpers. Help us weed out pests and infestations and keep our eyes on You. In Jesus' name. Amen.

"You can't make a silk purse out of a sow's ear."

"Do not be deceived, God is not mocked; for whatever a man sows, this he will also reap." Galatians 6:7

I come from a long line of beekeepers. My father, raised by his grandfather, and his great-grandfather were all beekeepers; possibly even more before then, but it is not easy finding history like that before 1880.

There are many fascinating things about bees and honey but perhaps most fascinating is how pure the honey is. Honey has been used to heal wounds since ancient times because of its anti-oxidant, anti-bacterial, and anti-inflammatory properties. If you drop something foreign into honey, it will push the object to the top rejecting it.

The kind of material that something is made from has the power to "make it or break it," including people. If we spend our time pouring junk into our mind, body, and soul then what we produce will seem ordinary or even spoiled. Unlike the honey, we will not have the power to push the negativity away. However, if we spend time in God's word, learning and reading, taking care of our body by eating and exercising – the ending result is strength and endurance.

God takes notes of the work we put toward what kind of person we want to become. While He still loves us regardless, He does bless us accordingly to the time we devote in taking care of ourselves according to His law (Daniel 1:17; Matthew 7:17-19)

Prayer:

God, thank You for blessing us. Show us examples to inspire us to become better as people and Christians. Let our actions be fruitful to Your kingdom and glorify Your name, In Jesus' name. Amen.

"Let your hair down."

"You crown the year with your bounty; your wagon tracks overflow with abundance." Psalm 65:11

Winter in the south is unpredictable. However, one thing is fairly certain, it is not likely snow. In my hometown, it only averages about two snow days a year and those are just a few snow "dusting" days, not enough to play in. As a child, I coveted the scenes on "white winterland" postcards.

One winter, a "perfect" snow finally came. Even though there was snow, the landscape of our farm made it nearly impossible to sled. The weather apparently excited my dad too because he connected my sled to my mother's 1992 Nissan Stanza, and drove like a mad man dragging me across 40 acres of fields. When he turned the wheel of the car, my sled flipped over on its side. I yelled for joy (and my life) that day and hold it as a dear memory in my heart.

Life has special moments that make living more beautiful. Jesus knew this and celebrated life with his friends and family. What beautiful memory can you recall from your own life? Share that story with someone and plan to make new memories with new people. Celebrating life is made better with others. People can become introverted or cut themselves off because they find it easier to deal with solitude than rejection or disappointment. God designed us to be together, grow together and celebrate together. Good connections connect us to Christ.

Prayer:

God, thank You for each day that we can experience afresh and for the blessing of people. May we celebrate together and be grateful for this day You have made. In Jesus' name. Amen.

"Honesty is always the best policy."

"Do your best to present yourself to God as one approved, a worker who does not need to be ashamed and who correctly handles the word of truth." 2 Timothy 2:15

Once as a teenager, I skipped school with friends and drove to Birmingham. In what has to be the worst luck, someone hit my car that day! Being young and caught up in something that I was not supposed to be near, I did not make a police report. Driving home, I started to think up the great lie that I would tell my parents as to why the side of my car had a huge dent in it. When I arrived home I told my mother that I came out of school and found my car like that in the parking lot. She immediately picked up the phone and called the school to speak to the principal. I knew that at any minute the administrator would tell her that "Elisabeth didn't even come to school today." So, I confessed to my mother. That was the last time I lied to my parents. The pressure was too burdensome.

Honesty is always the best policy. If you are having trouble in life (big or small), telling lies will only complicate the matter.

God places that moral compass inside of us and puts good people in our life for a reason. He does not want us to be stressed out because of "the web we weave." Whatever, burden and load you are carrying today – give it to God. Life does not have to rest of your shoulders.

Prayer:

God, Forgive me of the areas I have not been truthful. Place people in my life that hold me morally accountable. No matter what the outcome, help me to always choose what is right so that people may know me by my honesty and integrity. In Jesus' name. Amen.

"All good things come to those who wait."

"Wait for the LORD; be strong, and let your heart take courage; wait for the LORD!" Isaiah 40:31

When I began restoring my great-grandmother's house I was able to do many of the repair projects myself. However, there were some projects I could not do on my own. It was frustrating to feel so in need, call repair people, and no one show up for the job. A few times, I sat on the floor and cried thinking about all that had to be done and feeling hopeless about the lack of control I had in the situation. Eventually, I asked a friend to come install my hot water heater. He brought an "expert" with him to help do the job. The two of them installed the hot-water heater (to my great relief). When they finished the project, the expert asked if there was other work on the house he could help with. I gave him a tour of the house and a list from room to room of everything I wanted to change or update. By that autumn he helped me complete most everything on that list. During that time, I noticed that this gentle man was doing other kind extras, like watering the plants on my porch. The next autumn we announced our engagement. I didn't find out until we were married that he actually didn't know anything about installing hot water heaters. My friend called him an "expert" to introduce the two of us — what a blessing in disguise (actual disguise!)

There are a heap of things that we cannot control in life. God knows the concerns of your heart — pray and ask him to help your situation. The entire time this "expert" was working on my house, I was praying for God to open my eyes to be able to see the right husband for myself. Ask for what you need, in every way, and specifically to the Father.

Prayer:

God, thank You for loving us enough to listen and know every need of our life. Like a child, when we humbly ask for Your help, You know what is right for us. Give us peace in knowing You are already working on our resolution, in ways that we cannot imagine. In Jesus' name. Amen.

"A bad penny always turns up."

"We know that for those who love God, that is, for those who are called according to His purpose, all things are working together for good." Romans 8:28

My mother has a knack for owning strange, crazy dogs (See devotion for February 7 if you missed it.) After her beloved "Pepper" passed away, she adopted "Rowdy." Rowdy (so appropriately named) came to my mother's home with a scar across his face and a broken tooth. We initially met him while he slept ON TOP of mother's Cadillac. He was the very definition of "Rowdy" living. He loved tearing the trash can apart and spreading the debris across neighboring yards. Before she decided to take ownership of him, he would frequently scour the highway for roadkill and bring home a deer leg (or who knows what) to snack on during the day. When she sold her home, Rowdy came to live at my house, so he could continue enjoying country living. Even though my community is small and quiet, I only live a short distance to our local McDonalds. Once Rowdy discovered his love for McDonald's he camped out at the drive-thru, making sad faces at passing cars. I learned of Rowdy's Happy Meal obsession when a photo of him was shared on social media a few hundred times with a caption that said "someone dumped this poor starving dog off." From what the restaurant employees said, he earned about 25 cheeseburgers that day. There are also other quirks to Rowdy. He will royally freak out if he gets tangled in his own leash, and he doesn't like his paws touched. Even though some might call him "broken," I really love him! He has such a sweet shiny nose. He loves to go for walks and loves it when you scratch under his collar. He is not any more broken than the rest of us.

People have their hurts and hang-ups from the past. Most of us have strange quirks that we are accustom to and don't we all enjoy a rub behind the shoulders? Yet, in our brokenness, God still loves us. God wants us to live up to our potential and be happy just like what I want for Rowdy. He would be happier if he cut the "rowdy"-ness from his life, just like God wants us to have a cleaner, more fruitful life.

Prayer:

God, thank You for loving us despite our rowdy ways. Forgive us for the things that separate us from living a more fruitful, joyful life with You. Free us from our brokenness. Help us see what causes chaos in our lives and put it away. Give us Your peace and assurance that You are the great provider and will fill any void that we have. Thank You for all of your endless provision. In Jesus' name. Amen.

"A bird in the hand is worth two in the bush."

"Bless the Lord, O my soul, and all that is within me, bless His Holy name! Bless the Lord, O my soul, and forget not all his benefits, who forgives all your iniquity, who heals all your diseases, who redeems your life from the put, who crowns you with steadfast love and mercy, who satisfies you with good so that your youth is renewed like the eagles." Psalm 103:1-5

In my early 20s, I was interested in photography (back when photography was a real skill and included knowing what kind of film and lens to use). There was an older photographer in my community named Mike, and I heeded any advice he gave about cameras and photography. Mike gave me the best advice that I still use for special Kodak moments. "Do not become so obsessed with getting the perfect photo that you forget to look up over the camera and enjoy the moment." After that day, for all of the moments where I wished I had a camera to capture the moment, but did not have one, I decided to enjoy what I was seeing to the fullest (instead of leaving the scene to go hunt down a camera).

God's blessings are in front of our face. We become so obsessed with what we want and do not have that we forget to stop and enjoy what we do have. "Count your blessings" is an actual way of life and can be a movement to being fulfilled.

Prayer:

Dear Father, thank You for what You have given me today. Thank You for my station, who I am, and the people I know. We feel Your goodness actively working in our lives. Thank you, Lord.

"Nothing is certain but death and taxes."

"Whoever claims to live in Him must live as Jesus did." 1 John 2:6

I am fortunate to have stayed in the same small town my entire life. Some things have changed over the years. There are more buildings now in the town center. The school playground that I played on as a child (made from old tires and feet away from train tracks) is a vacant lot now filled with kudzu. And although quirky, there have been the same two trees that have stood alone in a field beside a local church. That might seem strange to note trees, but these trees are huge Oaks and are a focal point when driving through the little town. One of my best friends from school lived near the two trees, and I spent many years of my youth driving right beside them.

A few years ago, one of the trees fell. It was particularly a symbolic moment for me because my friend from school (that lived near them) also passed away. So the one Oak stood in solitude and has been an emblem for me and my own life. For years, it has stood alone but has enjoyed many sunsets until recently when it also blew over during a storm. For me, the message is so clear that nothing is permanent in life. Everything has an inevitable fate to pass away except your love for God. In 200 years from now, you may not be remembered, but the way you express God's love to others will continue to ripple through time if you make waves big enough now.

Prayer:

God, help us reach out to others in love through our smile, words, actions, and invitation. By using the creative gifts that You gave us, let us express Your love so that others may see that beauty and be inspired. In Jesus' name. Amen.

"Can't never could, Won't never will."

"As iron sharpens iron, so one person sharpens another." Proverbs 27:17

In my life, I've had a first-class seat to watching my mother being a "can-doer." In the 1980s, many women saw work reform in the workplace and dreamed of an independent life. My mother grew shoulder pads and business suits and went into real estate (at a time when there were 5 real estate agents in my county instead of 100). I grew up watching her sometimes struggle, but always finding a way to make every situation work. Her role as a confident female example enabled me to grow up with confidence as a young woman. If I needed a tree removed from my yard, I got my saw and went to work!

I will forever be grateful for all of the ways that women have been liberated. However, all of that "can-do" attitude can exhaust a person. God does not mean for us to carry the weight of the world on our shoulders. Even though He might have equipped us, it can be an equal blessing to stop, reach out, and ask someone for help. Working with others, not only releases a burden, but is a way to connect to others, learn about their interests and concerns, talk about God and make the Kingdom grow. If God meant for you to do everything yourself, He wouldn't have surrounded you with a world of people. He means for us to find a way to connect.

Prayer:

God, thank You for the people You place in my life. Place people directly in my path that we may productively work together while gaining friendship and strength. In Jesus' name. Amen.

"Ask no questions and hear no lies."

"Therefore, if anyone is in Christ, he is a new creature; the old things passed away; behold, new things have come." 2 Corinthians 5:17

In my 20s, I took a girls trip to the beach with my friend, Jessica. The Gulf of Mexico has been "the" go-to beach place all my life, and they are equipped for tourists. The sandy white beaches don't disappoint and are stocked with fun amenities. We both lathered ourselves up in suntan oil (even though I know wiser now) and headed out to the beach! After a while, we decided to rent a watercraft for 30 minutes. Even though neither of us had ever used one, we both knew how to swim, and the thought of carrying ourselves out to the middle of the sea didn't scare our young, naïve minds.

We both hopped on and instantly jetted out to the Deep Blue where the waves are BIG. Once out in the ocean, I found the big waves a bit intimidating. Our motor craft wasn't able to dash across the top of the water because the waves were so deep and rocky. I slowed down and when I did, we overturned.

As soon as we came back up, we swam to the craft to pull ourselves up. However, because we had lathered ourselves up so well in sun oil, we couldn't get a good enough grip to pull up on the craft. So there we were, floating in the middle of the ocean, too afraid to think about sharks, and waiting for the ski company to realize that our 30 minutes had lapsed. When a man eventually came, he wasn't able to pull our greasy hands and arms aboard either. The both of us barely pushed Jessica up but that didn't help me. I eventually held on to a giant banana raft that was 20 feet long and was towed into shore. Nothing was more exhausting and embarrassing than having the entire beach watch my banana raft rescue.

Life is adventurous and full of turns. Most people would agree that there is a time in each of our lives that we would like to forget. It is even possible that you have buried it so deeply in your heart and past that you don't even acknowledge it anymore from the shame felt.

Shame is something that each person has experienced (if they are honest with themselves) and that experience helps us connect to other people. (If everyone has experienced it, then why is it still so taboo?) Those experiences allow us to connect to the world, because they are part of real life. God doesn't want us to live in shame and fear. He can and will set you free from EVERYTHING through humble submission and honesty.

Prayer:

Dear Father, thank You for new beginnings. Thank You for allowing me to use my past experiences as a way to connect to others. I ask that You use, even the worst moments of my life as a way to reach out to others who feel alone and burdened by shame. Thank You for the gift of freedom. In Jesus' name. Amen.

"You've made your bed and you must lie in it."

"If we confess our sins, he is faithful and just to forgive us our sins and to cleanse us from all unrighteousness." 1 John 1:9

The expression "you've made your bed and you must lie in it" always brings to mind a time when I was about five. My mother had just put me to bed, and I heard a "buzz" under the covers. I quickly jumped out of the bed. I listened and ruffled the blanket and "buzz" – I heard it again! I quickly ran to my parents' room and exclaimed that I could not go to sleep because there was a bee. My mother went to my room and pulled the covers back to show me that nothing was there. I pleaded and told her, "YES, THERE IS!" She then explained that if I didn't get back in bed she was going to spank me.

It is important to know that up until this point, every night for the last couple of years, I protested going to sleep. So even though I declared there was a bee in my bed, it looked like all of the other nights when I was fighting going to sleep. Out of fear of my wrathful mother, I did get back into the bed where I was stung. Mother came to comfort me and felt awful sentencing me to a bee sting. However, the bee sting was really my fault, because for a long time, I had "cried wolf," not wanting to go to sleep. It eventually caught up to me, and I paid a price for it!

We all have made poor decisions at times which have resulted in an undesirable penalty. I wish I could say that I have only made the one mistake of never wanting to go to bed, but people are sinners. We sin. The good news is that God gives us a blank slate to start fresh. We might pay for our mistakes, but once we confess and have accepted responsibility for our actions, we are forgiven. God doesn't keep holding us accountable for the sins we have apologized for. He wants us to get back up, shake the dirt off and do better in the future.

Prayer:

Dear God, thank You for giving me another chance when I don't always deserve it. Thank You for your unconditional love. Amen.

MARCH 10

"Scratch my back and I will scratch yours."

"If one person falls down, another person can help him up, but pity anyone who falls and has no one to help them up." Ecclesiastes 4:10

Having friends around to help get a big job done always makes work easier. Although weddings can be a headache to plan, it is a blessing when bridesmaids are there to help and remember every detail. I remember for my sister's wedding I took photos for three hours to help capture her beautiful day. In turn, on the morning of my wedding, she helped me arrange nine boutonnieres and four flower crowns for the flower girls. Although the flowers were beautiful and smelled like a eucalyptus heaven and her wedding photos came out lovely, what I remember most is not the tasks, but the meaningful time we spent together. I enjoyed being there with her. Both of those days added joy to my life and memories.

Working alongside of someone doesn't have to be monotonous labor, it can be love. It can add beauty to an otherwise plain day.

Savor your time and experiences with others. God gave us people to help one another in listening, learning, laughing, crying ... all of the seasons of life. Missing the opportunity to spend time with someone might mean "missing the boat" and missing the blessing.

Prayer:

Loving Father, we thank You for the love You pour out on us! Thank You for the people in our lives and the seasons we share with them. Help us see every day as an opportunity to love others. In Jesus' name. Amen.

"He could squeeze the buffalo off of the nickel."

"The man who had received five bags of gold brought the other five. 'Master,' he said, 'you entrusted me with five bags of gold. See, I have gained five more.' "His master replied, 'Well done, good and faithful servant! You have been faithful with a few things; I will put you in charge of many things. Come and share your master's happiness!'" Matthew 25:20-21

I am sure you know someone that saves everything including glass jars and aluminum cans. For me – that was my dad. He never did without anything in his life but had a keen knack for reusing and recycling most everything. We occasionally would make a joke about him being a "tight-wad" because of the extremity for saving everything. For example, he always kept a pack of chewing gum in his shirt pocket, and if you asked for some, he would take out a piece and rip it in half, saving the other piece for later.

Being an American is a title that I think most of us are proud of, but it usually comes with an abundance of "stuff" we don't need. We are quick to throw away the old instead of reusing. What have you thrown away this week? I wonder how the world's perception of Jesus would have changed if he was well-known for throwing away abundance, wearing $200 shoes and eating caviar. Billions around the world are drawn to Christ by his transparent love for people and God, the Father, and nothing more. In what ways are you making your life like His?

Prayer:

Jesus, thank You for Your leading example on love. Shine light on the ways that You want us to change. In Jesus' name. Amen.

"A bad workman blames his tools."

"Then the LORD opened the donkey's mouth, and she said to Balaam, 'What have I done to you to make you beat me these three times?' Balaam answered the donkey, 'You have made a fool of me! If I had a sword in my hand, I would kill you right now.' The donkey said to Balaam, 'Am I not your own donkey, which you have always ridden, to this day? Have I been in the habit of doing this to you?' 'No,' he said. Then the LORD opened Balaam's eyes, and he saw the angel of the LORD standing in the road with his sword drawn. So he bowed low and fell facedown." Numbers 22:28-31

I have used many copy machines in my life. In the 1990s, they sucked in each page like they were dying of dehydration in the desert. (They even made a quick "SUCK" noise.) During each use it was inevitable that the machine would suck in 10 pages at once and make a "HACK" noise, similar to a cough. For this quote, copy machines seem to be the perfect "tool to blame," and I am unapologetically blaming them now.

Tools can indeed be awful, but they are helpful and have evolved from what was used yesterday. Be grateful even for the problems. Life is always changing. Always be ready with a cheerful and grateful heart to use all resources for God, especially in how we behave.

Prayer:

God, thank You for our tools, even the ones that don't seem to cooperate with us. Help us have patience and be grateful. May our labor glorify You. In Jesus' name. Amen.

"A picture is worth a thousand words."

"These things God has revealed to us through the Spirit. For the Spirit searches everything, even the depths of God." 1 Corinthians 2:10

One of my favorite photos of my dad is when I was about five years old. He had built a swing and said, "jump on." As I was preparing to swing, he jumped on top of the swing too and the picture was taken. For most of my life I have looked with such love at the photos of us, remembering how much he loved me. I don't have near as many photos with my mother. She was constantly working and as I got older, I frequently wondered why she chose not to share those moments with me.

Only after the birth of my son did I realize when I started taking pictures of my son with his father that my mother was not in any of the photos because she was the one taking the pictures! All of the feelings I had for decades about having such few photos of my mother came to light. When you see a photo or remember a moment in time, there is no possible way to capture all of the background details, off camera, just like my mother's presence that day, smiling behind the camera. Only God can see the big picture. If there is a portion of your life that leaves you feeling sad and forgotten, know that God has you in His sight. Only He is able to see the "Big Picture."

Prayer:

God, for the times in life where we don't always understand situations, give us hope and understanding. Give us peace and the assurance of Your love. In Jesus' name. Amen.

"A miss is as good as a mile."

"Watch therefore, for you know neither the day nor the hour that the Lord will return." Matthew 25:13

Camden, Alabama in a special place back in time. Old Antebellum homes sit on thousand-acre plantations, and the families that live there memorialize their family members by having a formal painting of the family commissioned that hangs in every living room. Off the side of Camden is a daily ferry that will carry passengers across the river to Gee's Bend (another old settlement that looks like it might have been the inspiration to a Mark Twain novel). Each day, people load onto the ferry and chug across for fifteen minutes to the other side.

Once, my friend Linda took me to ride the ferry across, but we had missed its departure by minutes! Anyone who has missed their flight at an airport knows there is not any chance of the plane coming back for you; the same goes for the Gee's Bend Ferry. Instead we decided to visit Gee's Bend by driving (a forty minute uneventful ride, each way.) I have always been regretful that we didn't make that voyage and get the experience.

Missing the God experience is the very same. We can be so close: a friendly person that volunteers, goes to church, and gives to charity, but if we do not know and love Christ as our Savior, the "ferry" will eventually depart and the opportunity will be lost. The best thing would have been to get there early and be prepared.

Prayer:

Father, thank You for giving us the opportunity to know You. I know that Jesus died for my sins. I ask You to forgive me of my sins. Come into my heart and life. I want to live for You. In Jesus' name. Amen.

"All good things must come to an end."

"In the beginning you, God laid the foundations of the earth, and the heavens are the work of your hands. They will perish, but you remain; they will all wear out like a garment. Like clothing you will change them and they will be discarded. But you remain the same, and your years will never end." Psalm 102:25-27

A few summers back my mother rented a beautiful condominium at the beach and invited me and my cousin. We grew up together and have "cousin stories" from a shared adolescence. When we arrived at the condo, we both were enamored with how posh it was. We each had a bedroom and bath to ourselves, and the entire condo was decorated in a beautiful granite.

One evening I made dinner for everyone. (I love to cook and everyone knows it – which might be the reason Mother invited me.) I was in the kitchen making pasta, I opened the lid to the pot to check on the noodles. When I went to put the lid back on the noodles, the lid was vacuumed onto the granite countertop! I calmly went to my cousin's room and said, "I need you to come in here. I have an emergency!" When she entered the kitchen, I told her what I had done and that the lid was now stuck to the counter. She looked at me, and we both knew in that moment that my mother was going to kill me! Would she lose the deposit on the condo? Was I damaging the countertop? Would that expensive piece of granite have to be replaced? I had so many unknown questions that I was horrified! If you know the wrath of my mother – you would have been horrified too! "What are you going to do?" my cousin asked me. "You have to help me fix this before mother notices – that's what!" I answered. Like an episode of Lucy and Ethel, we began scurrying trying to lift the lid with all of our might. My cousin (who only weighs just over 100 pounds put her entire body weight against the cabinet and pulled. Nothing! We opened the drawers and looked for spatulas to wedge between the counter and lid, but nothing could break that seal! About that time, my mother walked by and asked how it was going. "Finnne!" we chimed in harmony. My cousin eventually looked up on the internet how to remove the lid (with ice apparently!) We were both relieved and the entirety of dinner was spent silently trying to calm our nerves.

Life has bumps, grinds and hick-ups. A day at the beach can quickly turn into a nightmare that is seemingly out of control. God is always in control though. We can look back and laugh about the lid now. Whatever you are going through that feels like a rollercoaster, all rollercoasters come to a stop. Hang on to God until you get there.

Prayer:

Dear Heavenly Father, thank You for the fun times and memories. Thank You also for always seeing us through to the end. Regardless of how impossible and crazy times seem, You are with us. Send the Holy Spirit to calm and blanket us in peace. We trust You. In Jesus' name. Amen.

"Dead men tell no tales."

"Do you not know that in a race all the runners run, but only one gets the prize? Run in such a way as to get the prize. Everyone who competes in the games goes into strict training. They do it to get a crown that will not last; but we do it to get a crown that will last forever." I Corinthians 9:24

Perhaps one of the saddest parts of losing someone we love is the loss of hearing their thoughts, jokes, and advice on certain topics. My late father enjoyed sending his greeting cards addressed to friends and family addressed to fictional, comical people and names. For example, on the front of the envelope to his brother it would read: To the Smith Crazy Nut Farm. I enjoyed and miss those crazy antics.

God gives us life to fulfill tasks here on Earth. A large part of that role is developing relationships with people and shining light on the message that God is Love. When our time on earth is complete, the hourglass has finished its cycle. The good (or bad) that we leave behind in our footprints leaves an impression on earth for the future.

On some of the best game shows, competitors race to complete before the buzzer chimes in order to win the prize. That is comparable to the life we should live here on earth in finishing our task. Besides creating relationships, we are meant to love other people and follow the Gospel. We are the hands and feet of God.

Prayer:

Dear Heavenly Father, thank You for entrusting me to love and care for Your sheep. Equip me to know all the ways that I may serve You. In Jesus' name. Amen.

"Do unto others as you would have them do unto you."

"To all who did receive him, who believed in his name, he gave the right to become children of God."
John 1:12

While trying to plan a last-minute trip to Washington D.C., my best childhood friend and I decided to lodge with a group of older sisters that lived together and looked after their father. We didn't know any of them but looked forward to the adventure of whatever we came across.

We drove from Alabama in one day and arrived late at night. We anticipated that they may not even open their door being that it was so late. We were surprised that not only did they open their door, introduce themselves, ask if we had eaten, and give us a tour, but their amenities were abundant and were a blessing after a long drive.

They didn't know us from Adam's house cat, and we were surprised to sleep in our own private living quarters with a private bath. We woke up on our own time (which was appreciated after arriving late). When we entered the main part of their home, we were greeted with a huge breakfast and a dozen family members, including their 90-year-old father sitting around a table greeting us.

They were so kind and generous and refused to accept any kind of donation. It left me and my friend feeling humble and speechless that such kindness still exists.

It is easy to feel torn down and discarded living in the world. We live in a culture of *never pretty enough, never rich enough, never fast enough, never smart enough;* and that culture begins early in life. My first encounters of realizing that I might be considered less valuable than others started in elementary school where most all children usually experience name calling and begin creating a caste system.

God's goodness shines in the world like a rare beacon for the lost and unloved. The love and hospitality of those women were the likeness of Jesus, and it was so refreshing that it left us speechless that anything of the like still exists in our world.

They didn't know us, yet they trusted us in their home; gave us food, shelter, and spoke to us like friends.

I still keep in touch with them and correspond through seasonal cards which I always address to "My Liberty Sisters" (since they live in Washington D.C.)

God presents opportunities to us every day for us to unconditionally love others. We usually put restrictions on our love, how much we will allow ourselves to trust others, or the limit of our generosity.

God asks us to do unto others as we would do unto ourselves, but we don't put a cap on our own love, acceptance, or generosity. Learning to love others in the same way as we love ourselves can be enabled in our lives by asking for God's help.

Prayer:

Heavenly Father, thank You for the goodness and purity that still exists in the world. It is face-to-face encounters with Your Son, Jesus and is refreshing in this evil world. Bless those that bless, love, and accept others so freely. Help me in loving others in the same way. Take away my fears and help me trust others that need to be loved. In Jesus' name. Amen.

"Money is the root of all evil."

"You cannot serve God and money." Matthew 6:24

People are obsessed with fame and fortune. To an outsider visiting our planet, it wouldn't take long to realize that the human species wants money and to show it off to others more than anything else. Our T.V. highlights wealthy families living in English aristocracy, kings of Egypt, and even in modern times, such as, England's royal family, and the lifestyle of rich American housewives.

Usually with monetary titles you can buy nearly anything you want or need. However, money can't buy happiness. In difficult moments, it can be hard to smile and thrive when you feel inadequate, unloved, or unworthy. Since the beginning of time people have coveted gold and monetary treasures. They have crossed seas and slaughtered races for the opportunity to fill their pockets with gold. What if there was a kingdom that offered more than gold? God's Kingdom is labeled as "most high" and offers other treasures such as peace, joy, love, and goodness. You will not find those anywhere else. Everyone is invited to be part of this family. This means that on dark days when others tell you that you are not good enough − you are good enough because you have already been chosen. Remember also, that the way you exert your power and show grace is a reflection of God.

Prayer:

God, help me be love and grace in the same way that You have given those things to me. Silence my voice when I need to hear those that need to be heard and speak up when an issue needs action. Give me the wisdom I need in order to be a good example. In Jesus' name. Amen.

"It takes a village to raise a child."

"So then, it was not you who sent me here, but God. He made me father to Pharaoh, lord of his entire household and ruler of all Egypt." Genesis 45:8

I've always been a big believer in the saying "it takes a village to raise a child." Imagine my surprise when the whole world shut down for two years during the COVID pandemic. I didn't have a village to share parenting wisdom on topics like pregnancy and delivery. Community interaction has been limited. It also has broadened my respect for single parenting greatly, because not only did COVID limit their village, but they ARE the village.

No matter what you are going through, having a limited village is scary. Not only is a support system comforting while raising a child, but it is needed in all walks of life. In the Bible, Joseph (Coat of Many Colors) lost his "village" when his brothers sold him into slavery. He was later wrongly accused and put into jail where he waited for two years. He was finally brought to the King of Egypt, who loved him, saw his unique ability, and rewarded him greatly with endless resources. In Joseph's story, it took well over a decade for him to see the full-circle of God's plan. Living without any friends or family and put into prison, I am certain that he felt alone, betrayed, and forgotten at times. However, God is always with us and will bless his children in countless ways. Maybe it seems that you are without a village and without resources, but God has a plan to bless you.

Prayer:

God, comfort me during my most difficult times. Get me through the rough patch so that I might live to be witness to the blessing and glory of Your Kingdom. In Jesus' name. Amen.

"It's Greek to me."

"Either make the tree good and its fruit good, or make the tree bad and its fruit bad, for the tree is known by its fruit. I tell you, on the Day of Judgment people will give account for every careless word they speak, for by your words you will be justified, and by your words you will be condemned." Matthew 12:33; 36-37

It is so easy to have a misunderstanding with people. Communication is key and not everyone is good at it. According to the BBC (British Broadcasting Corporation,) women use an average of 20,000 words a day, while men only use 7,000. It can be argued that more words might help or hinder conversation. There is also the case of words that sound similarly. If you have a thick Southern accent like me, I am sure you have been asked more than once in your life if you said "Ranch or French" salad dressing, because southerners pronounce them similarly. A friend of mine named Lynn has her named frequently mistaken for "Lee Ann" because of her accent.

For those that speak a second language, most will agree that English is a difficult language to learn because of the different spellings and meanings of "won" and "one," "would" and "wood," "tire" (car) and tired. It is not just English that's difficult. I speak Spanish as a second language and have a difficult time pronouncing and remembering words like "cartera" (billfold) and "carretera" (highway). "Cabello" (hair) and "caballo" (horse) also sound similar. I have told many native Spanish-speakers, "I like your horse" more times than I would like to admit.

With all these communication blunders, it should come as no surprise that in the midst of conflict, tensions can rise quickly. People can feel angry, hostile, and afraid when there are important issues that need to be addressed. Additional stress factors like a bad health prognosis and financial issues make communication worse.

When is the last time someone spoke out of anger to you? Did you consider all of the factors that might be weighing on them in their life?

A person might also feel work-related stress and inadequate in some of the areas of their life. It doesn't make it "okay" when people snap or give sarcastic responses, but it is a big red flag that they are having communication issues, stress factors, and feel overwhelmed.

Instead of snapping back, take a step back. Give them space and let them know that they are being heard. People giving snappy answers is not a new thing. Jesus addressed them in Matthew 12:33; 36-37, "Either make the tree good and its fruit good, or make the tree bad and its fruit bad, for the tree is known by its fruit. I tell you, on the Day of Judgment people will give account for every careless word they speak, for by your words you will be justified, and by your words you will be condemned."

It is important, even when we feel overwhelmed, or when we think it is the other person's poor communication that has failed us, to go to them and try to reconvey the message with a humble heart. Even though we may have many differences and backgrounds, it will bless and strengthen the Kingdom to be in communion with others.

Prayer:

Dear God, help me when communicating and when interacting with people that are stressed out, aren't communicating, and possibly don't know the peace that You offer. Let my words, response, and actions in every situation be an example of Christian love so that others might know You. Use me, Lord. In Jesus' name. Amen.

"It will come back and haunt you."

"**Jesus answered him, "It is also written: 'Do not put the Lord your God to the test.'" Matthew 4:7**

A few years back, my family planned a trip to the beach. I was very excited to play with my niece and nephew on the beach; jumping waves and making sand castles. On the Friday before, I was finishing up a pottery piece I had been working on. It was (and is) the largest piece I've ever fired. I was inspired by nature, and I knew it was special from the beginning. Eventually, I left my ceramic piece to dry over the weekend as I loaded up the car and headed to the beach.

Our family time was everything I imagined it would be. However, while we were jumping waves, I had a horrible allergic reaction to something. My face and arms burned, and the salt water made the sting worse. Apologizing to my niece and nephew, I had to go inside and tried to wash off whatever it was that was causing me to suffer.

The allergic reaction continued and eventually, my mother asked, "you haven't been in any Poison Oak, have you?" I scoffed and laughed at the idea. She then asked if I had used real leaves for my ceramic pitcher – and I had. I had taken each leaf and pressed it into the clay and cut each leaf out, pressing it against the pitcher, playing in it for hours!

Sometimes in the midst of our carelessness, we suffer greatly for our actions. Sin is very similar in that it creeps up on you. It will make us suffer and it is our job to recognize it when we see it. Always be vigilant in guarding your heart, mind, and soul. What appears innocent may destroy.

Prayer:

Dear God, thank You for giving us the gift of the Holy Bible, so that we may know right from wrong. As we study it and put aside time to know You better, we ask that you place Christian people in our path to help equip and strengthen us. The devil is divisive. Help me to recognize him quickly so that I may live closer to You, unhindered, and unscathed. In Jesus' name. Amen.

"It is no use crying over spilt milk."

"The eye is the lamp of the body. If your eyes are healthy, your whole body will be full of light. But if your eyes are unhealthy, your whole body will be full of darkness. If then the light within you is darkness, how great is that darkness!" Matthew 6:22

One Thanksgiving, I made three dozen deviled eggs for our annual family gathering. I placed the egg container in an ice chest for traveling. When we arrived at my aunt's, I took the chest inside because I knew her refrigerator would already be full. An hour later when everyone was ready to eat, I opened the chest and two dozen of the eggs sat below ice water in a slushy, yellow mess! Someone has snuck into the ice chest to eat an egg and didn't put the lid back on securely!

We have all experienced some form of slushy deviled eggs in our life. When life throws us hard balls, we can't let it ruin the rest of our lives (or dinner in my case). You are still alive and how you respond to your bad situation affects your life. Me lamenting over the eggs in front of everyone, would have put a dent in the festivities of being "thankful." God has given each of us the choice of seeing the glass half empty or half full. God always restores everything that is lost.

What areas are you hurting from in your life and how will you respond to the Lord?

Prayer:

Oh God, I know that You love me, so I put my trust in You. Do with my life as You will, because I never had control of it to begin with. My eyes are on You because nothing else is constant. In Jesus' name. Amen.

"When it rains, it pours."

"Behold, I am doing a new thing; now it springs forth, do you not perceive it? I will make a way in the wilderness and rivers in the desert." Isaiah 43:19

The South during summertime is no joke! You better get ready to take at least two showers a day. One time on vacation, I thought I would be fancy by going inside of the hotel sauna. My first minute in there – NOPE! It feels exactly like summer in the South! Why would anyone want that?! I also can't imagine living in the 1800's with layers of fabric piled on over pantalets and a corset, without air-conditioning! Bless their hearts!

Life can feel like a ball gown during a southern July. We "feel in over our heads." When my daddy passed away, our family farm needed a caretaker. Even though people like to romanticize the idea of living on a farm, it is hard work! For a year, I fixed fences, cut the grass, threw hay bales, hammered ice in the water trough in 20-degree weather, herded cows when they "got out", pulled snakes out of the chicken coop - all while working a full-time job. It was exhausting! Even though we loved the farm, it became a burden and overwhelmed both us.

When life gets overwhelming and we think we aren't going to be able to handle the situation we are in, we should call on God. If you feel suffocated by a situation or like there is no way out of the current situation because "that's how things are now" – it is not true. No matter the situation or past, God offers a path to peace to His children that love him. God can make a way, out of no way! (I Corinthians 10:13; I Peter 5:7)

Prayer:

Dear Father, You know the difficulties I have and how I want to change. I need Your help. I commit my life and surrender to You. In Jesus' name. Amen.

"The longest journey starts with a single step."

"Follow God's example, therefore, as dearly loved children and walk in the way of love, just as Christ loved us and gave himself up for us as a fragrant offering and sacrifice to God." Ephesians 5:1

I tend to recall people according to things they have said to me. Some of my earliest remembrances is of my parents reinforcing, "Yes, you can do it" for things like learning to ride a bicycle. I remember my fifth grade science teacher, Sherry Cox explaining the importance of the forest and our class adopting an acre of the rain forest that year. When I was a teenager and having trouble with a classmate, my sister pointed out that "everyone wants to be liked," which helped me to see the classmate's point of view a little better and not dislike her as much. All of those statements had huge impacts on my life and the person I became. The words we say to people have power. They can build up or tear down. They can educate or ignite fear.

Palm Sunday was such a big movement in the Bible. It is Jesus taking His first steps towards His fate and future. What He would say and how He would respond was the most important part about Him.

Even though we are not Jesus, we are a reflection of Him. Our words are impactful and we might possibly say a phrase that someone remembers most about who we are.

Prayer:

Father, as we remember the profound impact the love and actions of Jesus had on people, we want to reflect that. Let us not live to please people, but instead seek whole-heartedly to reflect Your love and truth. In Jesus' name. Amen.

"Great minds think alike."

"I hope in the Lord Jesus to send Timothy to you soon, so that I too may be cheered by news of you. For I have no one like him, who will be genuinely concerned for your welfare. For they all seek their own interests, not those of Jesus Christ." Philippians 2:19-21

I've collected a wide variety of friends so far in life. I have lifelong friends that are punk-rockers, hippies, nurses, a mix of different ethnic groups, religious friends, history and art enthusiasts and home makers. If you know me and we are friends, you likely fit in one of those groups.

One of my friends that I met later in life, Joyanna, is one of my few writing friends. As an editor, she can read what I am trying to convey in my writing and make the best wording of it. Besides writing, she has a wide mix of other interests I similarly love, like meeting new people, God-searching, and other cultures. She is direct, honest, and I know she will follow-through on whatever she says. Perhaps one of my favorite things about her is she does not live according to what other people think is "cool." That was a difficult lesson for me to learn in life, so I feel very perceptive in finding people that are comfortable being themselves and solely living for God.

Who has God placed in your life? How would you describe them? What characteristics do they possess that make you a better person for knowing them?

Prayer:

God, with Thanksgiving in our hearts, we praise You for the friends You send that enrich our lives. Open our hearts to see life-changing attributes that we need to implement in our lives. In Jesus' name. Amen.

"Do not throw the baby out with the bathwater."

"Be alert and of sober mind. Your enemy the devil prowls around like a roaring lion looking for someone to devour." I Peter 5:8

Have you ever felt thrown away? More times than anyone would like to admit, people feel discarded when they aren't chosen for kickball in elementary school, their spouse leaves, or they lose a job. Feeling thrown away is a vulnerable, pivotal time in a person's life. No one seems to understand, and it is an emotion that only the person can address and deal with. In my own life, I have felt let down by people I trusted many times. It hurts. There is a mix of feelings such as disappointment and hurt.

In one of my favorite Christmas movies "It's a Wonderful Life," character, Bill Bailey gets to experience the world if he had never been born. His wife and mother were turned into cold, bitter people, his town was turned into a shameless town, and his beautiful children no longer existed. No one else in the world can be you. God created you for a reason. Looking down at our unique finger prints is a witness that God wants you to do things that no other person can do.

Frequently, the devil tells us lies to put us down. Perhaps you were "thrown out with the bathwater," but the world can always be changed, and for the better. God is counting on your determination to not give up.

Prayer:

God, May we be reminded that we are Your precious children. We declare that You are Lord and the truth will prevail. Be with me, Lord and keep me strong during the storm. In Jesus' name. Amen.

"Do not put too many irons in the fire."

"Behave wisely toward outsiders, making the best use of your time." Colossians 4:5

I once knew a woman that worked for a church. On Sunday mornings when people would stop to talk to her, she would stop and make time to talk to them. Even though she had 10 other things to do, she made sure the person that reached out knew that they had been heard and felt appreciated. Witnessing this is something that really changed my life. Up till then I always felt like rushing around for people was the best service and knowing her "stillness" changed my outlook on life.

Time is the most valuable thing on earth. People spend their entire life looking to become a millionaire, but time is far more valuable and many don't realize it until the end.

Since first meeting that woman some 14 years ago, I've noticed how other people spend their time is a direct reflection of their own inner peace and how they view others. Stopping to listen to people seems to be my favorite hallmark of my favorite people – because they are genuine and aren't driven by money. That is something rare and precious these days.

Use your time well, friends. Designating time for people is part of your Christian witness. If you have "too many irons in the fire" you will lose the window of time to share God with others.

Prayer:

Holy Spirit, quiet my soul in the midst of the world pulling on me. Silence the chaos and commotion around me so that I can listen to the needs and prayer requests of others and my own heart. May I use this inner-peace as a cornerstone to strengthen my relationship with God so that I can focus my attention on His will. In Jesus' name. Amen.

"To err is human, to forgive divine." – Alexander Pope

"Humble yourselves before the Lord, and he will lift you up." James 4:10

One of the most attractive qualities (in my opinion) is humility. It seems erroneous to ask the president or King of England to do anything lowly for me like washing my dishes or take out the trash; namely, because it is not likely to happen. However, Jesus knowing what was about to happen to him, sat on the floor and washed feet. He insisted.

I will never forget years ago on Maundy Thursday, my friend and former high school principal sat on the floor and washed my feet. I felt that she should not be washing my feet. She was elderly, cultured, admired by the community, educated and poised, and she held my huge, size 10 feet and bathed them. She held my feet in her hands with a smile full of love – that love left me speechless. It is that same love and humility that was abundant on the night Jesus washed the disciples' feet.

Jesus knew that one of the disciples was about to betray him and turn him in to the police. If you have ever been betrayed for any reason, you know that the first emotion you feel is anger – rage even. However, Jesus washed Judas' feet and had dinner with him. That is a love that is indescribable. It is only fair to say that it is the way that Jesus chose to love, because there is not an equivalent love standard. It is the kind of love story that last thousands of years, inspires, and gives hope.

In modern times some of the most common responses to Judas would have been, "don't ever call me again," but Jesus loved him wholeheartedly.

Prayer:

Dear Lord, Your love inspires us thousands of years later. You are the perfection of love divine! Forgive my trespassers as You have forgiven me. Soften my heart and let me look to bless my betrayers. In Jesus' name. Amen.

"The darkest hour is just before the dawn."

"From noon until three in the afternoon darkness came over all the land. About three in the afternoon Jesus cried out in a loud voice, *'Eli, Eli, lema sabachthani?'* (which means "My God, my God, why have you forsaken me?" Matthew 27:45-46

Years ago, I visited a Holocaust concentration camp in Czechia. One of the most horrible places of the camp was the isolation room. Even though I visited the museum nearly 70 years after prisoners were liberated and am of sound body and mind, the darkness of the isolation room would easily make the strongest person plead for someone to open the door. I can only describe it as the most pitch black of black and was so dark that for a moment I questioned if my eyes were open or closed, which made me stretch my eyes open wider trying to make out some distinction. It is easy to see how someone could lose hope in a place like that, but surprisingly hope is the very thing that kept many people alive. Survivors had hope that eventually a new day would come and the sun would eventually shine again.

During the crucifixion, Jesus experienced darkness. He dealt with accusations, shame, and physical abuse. However, God always has a rewarding ending and did not fail when it came to Jesus; creating Eternal Life for us all! There is new life at the end of every dark tunnel. Sometimes it can be so dark that you can't imagine finding your way out. Hold on because the dawn is on its way.

Prayer:

God, thank You for the new life that You give even when we think everything is over. Be with those that are afraid and unjustly suffering. Bring swift justice to the victims. Set glimmers of hope in our path to encourage us. In Jesus' name. Amen.

"Shrouds have no pockets."

"Do not store up riches for yourselves here on earth, where moths and rust destroy, and robbers break in and steal. Instead, store up riches for yourselves in heaven, where moths and rust cannot destroy, and robbers cannot break in and steal. For your heart will always be where your riches are." Matthew 6:19-21

When my father passed away, there were areas of my parents' house that were left untouched that served as a way to emotionally hang on to him longer. His workshop still had notes on the counter. The stereo was still dialed in to his favorite station. In his closet, all of his clothes hung perfectly as they had before his death. However, when my mother decided to sell her home, we both decided it was time to clean. I would hold something up and within 4 seconds it had to be "love it" or "donate." What took a lifetime for him to collect, took about a day to go through. During that sorting, I realized that there were many things that my Dad held onto for a "rainy day." In his closet were 10 pairs of brand new shoes that had never been worn, and gadgets that had never been out of the box. He would frequently say, "I am saving that for when I need it."

In Luke 18, Jesus told the rich ruler to sell all of his riches and give them to the poor. We should do the same within our own lives. You won't be taking anything physically to Heaven. What do you need to let go of today in order to live closer to God?

Prayer:

God, may I be unhindered by worldly possessions and money. Give me opportunities to see the people I can help, that more people might be blessed in Your Name. In Jesus' name. Amen.

"Love will find a way."

I give them eternal life, and they shall never perish; no one will snatch them out of my hand. John 10:28

Easter always marks the season for spring flowers, Easter lilies, open-toe shoes and wearing white! It seems like the yearly calendar would have been better placed with spring starting the year and ending at bitter winter. Fresh to old seems to be the natural progression of life. However, fresh, warm days are not how the greatest story ever told played out. Jesus suffered a brutal death. He was spit on and made fun of. He was stripped naked. His death was in agony, full of tears and lacking mercy. Especially after seeing the sky turn dark and the temple curtain torn in two, those days, full of mourners must have felt like they were living in the darkest of times. When Jesus Christ rose again what a joyous time that must have been; unbelievable for most! When I think of my deceased friends or family – what would I have thought only a few days later to see them again!?

What joy! Jesus' resurrection gives that hopeful joy to everyone. Whatever pain, suffering, torment, or sin that ails you, you can be relieved by the hopeful joy that Jesus gave.

Christ is Risen!

Prayer:

Resurrected Christ, all honor and glory is Yours! Praise God for the hope and life You bring to the masses. Forgive me, wash me clean, and claim me, Lord! In Jesus' name. Amen.

"Barking dogs seldom bite."

"By this we know love, that he laid down his life for us, and we ought to lay down our lives for the brothers. But if anyone has the world's goods and sees his brother in need, yet closes his heart against him, how does God's love abide in him?" I John 3:16-17

As I write this devotional, my precious dog, Dan, turns 15. He initially wandered up on someone's porch as a puppy. I felt so bad for him that they weren't watering or feeding him because "if you feed them, they'll never leave," so I took him! Needless to say, over 15 years, we have become the greatest of friends. As a puppy, I cuddled him. He helped me when I grieved over the passing of my father, broken relationships, listened when I voiced how frustrated I was with others; he is a "good boy." Over that time, we have moved three times. He has witnessed four presidents take office. He also witnessed the meeting of my future husband, our marriage, and the introduction of our newest addition to the pack, our son. However, in his old age, he has also decided that he hates everyone, including my husband. Every evening when my husband comes home from work and pulls into the driveway, Dan runs to bark and alert me that an "intruder" is here. Nothing seems to break Dan from the feeling that my husband is an outsider. However, when my husband goes into the backyard, Dan doesn't say anything.

My husband equally makes negative remarks when he is near Dan, like "is it not about time to eat, Dan?" They continuously jab at one another. A few times when I have been away from home, I have worried about them being together, but my husband always looks after Dan, feeds him, and so far, the dog hasn't bitten him. They have made a relationship out of their mistrust for one another. Even though I know Dan is not cuddling with him, I know he is still looking after the house and accepting his treats. They work together for the sake of our home, to protect it, and make it stronger.

In the same way, people are also very different. I can count on all fingers and toes the people that make me "nuts!" There are some that are too outspoken and some that don't speak up enough. Some are selfish and greedy and some don't take what they need to save themselves. As individuals, we are all unique pieces of work – puzzle pieces, even! Like puzzle pieces, we don't fit together well with other pieces, but we are all still needed to make the puzzle work.

God requires that we love and look out for each other. In Jesus' request to "feed my sheep" and to "clothe and feed" those in need, He didn't stipulate that our help be to those we "like." We are all meant to work together and sometimes it will look like a strange relationship, like the matching of the dog and my husband working together. To whom much is given, much is required and that includes putting our "bite" aside sometimes.

Prayer:

Father God, silence my hatred and dislike, so that I may love people fully in the same way that You do. In Jesus' name. Amen.

"Little pitchers have big ears."

"If anyone causes one of these little ones—those who believe in me—to stumble, it would be better for them to have a large millstone hung around their neck and to be drowned in the depths of the sea." Matthew 18:6

As a child, I remember giving my mother collections of flowers, rocks, and leaves because I could see how they were all beautiful and different, like pieces of art. When my own son was about six months, he loved seeing people wear printed shirts. Every time he saw a design, even if it was on his bedding, he would reach out and try to grasp the design in his hand thinking it was 4-dimensional. I am sure it was a disappointment.

The world is not always as beautiful as it first appears. Some things are inevitable for our children to be exposed to (I'm not looking forward to explaining world issues to my own son.

God, our Heavenly Father, always offers refuge to whatever we are going through. He created us to be the beautiful sensitive child that we are, who appreciates the beauty of the world but feels disappointment when the world hurts or ignores us. God cares. He is always there to listen and guide us.

Prayer:

Father, thank You for loving us. Protect and guide us in this evil world. In Jesus' name. Amen.

"You can't win them all."

"Therefore, if anyone is in Christ, the new creation has come: The old has gone, the new is here!" 2 Corinthians 5:17

When we put our "all" into a project or relationship it can feel devastating that "our best wasn't good enough." It feels like the end of the world, or the world as we know it. In those difficult moments one huge advantage that we have on our side is history. Looking back in history we can see that God uses everything, eventually for His advantage. Even the downfall of some of the most impressive empires like Rome or Ancient Egypt, liberated thousands of people, although I imagine the first few years after those events were difficult for everyone involved because they were learning a new way of life.

When change is involved it hurts, but eventually the clouds clear and a better opportunity arises. Letting go of the past can be difficult and you might even grieve your old lifestyle. There are countless accounts in scripture attesting to change and how difficult it was, (see Adam & Eve, Moses, Noah, Job, Daniel, David, Saul, practically everyone, and most especially Jesus).

As many tribulations as the Bible accounts for there are also as many verses letting you know that things will turn out okay in the end.

"Jesus Christ is the same yesterday, today, and forever." Hebrews 13:8

"Don't worry about anything, and in all your prayers ask God for what you need, always asking him with a thankful heart." Philippians 4:6

God knows what you are going through but will see you through the storm to a better future.

Prayer:

Dear God, thank You for always sticking with me in dark times. You know the details of my life. I trust You to make something beautiful out of my current circumstance. In Jesus' name. Amen.

"Tis better to have loved and lost than never to have loved at all." – Alfred Lord Tennyson

"From that time on Jesus began to preach, 'Repent, for the kingdom of heaven has come near." Matthew 4:17

Everyone grieves differently. Jesus, upon hearing of His cousin, John's beheading, left town, and went to live in another area to spread the message that "the Kingdom of Heaven is coming near." It was there in the town of Galilee, that He began forming His group of disciples.

John's death hurt and bothered Jesus as He obviously loved him. He had just baptized Jesus. (I remember my own baptism as one of the most holy moments in my life where the presence of the Holy Spirit surrounded us and could be clearly felt. The love was palpable.) Yet in Jesus' hurt and bereavement, He sought to spread the Gospel and complete the prophesy.

From my own experience, any time I have lost someone I love, I want to hide away from the world. It is healthy to change your surroundings if you feel like a blank slate will help, but it's important not to lose focus of continuing the Christian mission of spreading the Gospel. Jesus picked up where John the Baptist left off, telling everyone to "repent, Heaven comes," which is a task for every Christian, even in the midst of turmoil.

Prayer:

Dear Heavenly Father, thank You for the blessing and gift of baptism. We ask you to help us remember our own baptism or to seek out being born again. Help us during our difficult times of grieving. Heal our hearts through doing your work on Earth so that Your kingdom may be glorified. In Jesus' name. Amen.

"Uneasy lies the head that wears a crown."

"To whom much is given, much will be required." Luke 12:48

In my small community, we once had a beloved man that was mayor of the city for 30 years. He was a calm, level-headed man that was easy to like. As a young child, I remember telling him that one day I would be mayor when he retired, and he said, "well you better get ready for people to call you at all hours of the night and tell you their problems." Even though I think of myself as sympathetic to people's needs, those words really stuck with me that people must call him all during the night when water lines break or for other important issues. After he said that, I took particular notice in my life of watching celebrities who really needed a break from the limelight and unfairly blamed leaders who even went to prison as scapegoats. In some countries, rulers have even been put to death by the people.

However, in every station in life is the opportunity to change the world. We have each been given a set of cards to play in life. In all opportunities there will be difficult times. Being a manager over anything requires consideration and deliberation. In the Parable of the Talents (Matthew 25:14-30) when a group of people received different amounts of money, one person invested their money, while another one dug a hole in the ground and buried his money. How we use our resources and manage our blessings will directly influence the blessings to come.

Prayer:

God, thank You for life's many opportunities. Help me know how to select wisely and manage my affairs according to Your will. Let me always seek Your face when I have a difficult decision to make. In Jesus' name. Amen.

"Do not cross the bridge till you come to it."

"Delight yourself in the LORD,
and he will give you the desires of your heart.
Commit your way to the LORD;
trust in him, and he will act." Psalm 37:4-5

As someone who enjoys planning, I also enjoy planning my life (or trying to). When I was a teenager, there was a certain time that I hoped to finish school by, be married, reach certain levels in my career and savings, a time for children, purchasing a home, and the list goes on. However, life doesn't usually work that way. Even when some of these milestones come to fruition it can be devastating when things don't happen the way you would like them to. At certain periods during my life, having realized that I had not achieved my ideal milestone, it became depressing and at times even made me resentful of others that seemingly did not deserve it. The devil can be cunning in knowing what you desire and will turn your heart against the people around you.

In time, God will reveal life's path to you. The path may not be exactly the plans that you planned for yourself, but the ending result is always a prosperous and positive one. He will fill your cup until it pours over. He will always give you your daily bread. Until then, continue to pray in submission and obedience asking God for what you desire and that His will be done.

Prayer:

God, Forgive me of my resentment towards others. Help me to always trust Your perfect plan and look for the path that You set my feet. You know my heart in asking to fulfill my dreams. I trust You in steering my future and will go where You send me. In Jesus' name. Amen.

"Do not put off until tomorrow what you can do today."

"Be careful how you live. Do not be unwise but wise, making the best use of your time because the times are evil. Therefore, do not be foolish, but understand what the Lord's will is." Ephesians 5:15-17

Growing up, our home was in the middle of a hay field. My father took immaculate care of the field year-round, digging up any weeds, cleaning trash that found its way into the field (namely balloons that people release), and fertilizing it. A couple of times a year the hay was cut, and it was sold to people that had show horses. It was beautiful, quality hay. That might sound a little crazy to most people, but if you have ever spent any time on a farm with livestock, you know there is high-nutrient light green hay, and then there is awful, worthless brown dust that people pass off as "hay."

When it was time to cut the Bermuda grass, commercial tractors would let it sit out a day to dry. Giving the hay time to dry out keeps moisture from being trapped in the center of the bail. The next day someone would come with a giant rake and fluff the hay up in long rows for the bailer to pick up. At any point if it rains, it risks ruining the drying process because of the moisture. It is essential not to procrastinate.

The entire process is beautiful to watch and has been a reflection of Christian living in my life. Living a good, clean life is essential to making a good product and any variation in the process is dangerous. However, most things that are worthwhile in life don't come easy. Bailing hay is a week-long process, but preparing the fields is a year-long commitment. I remember when our cows got out into the hay fields; we had to herd them by foot, instead of using a four-wheeler so the tires wouldn't tread on the grass. Herding cows by foot across 60 acres at 6 a.m. leaves your shoes and socks soaking wet from the morning dew. All of that might seem excessive, but the ending result was excellence, and our hay was the "cash cow" that was sold to high-end show horses.

Living a Christian life sometimes requires difficult decisions in order to keep living and growing in the right direction, but the ending result is beautiful. Others in the community that are non-church going see how fruitful your life is. If you are mixing in poison and "bad seeds" it is much less appealing.

Prayer:

Dear Father, May we keep our eyes on you in our secular world. How we respond to secular music lyrics, an invitation to adultery, or when someone personally attacks us, speaks to how fruitful our Christian life is. Help us, Lord. Help us respond in a way that glorifies You. In Jesus' name. Amen.

"Cleanliness is next to godliness."

"Commit thy works unto the Lord, and thy thoughts shall be established." Proverbs 16:3

The warmth of every spring wouldn't be official without spring cleaning. A while back, I caught on to a popular trend of setting a timer to clean. If you set the timer to clean the bedroom for 10 minutes, then it becomes a race. You move quicker and are more productive. Of course, you can't clean the house in 10 minutes but if you designate 30 minutes a day to three rooms of your home, the changes are drastically improved and noticeable. I also find that if I am almost finished cleaning a room at the 10 minute mark, I will actually work 12-13 minutes to go ahead and finish the task so that it is done properly.

I am easily distracted. So I set a timer and devote that time to "devotion time" as well. Having my devotion outside with the sunrise means that I will probably bird watch and watch the sun rise, instead of reading a devotion, which is why I consistently need to set that time aside (literally).

In the same way that spring cleaning (and cleaning in general) keeps my life clean, organized, and with minimal drama and stress – reading my daily devotion keeps my emotional and spiritual well-being clean, organized, and minimizes drama and stress too.

Prayer:

Dear Heavenly Father, thank You for your blessings today. Lord, I pray for help with my time. Send me things You want me to learn so that I may spiritually grow and be prepared for what life has in store for me. I want to "spring clean my life" so that I can communicate easier with You. Anoint this designated time daily so that I may know Your will. In Jesus' name. Amen.

"Better late than never."

"I discipline my body and keep it under control, lest after preaching to others I myself should be disqualified." 1 Corinthians 9:27

Remember when your mother asked you to clean your room? I hated cleaning my room and would wait until she was mad about it, told my father, and he gave me the afternoon to clean it, or he would "clean it for me" which meant throwing it all away. Sin is made up of from the same fabric of my childhood – procrastination. I've known people that have smoked and drank promising to "stop tomorrow"; end a relationship after one more promiscuous, sexual encounter, and (applicable to my own life) "start my diet next week" after I eat all of this delicious food!

Self-discipline is not fun and always sounds better when started later. However, that is just one more chunk of sin tacked onto my back (and yours). Sin stacks up around our life to a point where we can't see over the top of the pile. It is better to attack it aggressively. Why has bleach, been such a beloved cleaning product for hundreds of years? Because it attacks and cleans without hesitation, making things "white as snow." No one ever asks for a weak or procrastinated cleaning product, because it is not the best.

God is not looking for perfection. He is looking for hard-work, passion, and dedication.

Prayer:

God, thank You for giving us free-will. Forgive us for our lazy behavior and sin. Help us clean our lives. Help us weed out evil as we claim strength, honor, and glory. In Jesus' name, Amen.

"Once bitten, twice shy."

"Bear with each other and forgive one another if any of you has a grievance against someone. Forgive as the Lord forgave you." Colossians 3:13

We have all had our run-in with something bad that happened. You might have fallen off a ladder and injured your arm decades ago and no longer climb ladders. Growing up on a farm, I slid under (and hopped over) many hot-wires. If you have ever been popped by one, it is an experience you'll never forget and has made me cautious of them for life. As adults, we have all kinds of encounters where "we put our foot down" and say that we will never shop at that store or eat at that restaurant ever again. That attitude also relates to other people. We might never want to go on another date with someone or to spend time with them again.

I am always surprised when visiting favorite hang-out spots from my childhood that some change so much that I do not recognize them. Everything in life is like that. I look back in my own life and think about all of the different phases that I have been through. We too, are always evolving. Someone that met me 20 years ago that didn't like me, might be pleasantly surprised today.

It's so easy to get in a tiff about name-calling or a political opinion, especially these days. God's memory is infinite. Do you think he is holding on to a tiff from five years ago or even yesterday? No, of course not! God requires that we forgive one another and move on just as He forgave us. People change and deserve forgiveness. Using the power of forgiveness is accepting the gracious gift of Jesus Christ's life on the cross.

Prayer:

Jesus, thank You for the sacrifice of Your blood for my offenses. Forgive me for holding on to the sins of yesterday and the past. I ask You to forgive the person that offended and hurt me. I forgive them. May You bless their life. Thank You for Your infinite love that never fails. In Jesus' name. Amen.

"Idle hands are the devil's playground."

"Every good and perfect gift is from above, coming down from the Father of the heavenly lights, who does not change like shifting shadows." James 1:17

Whoever originally came up with the saying "Idle hands are the devil's playground" never had a magnolia tree. There are few trees, shrubs or bushes that litter the yard year-round like a magnolia. My husband, who loves to keep the yard spotless, spends half of his free time bagging up the leaves. We use an average of 20 industrial sized garbage bags for the leaves every year. He eventually started raking the 10-foot leaf piles onto a giant tarp and pulling the tarp into the forest behind our house.

The tree was planted in the 1960's by my grandparents and has grown into a 60-foot tower that is 50 feet wide and dumps a truck load of leaves in the yard every week! I once mentioned to a group of friends that I would like to have it cut and was met with a mob of defense about how it is the most beautiful tree and a symbol of Southern culture. To date, we haven't had it cut yet, mainly because "it costs an arm and a leg" to have trees cut. However, the tree is "growing" on me. Even though it has been in the front yard all of my life, and I played on the branches when I was a little girl, I only recently smelled its flowers. The blossoms, which are nearly a foot wide, aren't easy to get to, but if you are fortunate enough to be able to reach one, the aroma is Heaven-sent! Whoever said, "stop and smell the roses" apparently never smelled magnolias, because the aroma with the flower display is unmatched. The blossoms also make for beautiful, stately flower arrangements. My tree only blooms in summer and autumn but in the winter, I find myself now making arrangements with the oversized leaves at Christmas time. This past Christmas I made an arrangement of cedar and magnolia branches around our mailbox with a red velveteen ribbon. There are few plants that stay green year-round, but the magnolia is always there. In the spring, we use the magnolia leaves dumped into the forest as an enormous compost pile for our garden. The magnolia is always causing a mess in the front yard, but giving everything she has.

My new found love for the tree has caused me to reflect on all of the things, events, and people in my life that I have not appreciated. We all consider certain people or things to be making a mess or driving us insane! Certain events can also test our limits. Not being able to cut down the tree immediately and having to live with it forced me to look for its good qualities and uses; everything and everyone has them if we are honest. All good things are from God and the tree is certainly a creation of His. Blessings are not always obvious.

Prayer:

Dear God, thank You for your creations! Life is always interesting and Your endless wonders always give us something new to discover and consider. Thank You for blessing us with things and people that help our lives, even if we might not always realize or appreciate it. Help us see the beauty in everything You have made. In Jesus' name. Amen.

"Every dog has his day."

"Remember not the former things, nor consider the things of old. Behold, I am doing a new thing; now it springs forth, do you not perceive it? I will make a way in the wilderness and rivers in the desert." Isaiah 43:18-19

About a year ago, a local rescue took in a beaten down, Beagle-mix named "Layla." She was horrified of people, refused to play, or even come out of her dog house. My friend, Cherie would periodically send me photos of Layla's rehabilitation with captions such as "she will allow us to pet her only when she is in her dog house." After many months, Layla eventually began to relax and enjoy life (possibly for the first time ever).

If there has been a traumatic event or abus in your life you can identify with Layla. Through finding love, Layla began to heal and it restored her life. I'm sure at one point she thought her abuse was a lifelong reality, but I can happily share that Layla is happy with a family now that loves her.

If you are currently living through an earthly hell – that does not have to be a lifelong reality for you. Being a Christian, which requires forgiveness, does not equate to being forced to live in an abusive relationship. God loves you and has a new plan. There are loving people that will love and support you. God can drive out the darkness.

Prayer:

Father, Give those hurting strength to see them through the battle. Help them make a plan to get to a safe place. Blanket them with your protection and love. In Jesus' name. Amen.

National Domestic Violence Hotline 1–800–799–SAFE(7233)

"Born with a silver spoon in their mouth."

"Your faithful love is priceless, God! Humanity finds refuge in the shadow of your wings." Psalm 36:7

"Having a silver spoon" in one's mouth has always baffled me. Silver has always been relatively cheap in my lifetime. The popularity of having true silverware has faded over time and these days people sell it at yard sales to make wind chimes and bend spoons to make bracelets. It is not exactly prized as it once was. It seems most everything loses its value over time – food, silk, pottery, Beanie Babies © anyone? People have lost their homes and lifestyles according to the world's varying worth.

One thing is always true and constant – the love of Jesus Christ. It may sound cliché to tell someone "Jesus loves you" but people need to hear it now more than ever. Life gives us whirlwinds with unstable economies, people lose their home, job, and children. People feel like they are at the end of a rope.

The real value to share with others is the love and hope of Jesus. Even though you know that family members already love you, it feels good to hear them "I love you." I ask my husband nearly every day if he knows how much I love him, because I want him to unquestionably know it. Likewise, even though many people have grown up singing "Jesus loves me," tell someone that Jesus loves them and affirm their belief. It is worth more than a silver spoon or "all the tea in China."

Prayer:

God, though I may lose everything worldly, I know that You are always with me and love me. May the message of Your love spread like wildfire so that the hopeless may once again feel alive and loved. May I share Your message of love with everyone. In Jesus' name. Amen.

"Better safe than sorry."

"Ship your grain across the sea; after many days you may receive a return. Invest in seven ventures, yes, in eight; you do not know what disaster may come upon the land." Ecclesiastes 11: 1-2

Last year, my husband decided that he would singlehandedly cut down 90-foot trees around our home. Seeing the trees cut was bittersweet. We love nature, but we also love our home. All it takes is one tornado to snap a tree branch, and our home would be gone with the wind. He managed to cut them all successfully but asked for my help with one. He connected chains to persuade it to fall away from the house. He also asked me to come and pull a strap and manipulate the direction when it began to fall. I told him that it seemed unlikely that I could change its direction considering how much it weighed, but would do my best. When the tree made a "CRACK" sound and began to fall, I pulled the strap with all my might. A huge limb started to fall down on the house, and scathed the corner of my porch; enough to knock a single shingle loose.

The Parable of the Talents is a great testament to take a chance on wise investments. The Lord will say to you, "Well done, good and faithful servant; thou hast been faithful over a few things, I will make thee ruler over many things: enter thou into the joy of thy lord." (Matthew 25:23) My small persuasive weight with the tree likely made the difference. It is not in my nature to take chances but not taking chances on God's opportunity might make you "miss the boat." Be prayerful in your decisions.

Prayer:

God, help me be aware of good investments and to use what You give wisely. In Jesus' name. Amen.

APRIL 15

"Money does not grow on trees."

"All these blessings shall come upon you and overtake you, if you obey the voice of the Lord your God." Deuteronomy 28:2

My late father was keen on the belief that if you want something you have to work for it. He saved nearly everything he earned and didn't spend money freely. He also particularly loved to see state prisoners outdoors working. He said that they were working and contributing to society, instead of being "holed up, watching T.V. and feeding off of tax payers." He also loved working outdoors, himself and thought it was good for mental health to be outside. For those reasons, any time we were driving alongside the interstate and saw a caution sign that said "State Prisoners Working Ahead" he would take up a quick collection of one-dollar bills and as we were passing them throw the handful of cash out of the window.

Although money doesn't grow on trees, we are all pleasantly surprised when a free blessing comes along. It is unexpected, and we don't deserve it–that's the reason it is so joyful and welcomed.

God's gift of eternal life is also an unexpected blessing. Just like the prisoners didn't have to pick up the money, it is choice when choosing to accept Christ as your Savior. Jesus Loves You!

Choose joy! Choose Jesus!

Prayer:

God, thank You for the fount of Your blessings! I accept You as my only Lord, and Savior. Be with me every day in everything and light up my path. In Jesus' name. Amen.

"While there is life there is hope."

"If you, then, though you are evil, know how to give good gifts to your children, how much more will your Father in heaven give good gifts to those who ask him!" Matthew 7:11

Several years ago, when I pulled up in the parking lot at my job, I was walking from the car to the business entrance and heard a child scream. It was alarming, but when I looked around I didn't see anyone. "AHHHH!" I heard it again, and was surprised to look up and see that it was coming from a bird on the power line. I thought it was funny, and said "AHHH" back to him. After that day, the starling started making daily appearances and we spoke to each other daily. He became very special to me. For the next year, he met me every day and became a symbol of hope and joy. When I left that job, I missed seeing him but was relieved to see other starlings in nature as a reminder that God has blessed the world with His creations. God's beauty and joy is not limited to one place. Last autumn, I was blessed during my afternoon walk, to be caught up in a chorus of starlings in a tree and felt enraptured by the Holy Spirit.

How much God must love us to put such joyful creatures here on earth! While the world is full of sin and misery, there is always the opportunity to choose and see the goodness in the world. Hope is alive and God gives us glimpses every day of the goodness that still surrounds us. It is up to us to see it and thank Him for it. All of the good things in our life are from God.

Prayer:

God, thank You for the beauty of the Earth. How loving You are to show us these things daily. Thank you, God. Amen.

"When in Rome, do as the Romans do." -St. Ambrose 347 AD

"God made the four young men smart and wise. They read a lot of books and became well educated. Daniel could also tell the meaning of dreams and visions." Daniel 1:17

It can feel impossible sometimes to be noticed for a promotion when surrounded by other people that seem more talented, prettier, and wealthier. Although they do quickly gain attention, God makes a distinction in the personality of Daniel that he was a Godly man, as well as, "healthy, handsome, smart, wise, educated, and fit to serve in the royal palace and taught how to speak and write the language of Babylon." (Daniel 1:4)

It's important to live accordingly to surrounding peers while maintaining a Godly life. Daniel was a loyal servant to the king, while remaining true to God. He never accepted the food or wine from the king of Babylon because he only wanted to eat and drink foods that were acceptable according to God. Because of his loyalty, God blessed him with wisdom.

Our culture is obsessed with gaining popularity to the point where we look like clowns, stuffing our bras with socks, making fun of other people to seem funny, and spending so much money that we lose everything we have. Keeping our eyes on God not only forms a well-respected lifestyle, but it also levels us and keeps us sane. Because of Daniel's loyalty to God, God blessed Daniel and made him more appealing to others.

Prayer:

God, forgive me for the times where I have lost sight of staying true to You. Help me connect with others that I would not usually associate with and to "do right by them" while also maintaining a life that is pleasing to You. In Jesus' name. Amen.

"Let bygones be bygones."

"In your anger do not sin: Do not let the sun go down while you are still angry." Ephesians 4:26

A few months after my husband and I were married, we had our first argument. He moves "like a bull in a china shop" and broke one of my cups that I had out on the dining table to clean. He immediately asked why I had such a delicate thing out on the table and in his rebuttaled anger, shoved a box across the dining table toward me. The box left a foot-long scratch mark on the wooden surface of the dining table (which I also love) which resulted in an even angrier version our argument. I remember telling him that the scratch would always be a reminder in history to "his ugly attitude." That has been the ugliest exchange that we have ever had with one another. At the end of the brawl, we both sat down and discussed why it happened the way it did, how it made us feel, and how we could have handled it better.

Over the years, the scratch on the table has changed into something different than what I first thought it would. At first it symbolized ugliness, hatred, inconsideration and a lack of self-control but over time, the more I reflect it means endurance, forgiveness, and ultimately – love. Lovers are often depicted on greeting cards as a beautiful couple embracing in a hug or kiss, but love is something much more complex. If you can prayerfully stick together, the most beautiful thing will emerge – a better version of yourselves.

Love, of course is not specific to couples.The way you interact in a customer service position is a form of love. The way you interact with your neighbor is a form of love – and they all require work, seeking forgiveness, and patience at times. Some situations seem impossible, but with God nothing is impossible.

Prayer:

Heavenly Father, thank You for turning the "scratches" in our life into something new and beautiful. Help us love and forgive one another in the same way You forgive us. Give us the right words and actions when we need them most. In Jesus' name. Amen.

"Kill two birds with one stone."

"Don't withhold good from someone who deserves it, when it is in your power to do so." Proverbs 3:27

I love when I cook something, and it is meant for two different meals. When I bake a ham, I am freezing that gorgeous bone for when I make dried limas or pinto beans. When I boil a chicken to make enchiladas, I am also freezing that broth to make tamales later. "Killing two birds with one stone" makes me feel like a winner!

Likewise, I appreciate when I am in public for people to be efficient. Time is precious here on earth. The world revolves around it (literally) and because people are so obsessed with making the most of their time, technology has evolved us into a multi-tasking addition. If you've ever needed someone to talk to and they kept checking their smart watch or phone, you understand.

In order to really show love to someone, share the message of God and be a friend you have to be 100% present with them. Even though I love to multi-task, it is not possible for me to make the dried limas and the baked ham at the same time. Making a good ending result takes time and has a certain process, as does being a good disciple and friend to someone in need. I'm so thankful Jesus didn't teach the parables while looking at His phone, otherwise the disciples wouldn't have thought He was serious. Putting time aside for someone is a rare thing by today's standards. It allows a person to know they are loved.

Prayer:

God, help me be intentional when listening to others when they need a shoulder to lean on. God, anoint my time to be used for You. In Jesus' name. Amen.

"Don't keep all of your eggs in one basket."

"I will instruct thee and teach thee in the way which thou shalt go: I will guide thee with mine eye."
Psalm 32:8

Over the years, I have seen several friends move away from my hometown. It hurts that they wanted to be somewhere else. While it does make me sad sometimes that I no longer see them regularly, God provides new friends for us to connect with. Having my friends live in other cities reminds me of the life of Jesus. He was always on the move, traveling town to town to teach about God's love. If Jesus went to my high school, he would have surely moved away by now. Moving and sharing God's message was a fundamental part of the Bible. If Jesus and His disciples had never moved, Christianity would have likely stayed in their hometown.

God creates a different life and path for each of us. We aren't all meant to move around but for some, there is an unexplainable desire to live in another area. We all have a different life to fulfill whether that be the teacher, student, mother, child, CEO or janitor. Sometimes it is difficult to understand why certain people are the way they are. They act and respond differently to situations, but be assured that if they are living with God that He has a different plan for them that they are following. Sometimes diversity is not being obtuse, it is just following your calling from The Great I Am.

Prayer:

Dear Father, thank You for the people that you place in my life. Watch over them and bless them, even the ones far away. Guide their footsteps on the unknown path. In Jesus' name. Amen.

APRIL 21

"Beauty is only skin deep."

"What matters is not your outer appearance — the styling of your hair, the jewelry you wear, the cut of your clothes — but your inner disposition. Cultivate inner beauty, the gentle, gracious kind that God delights in." 1 Peter 3:3-4

Growing up, our family dog, "Brownie" had one eye. Brownie was a great dog. She protected me once against a pack of wild dogs, escorted me to the creek daily, barked if any stranger came near, and listened to countless hours of my heart-wrenching testimonies during Junior High School. She had beautiful chocolate fur and big fat paws that had fine, silky hair between her toes. In a way, I feel that I was partly raised by her because I knew her heart and she knew mine. I loved her and no physical difference ever mattered.

God creates unconditional love so that we can experience connections without walls. For many people when they saw Brownie, they only saw her for her missing eye. For many dogs that saw a 10-year-old girl crying about "the cool girls", they probably thought they should steer clear of me. God connected the two of us and creates bonds and beauty with love.

For everything that you dislike about your body or someone else's, God has a window of opportunity that can be filled with love. You just have to accept it.

Prayer:

God, May I see and know love with my eyes closed so that I don't become confused with what popular culture tells us. Help us to truly love others in the same way You love and accept us. In Jesus' name. Amen.

"Don't count your chickens before they hatch."

"Two are better than one, because they have a good reward for their toil." Ecclesiastes 4:9

I love to make lists. It might seem petty, but I also expect others to keep basic order in their life by having a calendar– but not everyone does! On several occasions, I have known people who seemed successful and well-liked, but every time I called them or needed something from them they almost never returned my call to the point where I decided that they didn't like me. I filed them under "unproductive" and "disorganized."

However, I once heard one of them be spontaneously asked to speak at a church organization and give a sermon. He was only given about a four-minute time to collect his thoughts. During that time, I would have been a nervous wreck trying to think of something important enough to say, but he jumped on the platform and gave a deep, meaningful message. Where God may not have blessed him with the ability to plan and organize, He instead, gave him the gift of spontaneity. Those two gifts are in direct contrast to one another and where God needs some of us to plan, he also needs some of us to "go with the flow." My ability can be helpful, but life can change and God can change our course in a quick second. We are all created perfectly according to God's own hand. Instead of always racing to the finish line of our calendar, it is more important to race to God and seek His will and approval.

Prayer:

Father, May we center our time with You, that above our busy schedule we are obedient to your plan. Help us always see the blessings in people, including those that are different than us. In Jesus' name. Amen.

"By the skin of your teeth"

"Therefore, if anyone is in Christ, he is a new creation. The old has passed away; behold, the new has come." II Corinthians 5:17

It is heart-sinking when you fail at something you are trying to achieve. In the moment it feels like a turn of devastation, leaving you lost and not knowing what direction to take.

After I graduated high school, my first career choice was to become a nurse. At college, I met wonder people and friends for life. However, in my last year of school, I had feelings of uncertainty that made me question my role as a future nurse. During one of my clinicals, we had a patient come into the ER that was coding. Unfortunately, his veins were collapsing and they were not able to save him. Watching his family arrive and the mourning that unfolded is something I will never forget. I had also recently lost my father to cancer, and "nursing" started to sound like a call to death. I flunked out my last semester, and felt lost at a crossroads. I felt disappointed in myself that I was not motivated to finish something I worked so hard on.

The great news is that God never lets the story end in such a sad state. All of my low moments, caused me to seek out church and the "new life" that Jesus promises each of us. God used that low point to lead me to spiritually-mature people that influenced and helped heal me.

Prayer:

God, I pray for those that are hurting so much that they are unable to even pray this prayer. Touch and comfort them. Strengthen them. Allow them to rest and when the new day comes, allow them to see Your endless possibilities at new life. You are always with us, and I praise your name. In Jesus' name. Amen.

"Speak of the devil, and he comes."

"But as for the cowardly, the faithless, the detestable, as for murderers, the sexually immoral, sorcerers, idolaters, and all liars, their portion will be in the lake that burns with fire and sulfur, which is the second death." Revelation 21:8

Ghost enthusiasts have always been attracted to my old home. It is true that these walls have heard generations of stories, wars, famine, feasts and the many personal details of the people that have lived here. I have had cousins (and some strangers) approach me about having a séance at my home, or even a Quija board party. I always tell them, "I don't want to call the devil up at a place where I live." They always are quick to respond that they aren't calling the devil, they just want to try to talk to their "Aunt Pearl" or any of the old spirits that have once lived in the house.

In Leviticus, God says not to seek out mediums. Later in 1 Samuel, God kills Saul for his unfaithfulness and chanting Samuel up from the grave. It should come as no surprise that to see a dead person, speak or raise up is not natural and to be on alert. No one could know what to fully expect when witnessing such an event, or be certain that it *really is* their "Aunt Pearl." Demons are a very real thing and the Bible gives accounts of the possession of people. Calling up something you know is not of God should be obvious that it is an invitation for the devil.

Prayer:

God, cleanse us of this romanticized evil of seeing our loved ones again on Earth. Let us be happy that the dead are at peace. Comfort those that grieve with the hope of seeing their loved one again. May they be blessed with that reality in eternal life with You. In Jesus' name. Amen.

"Easy come, easy go!"

"By their fruit you will recognize them. Do people pick grapes from thorn bushes, or figs from thistles? Likewise, every good tree bears good fruit, but a bad tree bears bad fruit. A good tree cannot bear bad fruit, and a bad tree cannot bear good fruit. Every tree that does not bear good fruit is cut down and thrown into the fire. Thus, by their fruit you will recognize them." Matthew 7:16-20

In what I thought was the most horrible lesson in my youth, my father never gave out a free loan. If he loaned you money, it was discussed when and how you would pay it back, and possibly even with interest. When I turned 16, my mother bought me a car against his wishes saying, "she'll never take care of something she hasn't worked for." In the moment, I hated that "easy come, easy go" ideology but over time have come to realize it is the truth in most cases. The best things worth having are some of the things hardest to obtain. Long lasting friendships and marriages are ideal, but aren't easy. You have to work for them. Jesus really did "pay it all" in allowing people like us to come directly to Him; giving us access to the inside of churches and having eternal life! Like all relationships, God does need us to put in the "sweat equity" of becoming better people. Once we enter into a relationship, we cannot continue to live in sin. We have to actively work on our lifestyles by changing our habits, actions, and the way we respond to people. Those things can be hard work, but not impossible, especially when we pray for God's help.

Prayer:

Heavenly Father, forgive me for not putting in the time needed in devotion to You. Forgive me when I fail You. Help me be mindful in the way I live my life, publicly and privately, so that my relationship can become stronger and that others may know the amazing love of Jesus Christ. In Jesus' name. Amen.

"Every story has two sides."

"You shall not pervert justice. You shall not show partiality, and you shall not accept a bribe, for a bribe blinds the eyes of the wise and subverts the cause of the righteous." Deuteronomy 16:19

I have always admired judges for their service to the community. For years, I dreamed of serving on jury duty living out a real-life Perry Mason moment. My time eventually came, and I was called to go through selection. I was accepted and was excited to be part of something so important and interesting. When the defendant came into the courtroom, they read his offenses aloud, which I learned was child abuse. My heart sank hearing that, but what is worse is that once they called out each offence, he said "guilty" over and over again without concern. It is awful to hear someone blatantly confess to abusing a child "under the age of 12" over and over again. His face showed no remorse.

I like to think I am a fair and just person, but my admiration for judges grew that day. After hearing the defendant's expressionless confessions, I felt tears stream down my face. What a strong heart and soul a judge must have to listen to such horrors while remaining calm and "just" to all parties!

People frequently complain about politics and the state of our government, but you seldom hear "pray for our judges and leaders." The country's morale is based with them and they hear no less than some purely evil testimonies.

Prayer:

May God keep our judges and our country strong and straight, following in the light of the Lord. In Jesus' name. Amen.

APRIL 27

"Live and learn."

"'Martha, Martha,' the Lord answered, 'you are worried and upset about many things, but few things are needed — or indeed only one. Mary has chosen what is better, and it will not be taken away from her.'" Luke 10:41-42

Have you ever been sitting in your living room, vegging out only to hear someone ring your doorbell? Your hair is not fixed. You have zero make-up on. Children have seemingly set off a bomb inside your home, and let's not talk about the bathroom.

I think that most Southerners compare having company to the Biblical story of Mary and Martha. Most of us love to entertain, feed you a slice of our Hummingbird Cake and sit out on the porch to talk. However, not being prepared for the visit can land us running around our house (like Martha) throwing toys in the closet and closing bedroom doors. While the Bible makes multiple references to being prepared, Jesus is essentially asking Martha to "sit down and enjoy each other's company."

I have found few things in life as precious as people's time. If someone is coming to give you their time but is an unexpected visiting friend, instead of shutting the curtains (pretending not to be home) consider opening your door (and heart). What they have to say may be life-changing and is certainly a precious gift. They might not be Jesus, but Jesus would tell you that "whatever you did not do for one of the least of these, you did not do for me." (Matthew 25:45)

Prayer:

God, help us see that the details of our house are unimportant when someone may need our help. Instill in us the desire to bless those that come our way (friends and foes). Help us not dwell on so many physical things of this world. May we be full of Christian love and grace. In Jesus' name, Amen.

"A penny saved is a penny earned."

"For everyone who calls on the name of the Lord will be saved.' How then will they call on him in whom they have not believed? And how are they to believe in him of whom they have never heard? And how are they to hear without someone preaching?" Romans 10:13-14

I like to keep special mementos from my life in an old cedar chest. Among my collection I have photos, greeting cards that loved ones have given, and old love letters that belonged to my grandmother. Saving things is a nice way to remember and revisit an important time. It is the same reason people collect and rebuild classic cars. Saving these "classic" memories is a good way to also pass them on to future generations. It is important to find someone younger, who shares an interest and educate them on the importance of such a beloved item.

Sharing God's word is much like that. It can feel "safe" as a Christian to live in your bubble once you know about God, but it is necessary to share that message and its importance with someone who will remember that classic legacy.

How many times in your life were you truly grateful for knowing God's love and presence? What if those moments never existed for you? Who would you have turned out to be instead? All of that sad mystery will be projected on to tomorrow's future unless you share how great God has been to you.

Prayer:

Dear Lord, thank You for the many times in life that You have saved me. Give me the perfect way and words to witness in conversation with young people. May they be able to see the way You molded and shaped my life. In Jesus' name. Amen.

"Waste not, want not."

"As each has received a gift, use it to serve one another, as good stewards of God's varied grace." I Peter 4:10

One of my favorite things about ordering Chinese take-out (besides a night off from cooking) is that the restaurant packages the food in the best durable containers with a clear lid. I always wash and save the containers. One kitchen cabinet stays full of the containers year-round until Thanksgiving comes, and I am able to send friends and relatives home with boxes of neatly organized food in the free Chinese containers.

God gives us lots of "extra" blessings in our daily lives and those extras are meant to bless others. If you see that you have all of your needs met, pass the excess to another person. When my sister and I were children, our mother always taught us "not to take the last piece" of food on the table because it might be better served helping someone in need.

Likewise, God has blessed everyone with a spiritual gift and talent. When something is delicious, expensive or rare, society tells us to hold on to the item and hoard it. Every good gift is from the Lord. His excess doesn't need to be hoarded. If your gift is singing, use your talent to lead others to a spiritual meditation with God. If your gift is carpentry, use your art to inspire a Christian message. Not using your gift is worse than throwing away those Chinese containers! Use it for the glory of God.

Prayer:

Dear Lord, thank You for making others so interesting and gifted. Help us identify what our gift is and set a fire in our soul to make an impactful use that will help others have a spiritual encounter with You. In Jesus' name. Amen.

"Heard it straight from the horse's mouth."

"Your word is a lamp to my feet and a light to my path." Psalm 119:105

I love old church windows. Many of the older leaded glass windows show scenes from the Bible and were specifically meant to shed light on the life of Jesus to the illiterate. Not being able to read handicapped their ability to know exactly what the Bible's message was.

In modern times, most know how to read but it seems that many Christians are too comfortable to open their Bible during the week. It is dangerous to solely rely on someone else's reading of the Bible regularly.

The Bible speaks to us all differently. It has certain scripture that is meant for us to read during certain parts of our life. When we read it for ourselves, the Holy Spirit may prompt for us to continue reading in a different chapter. We may take away a different message than when an orator reads it.

One of my favorite childhood games was "Gossip" in which a line of children all whisper a secret phrase down the line. In the end, the last child never gets the correct message. Something as important as the Gospel should never solely rely on "Gossip." God has gifted us His Word to use as the ultimate living guide. Churches and study groups are bonus to this grand gift.

Prayer:
Heavenly Father, thank You for the Bible and all of the helpful tools like, churches, pastors, study groups, Christian movies, and art. The list of your resources is endless. Help me put aside time to read the Bible. Help me understand it and how it applies to my life now. Be with me in everything that I read and encounter. In Jesus' name. Amen.

"The grass always looks greener on the other side of the fence."

"You shall not covet your neighbor's house; you shall not covet your neighbor's wife, or his male servant, or his female servant, or his ox, or his donkey, or anything that is your neighbor's." Exodus 20:17

I make a trip to Guntersville, Alabama to my aunt's house several times a year. Guntersville is a beautiful spot on the map. I always enjoy driving through unaltered countryside and they have an abundance of it. Another thing they have an abundance of is–chicken! There are too numerous of chicken houses to count. While driving through recently, I saw a group of native birds standing outside one of the chicken houses. I am sure that a fair number of them get their food from the abundance of bird seed that the farmers are distributing. I couldn't help but wonder if some of the wild birds are jealous and think "boy, those chickens sure do have the life – being fed, watered, and a roof over their heads every day!" Of course, the irony is that those chickens are about to be served on every table in Alabama.

What do you see others have that you want? It doesn't seem fair that "ill-bred people" (an expression of my grandmother's) have more success than I do, are seemingly better liked than I am, etc. How could a "no-good fool" (another expression of my grandmother's) have such an abundant life?

I feel certain that local wild birds have similar thoughts about the chickens and wonder how they can achieve similar success. Remember that what can appear as success, might have you served as fried chicken for Sunday dinner. God always takes care of His children. Put your trust in Him and be content with your daily bread.

Prayer:

God, help us see the success of others as their own, separate life path. Help us look at our own two feet and find the blessings of where we are standing. Thank You for the ability to see the difference. In Jesus' name. Amen.

"Do not cut off your nose to spite your face."

"Don't copy the behavior and customs of this world, but let God transform you into a new person by changing the way you think. Then you will learn to know God's will for you, which is good and pleasing and perfect." Romans 12:2

My husband and I had been renovating and restoring our 125-year-old home for years when I found out I was expecting. It never bothered me before to have a screw gun, tape measure, ladder, and table saw lying around the house until I realized that I was about to have a baby racing around to explore it. I used my pregnancy as a ticking alarm clock as a countdown to how much time we had left to work on the house. Officially marking my baby shower date as the day on the calendar to have all tools put away for good. The time went quickly, but the week of my baby shower I was able to walk around and proudly look at our orderly, clean home and new nursery, ready to receive a new family member.

Since baby shower guests would be arriving within the week, I selected nice "easy listening" music on our television for guests to listen to while they were at my home. I made a few more walkthroughs and asked my husband if he would mind cleaning certain areas to make them look nicer. He likes to collect things and leaves them on the porch.

On the day before my baby shower, our WIFI internet went out, which is not a big surprise. My small town frequently is without internet for days and has shut down the schools, businesses and even hindered emergency rescue services. Not having WIFI meant not having music for my party, but I decided I wasn't going to be bothered by it. However, even after my baby shower was over, we went without WIFI for nearly a week! I finally called the company to come out and as soon as the service man got out of his truck he asked where the service box was. He said, "it is a box that has cables coming out of it." I immediately felt my face turn red as I confessed to him that I had my husband cut it off of our home because I didn't like the way the cables looked. He took a great, big laugh and said, "the wife said to throw it away because she didn't like the way it looked!" He installed another, but I paid for it dearly.

Sometimes life looks, and is, messy. We feel pressure to make our lives look a certain way and fit in with a picture-perfect society. We all have different backgrounds, with different personalities, talents, and learning abilities. There is a peer pressure from society for all of us to be the same, and the truth is, sometimes our "WIFI cables" stick out. They need to stick out because that's what makes them successfully operate. While an honest look at self-improvement is always a healthy thing, it is important to appreciate the way God made us. If God made you (or another) noticeably different than others–respect that. Move on and determine how to use that difference for God.

Prayer:

Dear Lord, help us not to be bothered by society's pressures and to only keep our eyes on You. Bad things can happen when we take our focus off of You. Help us see the good in every situation and more importantly, the assurance that all things work together for Your good. In Jesus' name. Amen.

"If you lie down with dogs, you will get up with fleas."

"The thief comes only to steal and kill and destroy; I have come that they may have life, and have it to the full." John 10:10

Every now and then I come across a few personality types that bring the worse out in me. These pot-stirrers are seemingly unprovoked and lie, cheat and slander others. What are the factors that make-up these ill-behaved people?

The Bible speaks of demonic possession and shows us how that can influence and take over a person's life. However, identifying demons and even casting them out is not always welcome. In Matthew 8:34, after Jesus cast demons out of two men, the demons flew into pigs that flung themselves into the lake and the townspeople asked Jesus to leave. Other people that are part of a bad situation might not be able to see the entire story and might favor the side of the demon. Jesus doesn't stay to argue and explain to the townspeople what really happened. He moves on to continue healing people in other towns.

We are all called to continue spreading the Good News, even after we are berated or criticized. As Christians, we should expect to be attacked. God equips us to move away from negative people and will continue to empower us with the gift that He anoints us with.

Prayer:

God, thank You for the freedom of clean living, away from the chains of evil and death. I pray for my protection when encountering evil situations and pray for all of the people involved, that they too, may know the truth. In Jesus' name. Amen.

"Opportunity never knocks twice at any man's door."

"This is how you are to eat it: with your cloak tucked into your belt, your sandals on your feet and your staff in your hand. Eat it in haste; it is the LORD's Passover." Exodus 12:11

One of my favorite childhood memories is when my mother would unsuspectedly say, "We are going to the beach. You have exactly five minutes to pack." Those words sent us into a frenzy, asking for help to find certain things. Mother would always respond, "I don't know, but if you don't find it we will buy another one when we get there."

Looking back, I'm not sure what would have happened if I used 30 minutes to pack. Would she have left me? Probably not, but I wasn't going to risk it! Great things can come any second, and it's better to act now rather than miss the opportunity.

In the Bible, when Moses is waiting for Pharaoh to give his consent for the Israelites to leave Egypt, he instructs everyone to not wait for their bread to rise. By not adding yeast, it was an outward display of being ready the moment God calls. They were also instructed to keep their shoes and clothes on, ready to leave at any moment.

What are you waiting for in life? Good and fruitful things can come to those that plan, but great and extraordinary things can come to those that jump to the occasion.

Prayer:

God, thank You for blessing me with a new day and opportunity. Show me the door and help me be bold enough to open it. Bless my endeavors and protect me and those I love. In Jesus' name. Amen.

"Where there is a will there is a way."

"One night the Lord spoke to Paul in a vision: "Do not be afraid; keep on speaking, do not be silent." Acts 18:9

My mother has the creative ability to find a way in every circumstance. When I was a child and without a toy, mother would draw beautiful paper dolls to help the time pass. For Christmas one year when my father was sick in the hospital, she promised me a Christmas tree. When we purchased it the man (who I'm old enough now to realize wasn't a gentleman) said that we had to have rope and someone to tie it down on our car. Mother opened her sunroof and said "stick it through the sun roof" with a smile. Even though we picked pine needles out of the car from then on, we had a Christmas tree. As an nine-year-old, it was a fun experience to drive down the road with a tree sticking out the top of our car. Finding a way in every circumstance also helped her in life as a saleswoman. Looking back on those times, especially as a mother myself, I realize that some of her actions were out of fun, and some were from necessity. God gave her the talent of creativity because He knew she would use it for good.

In the Bible, there are many people mentioned that God made a way for them. It didn't matter what the circumstances were. If they were slaves, He set them free. If they were starving in the desert, He sent them food. If they were trapped by the sea, He parted it to allow them to pass. Most importantly in the New Testament, when people were condemned, Jesus gave them a new start in life and eternal life. Whatever the circumstance you find yourself in, God will make a way.

Prayer:

Lord, thank You for blessing us with creativity. All good things come from You. Thank You, for freeing us from death with the gift of Your son, Jesus Christ. All honor and glory is Yours. Amen.

"You can lead a horse to water, but you cannot make it drink."

"For all have sinned and fall short of the glory of God." Romans 3:23

By most accounts, I am a dog and bird person. Imagine my disbelief when my husband recently sent me a picture of an infant kitten than was found at his job site. The kitten barely had its eyes open and judging by its age would need a great deal of care. I have never had a kitten and knew nothing about how to care for it. Still, I couldn't bear the thought of the poor precious puff ball dying without its mother or anyone to care, so I took it in. (For the readers that don't know, kitten care is not for the weak. They require assistance in going to the bathroom and feeding every two hours.) What's even more amusing is that cats are a bit antisocial. You can call them for hours, and they will not come. Sometimes if you pet them, they might bite you depending on how they feel. The little black ball of fur weighed 10 ounces and even though I wrapped him up in a towel, he stuck his miniature claws out in defense. I pried his mouth open to squirt some of the milk in, which was spilt half of the time. I wanted him to thrive. I wanted to be his surrogate mother and love him, but by all actions, he refused. Eventually, he came around. He got fatter and purred from time to time.

God wants to love you. Instead of wrapping us up in a towel and force feeding us, He gives us the freedom to come and go. What areas do you blatantly try to deny God? Is it listening to profane lyrics that make you feel tough? Do you swear at other drivers on the freeway? Do you over eat? We all are sinners and have sinned, but living right and close to God can be the difference in our survival. God is not force feeding you because He expects you to know the difference and change.

Prayer:

God, I acknowledge Your love me. Forgive my rebellion. My actions don't always reflect my love for You. Help me know Your will for my life and live in accordance. In Jesus' name. Amen.

"Birds of a feather flock together."

"I have said these things to you, that in me you may have peace. In the world you will have tribulation. But take heart; I have overcome the world." John 16:33

Post COVID has been difficult to acclimate to. In 2021 while traveling, at nearly nine months of being pregnant, I desperately needed to use the bathroom. I parked at a popular chicken fast food and managed to waddle to the door to use their restroom, only to find the door locked. Someone came to the door and told me that their facilities weren't open due to COVID. It is not just bathroom facilities; it is finding a new norm of friendship. Some of my once free and untethered friends that once traveled across the country, now have anxiety about being social or even coming to my home to visit. It is hard to see and know where the line is and what the correct thing to do is. "Birds of a feather" don't necessarily flock together anymore. They might be afraid of one another.

While the worst of COVID seems to be behind us, we will always face uncertain times. During those times, we can only look to the Lord. Those that don't look to the Lord don't have anywhere to look.

Philippians 4:6 says, "Do not be anxious about anything, but in every situation, by prayer and petition, with thanksgiving, present your requests to God."

Prayer:

God, thank You for the peace and refuge You offer us. May we look to You during scary times. May we respond to the world with Christian love. In Jesus' name. Amen.

"The straw (or drop of water) that breaks the camel's back."

"Look at the birds of the air: they neither sow nor reap nor gather into barns, and yet your heavenly Father feeds them. Are you not of more value than they?" Matthew 6:26

Last summer, I found myself safeguarding a small swimming pool of old water. A group of frogs found this swamp water to be a hidden diamond and left me hundreds of baby frogs. I watched for weeks as they grew from a tiny little bead into a microscopic frog with a fin tail. To many it may sound murky and dirty, but it reminded me of my childhood and gave a life-giving gift to me to nurture and watch God's miracle unfold daily.

One day, a summer rain came. It was refreshing and made me happy that the tadpoles were getting fresh water from God's garden. I opened my backdoor and to my horror the pool was full and about to let the water gush out. I went out in the rain and could see the tadpoles at the rim, excited, jumping to get out. I knew that if the pool had any more water, they would all pour out onto the ground and die. I sat in the rain with a cup lowering the water level. They were all saved that day.

God cares for us in the same way. When we are too eager, He lets the water out. We may not know it at the time or sense His presence, but He is watching with His cup. Trust that He will make all things right and "lower your water levels." 1 Peter 5:7 reassures that "He cares for you."

Prayer:

God, in stressful times may we be reminded that You are with us; watching and protecting. In Jesus' name. Amen.

"Every cloud has a silver lining."

"Praise the Lord. Give thanks to the Lord, for he is good; his love endures forever." Psalm 106:1

Events or ill-minded people sometimes eat at our hearts. Most of the time there is not much control that we have over what an ill-mannered person says to us, puts on social media, or has created to try to take away our peace. Sometimes these acts are intentional and meant to wound us and sometimes they are not. Whoever or whatever the culprit, it affects our personal life and health. I recently found myself stirring late at night, unable to sleep thinking of such a person, and the misery they bring to the world.

I called out to the Lord, and He heard me.

No matter what wall or giant you are up against know that God cares for you in your situation. Give thanksgiving to the Lord, always! So, I lay in my bed and gave the Lord thanks, naming each thing I was thankful for. I started with things in my bedroom that were in front of me (because those were easiest for me to see in that moment).

"I am thankful for my bed. I am thankful for my husband. I am thankful for air conditioning. I am thankful for my clothes and for my home."

Soon, I was fast asleep because the Lord lifted my burden.

Take this time to list what you are thankful for. Do not limit yourself to a number.

Let this list of thanksgiving be our prayer.

"Every tide has its ebb."

"Again Jesus spoke to them, saying, 'I am the light of the world. Whoever follows me will not walk in darkness, but will have the light of life.'" John 8:12

Light is always helpful. As a child, I had a plush toy GloWorm ® that I could squeeze when I was afraid. I knew the light would ward off any evil monsters. As an adult, I know that a night light will help me find my way to the bathroom.

One of the main reasons that non-believers give for not being a Christian is "if God existed, He wouldn't allow bad things to happen. Where is He during dark times?" A heard a wise pastor give the explanation once in a sermon that "Earth is not Heaven." This world is a place of choices, consequences, and chaos. Heaven is reserved as a reward for believers. There will always be murder, death, sickness, greed, turmoil, and pain here on Earth. Thinking about all of the darkness that lives here can be overwhelming, leaving you to feel trapped in it. When we call out for God's help and don't feel His presence, many see that as God ignoring and abandoning us, including Jesus during his crucifixion.

God offers us an escape with his Word, Truth, and Light. Jesus told the people that He was the "light" in the midst of His own turmoil. God's followers in the Bible are rewarded after their suffering. It's important to remember during our trials, God is with us and will prevail. Until you feel relief, seek light by reading the Bible, worshiping God, and praying. The best is yet to come!

Prayer:

Light of the Darkness, help me through my difficult times. Give me strength with glimpses of light at the end of the tunnel. Send angels to encourage and help me fight my battles. All honor and victory is Yours! In Jesus' name. Amen.

"Ignorance is bliss."

"I have been crucified with Christ and I no longer live, but Christ lives in me. The life I live in the body, I live by faith in the Son of God, who loved me and gave himself for me." Galatians 2:20

As a parent, there are so many things that I don't want my son to know (at least not yet); news of murders and racism are a few examples. In Genesis, Adam and Eve were forbidden from eating of the Tree of Knowledge. I can understand how the knowledge of how dark and evil the world is, is not something any loving parent would want their child to know, yet God gave them free-will to choose in receiving that knowledge (which Adam and Eve did).

There is still an endless fount of knowledge that we still have the will to choose. Any time you seek out things you shouldn't, you are exploiting your own innocence. Examples of self-exploiting are looking up pornography on the internet and dressing provocatively. It opens up a new realm of suffering that you or the people around you will endure.

Prayer:

Dear Father, thank You for your never-ending love. Thank You for wanting to protect us from the evil in this world. Forgive us for our sins and the ways we disappoint You. I want to live for You. May my life reflect that. In Jesus' name. Amen.

"It's raining cats and dogs."

"Again Jesus spoke to them, saying, 'I am the light of the world. Whoever follows me will not walk in darkness, but will have the light of life.'" Matthew 8:27

I have never witnessed cats and dogs raining from the sky but nearly witnessed it raining frogs. About ten years ago, it rained more days in the month than were dry. Fortunately, the rain didn't cause flooding or any damage, but it did cause an influx of frogs mating. As I was driving home, I realized that the "drops of water bouncing off the street from impact" were not drops but tiny frogs. There were thousands of them, and it was impossible to not hit them as they plagued 80 percent of the street. The frog plague lasted for days and seemed only to be in my neighborhood.

Looking back, it doesn't even seem real! It has made me consider the plagues and supernatural occurrences in the Bible. Could the Jews believe their eyes when Moses was advocating for them? What must the world have been like when Noah witnessed the flood? Did he see herds of critters running across the fields searching in desperation for higher ground? God's hand is powerful and omnipotent. Sometimes when we see natural wonders of the earth, they are reminders of how powerful He is. The earth is God's creation. He breaths and the winds obey. The magnitude of His power is a marvel that we forget when we focus on our own problems. Remember that every plant, tree, sky, and sunset belongs to Him. Your breath was created by Him. NOTHING (relationships, health issues, finances) are so big that He will forsake you. Trust in Him.

Prayer:

God, we love you! Your creations inspire the world's best artists. Thank You for the wondrous seasons of frogs, and all of the serendipitous moments You allow us to witness. Let us remember in that inspiration the magnitude of Your love. Take our concerns and blanket them with Your peace. The promise of Your love is in every sunset and sunrise. In Jesus' name. Amen.

"Look before you leap."

"For all have sinned and fall short of the glory of God." Romans 3:23

You will never find me jumping out of a plane or on a roller coaster that is "death defying." God creates all types of people. I think that it is wonderful that some people are thrilled by adrenaline; I am satisfied with the assurance of safety. While some might call me a "fuddy-dud," I really admire those brave enough to go "where no man has gone before." I realize that some of the United States' greatest moments has been in valiance; winning wars, going to the moon and overcoming terrorists. Some of the most traditional jobs such as law enforcement and emergency medics take risks to save other's lives.

I can't imagine someone that is afraid of heights, electing to go into the 10th floor of a burning building to save people, but I know it happens. God has equipped each of us to be the different person we are, but with whatever our "calling" is, we are responsible for our own safety. Praying for our own safety, safety of others, and being spiritually ready to take on monsters in any form requires every person (especially those with an adrenaline job) to be "prayed up" for battle when entering the battle field.

Seeking the Hand of God in everything will give each of us the strength we need to get through whatever the task.

Prayer:

God, Bless those that protect us through the military and service workers. Thank You for people who are brave enough to take on any battle. Protect and equip them for what is ahead. Help each of us in our profession. Be with us, in Jesus' name. Amen.

"Slow and steady wins the race."

"Do you not know that in a race all the runners run, but only one gets the prize? Run in such a way as to get the prize." 1 Corinthians 9:24

Picking out a new swim suit is hard because we see all of our flaws; where we lack shape or have too much shape filling in the bathing suit. We are our worst critics, and it is a reminder that, perhaps, we did not "stick to our guns" during our New Year resolution to lose weight and live as healthy as we should have. This reminder of failure can feel similar to the same failure we experience as sinners trying to live a Christian lifestyle. Living life as a Christian is an ongoing battle, just as not eating all of those French fries is an ongoing battle, but it IS obtainable! "Slow and steady wins the race" is a reminder to keep going! In any race, there are obstacles and a strain the runner experiences. Not everyone gets to the finish line in the same time frame as others, but not giving up is an essential part of achieving any goal.

If you realize that you have failed in achieving your ideal summer time body, the best option is to "get back on the wagon. Equally, if you know you are living a life with some sin mixed in, "get back on the wagon" until you become the best version of yourself and one that is pleasing to God.

Prayer:

Father, forgive me for all the ways that I fail You. I want to live a life that pleases and glorifies Your Kingdom. During my moments of temptation let me be bold enough to choose the path that I know is Yours. Bless me with glimpses of how my life is changing for the better so that I may be blessed along the way. Thank You, God. In Jesus' name. Amen.

"Ask and you shall receive."

"Oh, that you would bless me and enlarge my territory! Let your hand be with me, and keep me from harm so that I will be free from pain." 1 Chronicles 4:10

Time has a way of making us forget the milestones that we have made. I recently watched a video of my infant son of when he could just barely lift his little head up and made a loud screech of joy. Milestone parenting teaches about developmental leaps that the child experiences as they get older. A young child might have difficulty grasping things, which is why pencil companies make those fat markers and pencils to hold onto. Naturally, as they get older, their articulation becomes finer. Watching these developmental leaps in my son's life sparked my interest to ask "when do the leaps end?" When questioning my own life, I know that I am smarter and wiser than I was when I was a young adult. It is a fair assumption that our entire life is made up of developmental leaps.

In the Bible's, Prayer of Jabez, (among many other Biblical characters) he prays for God's continued blessing in life. In the same way, you have to ask for what you need. We should continue to ask our Heavenly Guardian to help and deliver us. As a parent, I know I feel delighted when I hear my son call for me. Nothing is more beautiful than to hear him say "Mumma." God also delights in the sound of your voice calling for Him.

Prayer:

Father God, I ask You to bless me and enlarge my territory! Let Your hand be with me, and keep me from harm so that I will be free from pain. Let the wonders of Your Majesty radiate from my life so that others might find joy and hope. In Jesus' name. Amen.

"The devil is in the details"

"Teaching them to obey everything I have commanded you. And lo, surely I am with you always, to the very end of the age." Matthew 28:20

Several years ago, I bought an antique Sunday dress hat that was cream with a pink pastel brim. Inspired to wear it for Easter Sunday, I decided that I would make a dress to wear with it. (Mind you, I've never made a dress in my life!) I went material shopping and bought the most beautiful pink linen fabric that matched it perfectly. I didn't have a dress pattern, but thought "who needs a dress pattern?! I am creative!" (Those sewing shows on T.V. don't help! I always think I am capable after watching them!) In the most awful offense against linen, I laid the material on the floor and tried to trace my body with a marker which resulted in me looking like a giant Easter egg potato sack! The next day, I went back to the material store and bought another $40 of linen to take to a proper seamstress.

God gives us tools to help us in life, and sometimes we are so stubborn in our humanly ways that we suffer by our actions. Looking back, I should have at least bought a dress pattern since I had no prior dress-making skills.

There are so many actions and areas of our life that we mess up because we refuse to ask for help, namely our relationships with family, friends, and ultimately our connection with God. God gives us "dress pattern" tools like the Bible, church, small groups, and Christian people we can connect with– everything we need to make a solid Christian lifestyle. How and if we use His resources will decide on how well our Christian "dress" turns out. Hopefully, it will turn out to be one that people feel inspired by and see as beautiful.

Prayer:

God, help me use my creativity in the right channels instead of creating a stubborn disaster. May I always seek your face by using the tools You so lovingly give. In Jesus' name. Amen.

"The early bird gets the worm."

"You prepare a table before me in the presence of my enemies. You anoint my head with oil; my cup overflows. Surely goodness and mercy will follow me all the days of my life, and I will dwell in the house of the LORD forever." Psalm 23:5-6

God has an endless talent for creation. If there ever was an "early bird," it was my great-grandfather. "GrandDeddy" was already an old man when I met him. I mostly remember him being in his 90's and having the ability to run circles around all of us. He and his family were from Appalachia, which is still a unique Southern experience that you won't find anywhere else in the United States. His "people" lived in the mountains and he lived the entirety of his life on the side of a mountain, which he owned. As a child, it was a magical place to visit. He hunted for Ginseng in the 1960's before it was popular and sold it to Chinese marketers and traded furs. They had a wide scope of things at their home that you rarely ever see. A natural spring was on their property, and he built a wooden trough to carry the water closer to the house. He always kept half of a dried coconut beside the spring so it could be used as a drinking cup. Not only did I enjoy drinking water from the earth out of a coconut, but he had an apple orchard and honey bees. There was a wooden bridge which carried you to the cow pasture – so many great wonders to revel in! My great-grandmother, "Mama" would get up at 5 a.m. to make homemade biscuits, and it was always paired with GranDeddy's honey. He was young in spirit and body. He would step up on a wooden box to "buck dance" and always had a funny folk song to sing.

"I got a rabbit in a log, and I ain't got my dawg. How will I git em? I know! I will git me a briar and twist in his har'. That's a way to git em, I know!"

Even though he was unique and their home was magical, many other people and places on this Earth are wondrous. In multiple parts of the country and world, the ocean glows at night because of red tide organisms. Humpback whales travel 16,000 miles each year (the earth is only 25,000 miles in circumference). Antarctica also has 8 million year old ice glaciers.

God created all of these places and people. The human mind cannot understand all that the universe offers. We get so upset when we don't have control of a situation. Some people are afraid of dying and what comes after death but God, the wondrous Creator has already made a powerful display of His ability. It is all around us in the people we have met, their abilities and the miracle of nature around us. Whatever problem you might be facing, God the Creator has encompassed your life with miracles. You need only to open your eyes.

Prayer:

Dear Father God, Thank you for the miracle of Your creations. It is comforting to know that not only are You known as Healer, but You created all of the world's healers and medical staff. Not only are You known as the Artist, but You created all of the world's artists. You are the center point for everything good in the world. Thank You for the blessing of getting to know the people in my life and the miracle of nature that surrounds us. May we trust You and Your future for us. All of this goodness is Yours. In Jesus' name. Amen.

"Have your cake and eat it too"

"Finally, brothers, whatever is true, whatever is noble, whatever is right, whatever is pure, whatever is lovely, whatever is admirable—if anything is excellent or praiseworthy—think about such things." Philippians 4:8

When I was a young adult, I was under the impression that I was living my best life without God. I chose to live that way, so I wouldn't be confined by the endless judgements and rules governed by the leaders of the church. Looking back during those "unconfined" days, I realize that I was confined by that opinion of the church alone. It governed too much of who I wanted to communicate with, and more importantly, I always felt a weight of oppression and lost hope living a life without God.

Creating a relationship with God not only liberated me and gave me hope, but it also helped me discover more of who I am, who He created me to be, how to collaborate with others, how to respond correctly to bad situations, and help others learn more about who they are meant to be.

Many non-Christians refuse Christianity with the reasoning that "it is not scientific enough." Becoming a Christian did not give me the answers to all of my questions about life, but I didn't have them before. So "nothing gained, nothing lost." What it did give me was the grace and peace to understand that God is THE powerful, Almighty and that it's okay not to have the answers to everything. Choosing to feel the sunshine on your face and feeling its happy warmth is much better than living a life constantly searching for where the sun comes from.

Prayer:

O Creator, God, thank You for taking away the burden of constant worry. Sometimes we miss the forest for the trees in our face. I give You praise for all that is good. In Jesus' name. Amen.

"You can't judge a book by its cover."

"And the peace of God, which transcends all understanding, will guard your hearts and your minds in Christ Jesus." Philippians 4:7

Lantanas are one of my favorite flowers. They are so happy and hardy and go through a huge transformation each year from practically being non-existent at ground-level into a huge bush of multi-colored button flowers. When we found out we were expecting a baby, I even loved the name "Lantana" if it was a girl, but my husband didn't like the name and it wasn't a long-lived idea. However, even though it is a garden plant quite near perfection, if you pick the flowers, it gives off the most awful, putrid stink.

That is the ideal example of Southerners when we forget our Christian living and heritage. There is not anything more charming than a Southern smile and pecan pie, but the first time we push people away with anger, our sharp tongue or sinful actions it casts an awful pungent shadow over our life. We all are imperfect people, but living a lifestyle that pushes people away can confuse others on who we are, what a Christian is, and if they want to become one. Building God's kingdom means loving and encouraging others while waiting for the power of the Holy Spirit to speak to them. Our goal as Christians should always be to live and lead a life which will bring others to know God's love. That doesn't mean that we are living a perfect life.

The next time we experience chaos may we remember to deal with it like the fragrance of a rose, versus the odor of lantana. It could mean Eternal life to someone that is watching.

Prayer:

Father, help me to respond as Jesus would and not lash out in anger. May I be reminded that the world is full of "lantanas" when people are desperate for "roses." Send your Holy Spirit to move through me and my life and weed out all that gives disease to my soul. In Jesus' name. Amen.

"A stitch in time saves nine."

"Have I not commanded you? Be strong and courageous. Do not be terrified; do not be discouraged, for the LORD your God will be with you wherever you go." Joshua 1:9

Once while planning an evening ball, I spent so much time focusing on the event details beautiful that I forgot to find an dress to wear. Being that it was the last minute and I didn't have a dress, I decided to make one. I bought pre-sequined fuchsia fabric and somehow made a pretty decent gown that I was proud to be seen in. (Perhaps trying to make my Easter dress the previous year gave me some pointers.) However, one thing I did not have time to do was to sew the dress, so I used the next best thing−my stapler! I made sure to double staple and did a pretty good job. However, later in the evening my gown that had a modest slit at the leg, became a slit that made me nervous. (It was a moment, that I am sure Cinderella also felt when her gown was about to change back into rags). Luckily, I had the stapler nearby and reinforced it.

Our Christian life is the perfect Cinderella example. Everything might be beautiful and you might just be living a "stapled" kind of life, barely getting by, but that is dangerous. Living a life that is on the borderline of falling apart, might actually fall apart. That can mean death. It can also mean setting an example to friends and family and generations of loved ones also living a life destined for Hell. God offers us deliverance and hope for the future. We do not have to wait until we are "in a pickle." God is the cornerstone.

Prayer:

God, thank You for giving us a solid future that we can depend on. I want to align my life with living right and by Your Word. I am ready to seek Your face and will when making choices for my daily life. In Jesus' name. Amen.

"An apple a day keeps the doctor away."

"Yea, though I walk through the valley of the shadow of death, I will fear no evil: for thou art with me; thy rod and thy staff they comfort me." Psalm 23:4

Even though I know that apples are a healthy nutritious choice for my health, I haven't ever known anyone that has lived a long life by eating "an apple a day." Instead, I know several older adults, all practically centenarians and they all agree on their secret to a long life–"just keep moving!" It makes sense that in most all cases of near death experiences the will to live would be prolonged with a person's goal to continue to move, and would even aid the cases, like surgeries that need exercise in order to heal properly.

Feeling spiritually broken also feels like being physically broken and like the end of life. Sometimes life gives us unexpected circumstances that leave us feeling like "this is the end of life," and we actually have the urge to lay down and not get back up. Spiritual longevity is the same as physical longevity in the sense that sometimes life hurts, but we have to keep on moving to get through the hurt and hard times. "Just keep moving" is a way of living to get past the spiritual attacks and blows that the devil throws at us. God promises us a brighter tomorrow and future, but we have to keep moving to get there. Until tomorrow comes, praying, reading God's scripture, and reaching out to a Christian friend and sharing the issues you are dealing with will help you get through today's hurt and pain.

Prayer:

God, give me the strength to get through today. Comfort me and send Your angels to protect me. I surrender and place my trust in You. In Jesus' name. Amen.

"There is more than one way to skin a cat."

Immediately Saul preached about Christ in the synagogues, that He is the Son of God. Then all who heard were amazed, and said, "Is this not he who destroyed those who called on this name in Jerusalem, and has come here for that purpose, so that he might bring them bound to the chief priests?" Acts 9:20-21

High school seniors across the country are feeling the pressure to discover the next step for their future. It is important for everyone to have a plan for their life but important to remember that life does not always turn out the way you planned. The success you have planned for your life might be different than the success God has planned for your life. People (of all ages) usually feel devastated when their career path does not turn out the way they imagined. God uses such moments to help mold and re-direct each of us to where He wants us to be. Even though it is a painful molding, the blessing will be richer in the end. Everyone in the Bible had a different life before they lived closer to God, and eventually, they blossomed into something momentous. The end result produced something beautiful.

Crossroads in life are usually difficult ones. Ask God for help with what burdens you about the upcoming changes. God knows and understands how you are feeling. His plans are for you to live a more prosperous life than what you are currently living–you need only to trust in Him.

Prayer:

God, I know You are with me. Restore me with the joy of what is to come and the excitement of a new adventurous chapter. I submit everything in my future to You and ask You to guide me. In Jesus' name. Amen.

"The longest day must have an end."

"But seek first his kingdom and his righteousness, and all these things will be given to you as well." Matthew 6:33

When a multitude of little things keep building up, it is hard to keep calm. Recently, my husband, whom I greatly love, was working on an outdoor project. After a while, I went to check on him, and he was inside the house cleaning with a toxic spray that made the entire house smell like spray paint. (Never mind our child breathing in toxic fumes!) Second, I had been hiking the day prior and posted a nature selfie online from my walk. My hair wasn't fixed. I wasn't wearing any make-up, and my mother let me know that my public photo looked horrible. Third, my sister called to let me know that she was canceling her plans with me for the following day. Does this sound vaguely familiar?

Sometimes life leaves us feeling overwhelmed, frustrated, and even angry. My immediate reaction is to find solitude and step away from the world's chaos. God knows that our world is chaotic and that we need spiritual time to refresh. "Keeping the Sabbath Holy" is important to our sanity as it is to God's sanctity. God asks us to keep our eyes on Him in the midst of everything. Regardless what the world is saying (or sometimes screaming), God is our provision, which includes our peace. Remember the popular fire drill, "stop, drop and roll"? When you feel a volcano of anger about to erupt, "stop, drop and pray."

Prayer:

God, help me in my worst moments when I am lacking patience and the reflection of Your love. In Jesus' name. Amen.

"An ounce of prevention is worth a pound of cure."

"For God alone my soul waits in silence; from him comes my salvation." Psalm 62:1

If you have ever ran out gas, it probably taught you a valuable lesson. Maintenance is important. Servicing a car has several factors that have to be maintained (adequate levels of oil and coolant, tire pressure, etc.) Equally, our lives and bodies are systems that require maintenance, care, and proper fuel to keep on going. A friend that gardens recently experienced heat exhaustion while not properly hydrating and staying cool. The heat exhaustion resulted in him having a headache that lasted for days along with muscle cramps, leaving him unable to take any kind of medicine until his system recovered.

Lessons such as car maintenance and staying hydrated help prepare us for things that are important.

We all need spiritual maintenance, so when "it is time to sink or swim," we can swim. Life is always going to have whirlpools that are difficult to swim out of, but staying current with spiritual maintenance keeps our mind, spirit, and body in sync with what God is communicating to us. If we are receptive, the Holy Spirit will communicate that certain areas are safer and more life-giving than others, while some things are to be avoided.

Prayer:

God, May I be devoted to You in reading scripture, praying, and worship. Direct me on how to use my time effectively, so that I might be saved when worldly moments encompass me. In Jesus' name. Amen.

"Curiosity killed the cat."

"For the wages of sin is death, but the gift of God is eternal life in Christ Jesus our Lord." Romans 6:23

There is something about buttons that fascinate children. I try to share my phone calls with my son by putting the calls on speaker phone, but as soon as he sees the big red "END CALL" button, he is drawn to touch the screen. When I was a child (before cell phones existed), I was intrigued by the button located in the supermarket meat section. To my mother's dismay, I loved pressing the button and a man appearing in a white coat to take my mother's meat order (except she didn't have one). Temptation is always smartly disguised. It comes in the form of a button to children, but to the rest of the world, temptation is always paying attention to what intrigues us. It knows the inner workings of our lives and how to lure us in. Peter said in I Peter 5:8, "Be sober-minded; be watchful. Your adversary the devil prowls around like a roaring lion, seeking someone to devour."

Temptation can appear in the form of vulnerable people around us, chemical substances, or gambling. It can literally shape into anything that takes your focus, love, and devotion off of God. When a blessing comes to the door, ask "does this takes my focus, love, and devotion off of God?"

Prayer:

Heavenly Father, I ask You to be with me during temptation that are to come. Give me strength and surround me with Your angels. Put my mind and hands to work so that nothing evil can catch my attention. I adore You. In Jesus' name. Amen.

"Don't beat a dead horse."

"If anyone will not welcome you or listen to your words, leave that home or town and shake the dust off your feet." Matthew 10:14

Perhaps the most difficult thing to deal with in modern times are people around us with an opposite viewpoint. I don't remember opposite viewpoints as being such a deal breaker when I was younger as I do now. There is so much animosity, heat, hate, and disregard for other people that even I have a difficult time in the moment remembering how much God loves the other person (or why).

When I was a child there was an older couple that lived nearby. They were always cold and stone-faced. After our home burned down and we moved away, the couple paid a surprising visit one day with several boxes of goods. Being a small child, I don't remember all that the boxes included. What I do vividly remember is a tie-dye Mickey Mouse shirt. Our home burning meant that I had been wearing a few outfits that were old and not my size. That Mickey Mouse shirt was one of the most beautiful things I have ever seen, and I can still see it perfectly. After that day, I saw that old, "mean" couple in a different light. They still seemed grumpy and didn't have much to say. I am sure that we didn't have much in common but that Mickey Mouse shirt was evidence of love in their heart. We had found a common thread and I liked them – not because I got a free gift from them but because they had shown me love. That love spoke louder than any opposite viewpoint they had.

Prayer:

God, thank You for love and decency that comes from You. Regardless of our worldly feelings and opinions, let us put everything aside that keeps us from presenting your love and decency to others. God, bless the good people that continue to do good deeds regardless of their opposite viewpoints. In Jesus' name. Amen.

"Every dog has his day."

"Therefore, judge nothing before the appointed time; wait until the Lord comes. He will bring to light what is hidden in darkness and will expose the motives of the heart. At that time each will receive their praise from God." 1 Corinthians 4:5

I recently saw an old classmate at the supermarket named "April." We all associate people from our past with certain memories and events, and to me April was the girl that I shared a math class with in the 8th grade. She was always loud and unruly. We never got along. One day, she threw a wad of balled-up notebook paper and intentionally hit me in the back of the head with it. Which I, in turn, picked the paper up and threw it back at her. The teacher (only seeing me throw the paper) immediately assigned me to write the glossary as a punishment. I never forgot it. For years after that incident, our dislike for one another continued. I once was also assigned to sit behind her and could see bugs crawling in her hair (only a foot away from my face) which only increased my dislike for her.

Now adults, I was glad to see that we were cordial when seeing one another. Upon leaving, it made me consider all of the difficult situations and trials she must have had as a child. All circumstances that I couldn't have possibly have known at the time. What are the people we dislike going through? So many factors in a person's private life play in to how they respond in public.

Prayer:

God, help me have grace and show love when I deal with difficult people and remember to pray for their life and situation. In Jesus' name. Amen.

"Familiarity breeds contempt."

"My command is this: Love each other as I have loved you. Greater love has no one than this: to lay down one's life for one's friends." John 15:12-13

One of my favorite things about vacation is being with my family. However, when we all get in the car together it feels like a bunch of wild cats in a sack. My husband sits in the back of the car with our son, so any time I want to ask him something I have to yell and repeat it three times until he realizes he needs to take his head phones off. One of the things that he loves to do on trips is pick apart sunflower seeds, which consists of him spitting them out into a cup. I LOATHE finding the empty kernels in my car afterward. My dear, sweet, mother is sweet until she has car rage, while I am driving, making negative motions to other cars and trying to hold the emergency handle on the roof. I feel that my driving is superior to most, except for all of the times that I forget to put the car into park or nearly roll the windows up on their fingers.

People can get ill-tempered when they are around each other for too long. This lesson doesn't just apply to my family. Everyone is like that. I Corinthians 16:14 says, "Let everything you do be done in love." Surely vacationing is initiated by love, but love is not just for part of the journey. Love is in the details of how we get there and how we spend every moment together.

Prayer:

Father, forgive us for our moments of weakness and ill-temper toward others. We ask for help in knowing how to respond in grace and love to all situations. Give us the correct words so that everything we do and say may be a reflection of You. In Jesus' name. Amen.

"Fortune favors the bold."

"Now faith is being sure of what we hope for and certain of what we do not see." Hebrews 11:1

It's no secret that if you want something in life, you have to go get it yourself. Being "bold" can be scary sometimes because you don't know if you will be the recipient of what you are looking for and it can mean taking risks. Sometimes you have to take a chance in order to reap the rewards. Even though this is usually associated with earthly wealth and riches, it is also true of Heavenly and spiritual wealth. Having faith in God's existence is a leap that some are afraid to take.

One of my favorite characters in the Bible is the Proverbs 31 woman, whom I admire. All of the ways that describe her are admirable but the attribute most notable to me is verse 25 that says," She is clothed with strength and dignity; she can laugh at the days to come." "The days to come" is a very wide statement considering all that is announced with wars, pandemic, recessions, food shortages, and mass shootings always at the top of the daily news. Her "laugh" is not for lack of love and concern, but is based in her faith and trust in God. That same faith has kept me calm and still in the worst times in my life. God's peace is unwavering and constant because He is always with us.

Those who are courageous are often the most successful and that also comes with fearlessly trusting in God.

Prayer:

Heavenly Father, I put all of my cares and fears at Your feet. Clothe me in strength and dignity. Strengthen me during difficult times so that others might see my faith and loyalty to You. Use me as a beacon for those who are failing and weak so that they may come to know You. In Jesus' name. Amen.

"Haste makes waste."

"For you are a people holy to the LORD your God. The LORD your God has chosen you to be a people for his treasured possession, out of all the peoples who are on the face of the earth." Deuteronomy 7:6

One of the worst goof-ups that I occasionally make cooking is not checking the spice shaker before I sprinkle in seasoning. On more than one occasion, I have poured a quarter cup of oregano in my pot (or worse) because it was free pour instead of the perforated sprinkle shaker. Once there is that much seasoning in the pot, the only thing you can do is pray for a decent outcome for dinner.

Every time it happens, it reminds me of the children's devotion of too much toothpaste squeezed outside of the tube. It is impossible to put the paste back in the tube once it's out.

When we say hateful things in a heated moment, it makes us look like oregano soup or squeezed toothpaste. There is no way to retract it once it's out. Being a child of God, we are asked to be an example to others and that is conveyed by how we present ourselves in public (and private). In any argument it is always best to start with a prayer, not oregano, not toothpaste, and definitely not a sharp tongue.

Prayer:

Dear Lord, "button my lips" when I feel compelled to "let someone have it." There are plenty of people on this earth that have a difficult time and are living in chaos without me adding more chaos into it. Help me to love and understand the other person, but if I can't understand, help me walk away in love. In Jesus' name. Amen.

"He's sitting on the fence."

"Cast all your anxiety on him because he cares for you." 1 Peter 5:7

One of the worst trials in my life came at the beginning of the pandemic. I had a health scare and felt too isolated to try to speak to friends about it. For the first time in my life, I had a difficult time praying and finding words to even say to God. Listening to worship music (while all positive and encouraging), the lyrics reminded me that "no, everything might not be okay." I found myself wrapping myself in the isolation of COVID and used it as a reason not to talk or engage with others because I didn't want to think about it. Doctors gave an option to have more tests made, but on a fluke mistake, the lab sample was lost in a winter storm on its way to California, and we waited for nearly a month for some kind of reassurance.

During quarantine, one of the only things anyone could do was go for walks. I began taking long walks and bumped up my exercise, praying all the while for God, to "please give me peace and let me know everything will be okay." One day shortly thereafter, I passed an old abandoned house that I had been past every day for 30 years. On that day I saw a Christian plaque hanging on the porch that read, "Salvation belongs to the LORD; may Your blessing be on Your people." Psalm 3:8

I had never noticed the sign until then and immediately felt relief in realizing that "salvation" or being safe was something that directly came from God. Whatever we are facing and whatever "evidence" we have that our world is crumbling, God is still God. Salvation is His alone.

Prayer:

God, Heal my mind, spirit, and body. Take away my fears. Where You lead me, I will follow because I know You are always with me. In Jesus' name. Amen.

"Jumping out of the frying pan and into the fire"

For we are God's workmanship, created in Christ Jesus to do good works, which God prepared in advance for us to do. Ephesians 2:10

When I asked my husband to install some new light fixtures in our old house, he went up to the attic, and I wasn't prepared for what followed. He came back down and said that all of the electrical had to be replaced because squirrels had devoured it. He also discovered that at some point the chimney had cracked and soot covered the entire attic space. There have been times when fixing our house that I have sat on the floor and cried wondering, "what have I gotten myself into?!" Life has a way of doing that. Not only just fixing the house, but sometimes life can feel like a labyrinth that I am trying to find my way through with a blind fold on. Even checking my email sometimes becomes an ordeal with not knowing the correct password, getting locked out because I entered the wrong password too many times, and proving that "I am not a robot." When I feel overwhelmed and exhausted by it, I remember Jesus in Gethsemane–an image I so closely relate to, that I keep the print in my living room.

Jesus, the Son of the Living God, also felt exhausted and stressed about the world in Gethsemane. Jesus offers us comfort and respite during our chaos and confusion because He knows about it better than anyone. He offers hope, rest, and renewal in exchange for your love and loyalty. Lay your cares at the foot of the cross. He cares for you.

Prayer:

Jesus, help me in my confusion and endless exhaustion. Guide me in my walk and decisions. Strengthen me and be with me in everything I do. In Jesus' name. Amen.

"Shape up or ship out."

"No temptation has seized you except what is common to man. And God is faithful; he will not let you be tempted beyond what you can bear. But when you are tempted, he will also provide a way out so that you can stand up under it." 1 Corinthians 10:13

I have had several friends and family that had a substance abuse problem. Whether drugs or alcohol, substance abuse is a disease, like Diabetes or Hypertension. It has to be addressed and treated like a disease daily. What is more difficult to identify, is the way we choose to respond to our loved one's problem. When personal items become damaged or stolen, it is difficult to know how, or if you should continue in a relationship with them. Anytime a relationship tie is severed it hurts.

God gives several scriptures to help us navigate on how to deal accordingly. He asks us to "forgive seventy times seven" (Matthew 18:21-22) but at the same time says to treat them as a Pagan or Tax Collector if they refuse to listen (Matthew 18:17). It can be hard to shut off contact with a loved one who has toxic traits. Matthew 18 is a guiding light on the topic. What is for certain in making the decision is that it should be done in love. Even if you no longer communicate with someone who refuses to change, it doesn't mean that you can't love them, pray for them, and bless them. During this difficult time ask for God to bless you with wisdom, peace, and strength.

Prayer:

God, Help me know how to respond (or not respond) to my loved ones with a substance abuse problem. Help me address it with love in a meaningful way. Soften the heart of my loved one that they might feel compelled to do right and change. Strengthen me, Lord that I might respond to this with Christian love. In Jesus' name. Amen.

"Those who live in glass houses shouldn't throw stones."

"Humble yourself before the Lord and he will lift you up." James 4:10

When I was 19 (before I had good common sense), a friend and I went shopping in downtown Montgomery. When we were walking in the parking lot, the most hideous car I have ever seen was parked next to ours. I said, "check out this nasty, pink diarrhea-colored car!" In the next 60 seconds, I must have turned white as a very large, scandalous woman opened the door to the pink car and asked, "what did you say about my car!?" I shriveled into a hole somewhere as the woman gave me a very clear, memorable message about how she had worked hard to pay for her car and she was proud of it. When she was finished, I have never wanted to run away so badly in all of my life.

Even though it was a traumatic memory (and I consider myself lucky I didn't get bopped on the head), that woman's words became ingrained in my memory forever. After having several embarrassing moments of my own with cars (breaking down on the side of the road, having to change a tires, and belts screeching in the rain,) I have realized she was right to scold me. While I thought I was being funny–I was being hurtful. Where the woman should have felt pride–I made her feel anger. Our words are powerful. In our brief time on Earth, let what comes out of our mouth be Godly and empowering.

Prayer:

God, May my words always be a reflection of You. Forgive me for looking to be above others and my hateful comments. Show me how to love others the same way that You love me. In Jesus' Name. Amen.

"If you can't beat them, join them!"

Other seed fell among thorns, which grew up and choked the seedlings. Matthew 13:7

One of the most identifiable trees of the South is the lovely Magnolia. My great-grandfather planted the one in my front yard 70 years ago, and it now takes up a large part of the front yard. At Christmastime, our family and friends cut some of the lower branches to use for decorating. We also enjoy its shade on summer days. However, just as lovely as it seems, it shades the yard so much that it kills all of the grass, leaving the front yard to be an unwelcoming dustbin. It also makes truck loads (no exaggeration) of leaves to collect weekly. It is not wise to ignore the leaves because they quickly mound up becoming hundreds of teacups of rain water that you have to walk through to check the mailbox. One summer, while trying to rake and bag all of the leaves, I was nearly bitten by a copperhead (the same color as the leaf) which hid under the leaf pile. Imagine my surprise!

I find that the magnolia is great metaphor for people. People can be ever so lovely, with the ability to write poetry and inspire millions just by speaking, but also have roots and leaves that crowd out beauty. Our action and words are equivalent to the magnolia leaves. If we do not take care of what we say it causes so much hurt and ugliness that any beauty that we have to offer is quickly forgotten. The power of a one-line remark can devastate someone for life. We misjudge our hatefulness as being witty and more intelligent.

Prayer:

Lord, plant the seeds of Your wisdom and beauty inside us. Let our words be the loving words of Jesus Christ. In Jesus' name. Amen.

"Imitation is the best form of flattery."

"The heavens are Yours, the earth also is Yours; The world and all it contains, You have founded them." Psalm 89:11

Can you imagine that the raindrops trickling down from the sky are musical notes from an orchestra? Even though a different tune, it is unique as an original song and masterpiece. God has created a natural symphony if we are ever mindful enough to stop and listen to it. The wind rustles and leaves crackle down the street. Birds tweet and flitter and the audience of a family of deer hushes to listen. Thunder rolls in the distance and percussion grazes the instruments gently waiting for climax just by the wave of the Creator's hand.

The mighty Lord has equipped you to sense everything that you can feel, see, smell, touch, taste and know. He has prepared everything here to draw your interest. That even the blackest dirt beneath your feet that you care nothing for, can grow enough food to feed and clothe the world. The very being of who we are as humans is a result of His creation. When we hear raindrops and see nature, we are inspired to write a symphony. When we see his celestial sunsets, we are inspired to paint and form poetry. His splendor is so great that even when you don't pay Him attention, He still cares for you.

Prayer:

Good Lord, We run through the fields and sing Your name. We touch the durability of the bark of trees and know You have given so much attention to detail here for us. We will sing and share Your love with those we meet. You have given us our senses so that we may know this goodness and we adore You. Amen.

"Guard your heart."

Balaam answered the donkey, "You have made a fool of me! If I had a sword in my hand, I would kill you right now." The donkey said to Balaam, "Am I not your own donkey, which you have always ridden, to this day? Have I been in the habit of doing this to you?" "No," he said. Numbers 22:30

Although I love people, it can be alarming to hear the lies, profanity, and foolishness that people use so loosely. All of the evil words that we hear on a daily basis can become numbing as we become accustomed to it in our culture. That recklessness muffles (and can even drown out) the sound of God and His will for our life. As Christians, we have to always be alert and guard our heart and mind – there are an endless number of people like Balaam in the world.

However, during unsettling times when we are having a crisis, it is comforting to know that God can and will get His message to us through any means necessary. In the Bible, God uses Balaam's donkey to turn around and try to correct his bad behavior. Nothing is too big or difficult for God in communication and He can completely change the outcome of our situations. We need only trust in Him.

Prayer:

O Father, prepare my heart when I am near people that are misguided and reckless. You gave your message to a donkey. So then, help me listen for Your will. Help me decipher the truth from the insults and evil of the world. Only You know my heart and how to capture my attention. I am in Your hands. Empower and strengthen me with Your armor that I will know Your truth and will when I hear it. In Jesus' name. Amen.

"Let the cat out of the bag."

Wait for the Lord; be strong and take heart and wait for the Lord. Psalm 27:14

Any time our life situation gets rocky, we feel overwhelmed and have a tendency to think that God has abandoned us, but nothing could be further than the truth.

When the rain pours and the wind bends the trees, we scurry to areas of safety and hope for protection. In nature, the animals and insects also seek shelter under leaves and under corners looking to keep safe. In all things we look to the Lord for His protection. When heavy rains come, we wait for the Earth to drink it in. We know God loves us and that we will come out unharmed with Him in the end.

After the storm passes, the clouds always break, and the song birds fill the trees rejoicing once again. The bees are free to carry their pollen. The breeze is cooler and feels good against our skin. Gardens grow rich with produce and our harvest is full. Rain has watered the parched, dry soil and all of nature is vibrant and green again after seasons of heavy storms. God's provision has been made and all of nature knows it. Whatever storm we are experiencing, cling to God as your refuge and wait for the blessings to come.

Prayer:

Father, we praise You. When we have lost everything, we will praise Your name because with You, we know we have everything. In difficult times, lift our hearts and spirits that we may always keep our eyes on You. In Jesus' name. Amen.

"Time is a great healer."

"If anyone will not welcome you or listen to your words, shake off the dust from your feet when you leave that house or town." Matthew 10:14

Other people's words have a strong impact and effect on our lives. Whether their criticism is meant constructively or not, other's opinions can feel like knives into our soul. Whatever the situation may be, it is always important to remember your value and self-worth. Hold firm to the person God is trying to mold you to be. If a person tries to tear you down, shake them off. Live your life righteously and no one will be able to discredit or damage your future. For you are a child of God, of the most high. You are royal. No one can discredit that.

Equally, you should act accordingly–in love, truth, and grace. If you are being attacked and are in the line of fire from people who aren't walking with God daily, don't be surprised! Don't go after them or try to attack them. Live your life in a way so that when people hear lies about you, they know they are not true. Your Christian life will speak to your integrity.

Prayer:

Dear God, Protect me in the presence of my enemies. Deliver me and keep me safe. I pray friends and family are able to know the difference and truth about me when hearing anything evil against me. In Jesus' name. Amen.

"Up the creek without a paddle"

"Give thanks to the LORD, for he is good. His love endures forever." Psalm 136:1

One of my favorite things during my youth was to cheer in the stands at pep-rallies for football games. All of the different classes would cheer across the gym to see who would win the Spirit Award. Students made signs, filled soda cans with rocks to shake them, and painted their face to show their school spirit.

Even though I don't even remember the last time I yelled or cheered for anything, those were precious times. In our youth, we were all so eager to make a fool out of ourselves to show our passion. Somewhere along the line, adults lose their passion for cheering. Cheering as a Christian translates to "praise the Lord for His goodness!" We definitely need that!

He alone does great wonders. He made the heavens and the oceans. His love for you is as deep as the sea. Mankind cannot even travel to the depths of God's oceans. He is worthy of praise.

When you are feeling down and feel lost to sea, trust that the Lord is with you. Praise His name and sing to Him! He is wonderful! God will prevail and never leave you. Look to the heavens and declare His name!

Prayer:

Thank You, God for Your grandiosity and almighty power! You are everything! I sing Your beautiful name, Holy and Powerful God forever! Amen.

"Ugly is as ugly does."

"Search me, God, and know my heart; test me and know my anxious thoughts. See if there is any offensive way in me, and lead me in the way everlasting." Psalm 139:23-24

If we are honest with ourselves, we all know some part of our life that is less than perfect. Whether it is the way we spend too much money, yell at drivers on the freeway, eat too much pie, or loathe people we have to communicate with on a daily basis.

We all have sin and fall short before the glory of God.

While we are in the act of those bad habits, we love to redirect our sin onto others making it someone else's fault. The person that overspends says, "I wish my husband wouldn't upset me making me buy that new $200 purse." The road rage driver says, "look at that stupid driver that merged without using a turn signal!" The overeater says, "I can't eat at Aunt Carol's house. She makes me fat and I overeat." The jealous co-worker says, "she doesn't deserve a promotion."

Sin is ours to reject or accept. Others around us might encourage us to sin, but it is ours for the taking or leaving. We ask forgiveness for the evil resentments and hatred we feel for others.

Prayer:

Search me God and know my heart! Take me and wash my heart and mind from wickedness. My sin rots my flesh and I have been less than the greatness You made me to be. Teach the ways I may bless and love everyone I encounter. Let my prayers, presence, gifts, service and witness be used for You and Your kingdom. In Jesus' name. Amen.

"You are going to miss the boat."

This is what the LORD says: "The people who survive the sword will find favor in the wilderness; I will come to give rest to Israel." Jeremiah 31:2

For people that live in the countryside, it is not a surprise that the countryside offers a beautiful peace. Growing up my favorite moments were listening to the deep bellows of frogs down in the holler', catching lightening bugs as well as listening to crickets and katydids chirp and sing in the fields and trees. It was like watching a beautiful symphony come to life every evening right after a magnificent sunset. Since then, even though I have experienced some amazing sights, those early days of childhood living on the farm are untouchable. There was a Godly peace that lived out in the woods, and I have always realized that many war-torn refugees would be desperate to experience it. It is a gift to have experienced it.

However, most of the world is usually more eager to seek out adventure and action. Rarely does one find a person that says "I am headed out to the forest to relax and reflect on God's goodness." Our world would be a better, peaceful, loving place if we looked for the peace always in our lives. God offers it and everything we need. As humans, we are always so afraid we are "going to miss the boat."

Prayer:

God, thank You for the respite You give us in nature. I praise You for the suffering that ceases in Your presence. For the brokenhearted and those suffering, may they find a restful haven in You. In Jesus' name. Amen.

"Caught between a rock and a hard place"

"She is clothed with strength and dignity; she can laugh at the days to come." Proverbs 31:25

Of the many wise teachings and instructions from the Bible, I have always admired the "Proverbs 31" woman for her lead to us all. Most notably, when times are hard "she can laugh at the days to come." During my life (and for most of us) times have been difficult sometimes economically, sometimes politically, and yet, the Proverbs 31 woman can laugh. The reason for her laughing is not because she is a child or careless, but because her faith is so strong in God that she KNOWS He will deliver and rescue her in whatever issue arises.

Looking back in my own life, I have been scared at times of how I would pay a certain bill, of an illness that was overtaking a family member, of the hatred spreading around politics ... of many worldly things. The Proverbs 31 woman is a reminder to put your worries and EVERYTHING in the hands of God so you can enjoy the day and put your energy in something more fruitful for God's kingdom; Holy advice not just for women, but for everyone.

Prayer:

My Father, when times are wrong and suffering, I will cling closer to You. When people have only hateful things to say about others, I will seek Your face. When hateful words fill the mouths of our leaders and mentors, silence any hate in my heart and let me find refuge in Your presence. Mold and make me, Father so that my thoughts and words are Yours, not what I have learned on this Earth. When the mob groups together and seeks vengeance and action. Help me identify and see the cause of division and put the disaccord to sleep. In Jesus' name. Amen.

"God is good all the time. All the time, God is good."

"Do not conform to the pattern of this world, but be transformed by the renewing of your mind. Then you will be able to test and approve what God's will is—his good, pleasing and perfect will." Romans 12:2

When traveling abroad, I met a person that most Christians would identify as a "Samaritan." When I describe him as a Samaritan, I don't mean "the good Samaritan" I am referring to the deeply rooted hate and disgust that most Jewish people had for Samaritans during Jesus' time. During my encounter, I was scared because I had heard that he was different than me. I was warned by my parents during childhood to stay away from "people like that." I had heard these things from people I loved so I believed and knew them to be true:

> *"Samaritans are lazy. They do not bath. They lie and will steal from you. Anyone socializing with a Samaritan would be considered an outcast. Unemployable. Anyone that married a Samaritan would no longer be accepted by their parents. Samaritans are not intelligent. They do not have the mindset for endurance. Samaritans were a waste of good space and resources, and bled dry the well from which we drank. Samaritans are dangerous and will kill you. They want to kill all of us."*

I looked away at the sky when I saw the Samaritan looking at me. Were his plans to rob or attack me? Would he kill me to please his god?

The Samaritan talked to me and I learned a great deal about his life. He was from a war-torn area, watched his parents be murdered by rebels, and had traveled hundreds of miles as a child, alone, to get to a country free from oppression. He was without religious conviction because it was in the name of "religion" that his parents were killed. Although our time together was brief, it was an opportunity to share that the Christian God offers hope to everyone.

Navigating new relationships and conversations is our mission as Christians. If God is for us, who can be against us? (Romans 8:31)

Prayer:

Dear God, help me see all people as a child You created. Free my mind from the hate that the world has taught me. I will praise You in the way I open my heart to others. My mind and heart cannot be for You, if they are against another with hatred. In Jesus' name. Amen.

"Don't be a worry wart."

Peace I leave with you; my peace I give you. I do not give to you as the world gives. Do not let your hearts be troubled and do not be afraid. John 14:27

I love opening my arms to receive my incoming toddler. As he gets older and his confidence builds, the days of holding him all day are becoming less. I love that his independence is growing but love to cuddle and hold him when he needs it. Every person needs someone to hug them and get them through difficult times.

Even the most "perfect of people" still need to be comforted at times. I have known several people that seem emotionless. Everyone needs someone to lean on. That person could be a friend, co-worker, or acquaintance. God did not give us other people in vain.

When situations seem impossible and others do not have any advice or comfort to give, God is always there and able. No one will ever love you more and be willing to hear your situation. Just as I will always be here to watch and catch my baby if he falls and wants a hug, God loves when we embrace Him.

Prayer:

Lord, You are He who loves me the most, and I love You. Comfort and bless me. You know my life and all of the hairs on my head. I trust Your will for my life. In Jesus' name. Amen.

"Perfection is the enemy of good."

"Humble yourselves, therefore, under God's mighty hand, that he may lift you up in due time. Cast all your anxiety on him because he cares for you." I Peter 5:6-7

I have always enjoyed writing. In junior high, I enjoyed writing short stories. In high school, at the request of my English teacher, Mr. McKee, my class kept a daily journal, which eventually led me to writing for a church and then newspaper.

Who can say how many words I write and type!? My published writing easily equates to a few hundred thousand words a year. At times when I publish something, there is always a group of people that seemingly find delight with errors or grammar mistakes, as if to say "I am smarter than you because I found your flaw."

In every way of life, personally or professionally, there will always be error. In your personal relationships, you will "goof up," you will say the wrong thing or make a bad action in error. In your professional life, we are only human and error should be expected. What is not expected are people finding joy in your mistakes. As Christians, God asks us to act in love and humble our hearts. Finding joy in the mistake of others does not make you look smarter. It brings to light that you have a need to compare your own knowledge with others. God is almighty and His knowledge is greater than us all. Humble your hearts so that God may teach you something new.

Prayer:

Father, at Your feet I humble myself. Help me find forgiveness and love for all of Your children. May everything I say and do be a reflection of Your love. In Jesus' name. Amen.

"Well begun is half done."

"I will meditate on your precepts and fix my eyes on your ways." Psalm 119:15

When taking a road trip, I like to begin driving early. No matter if I am going to the local state park or to the beach, setting out on the road at 7 a.m. usually ensures less traffic, which means safer road conditions, more time to enjoy our destination, and that we are not tired and nagging during the journey.

Even though, living a Christian lifestyle is not a physical destination you get to at the end of the day, it is a journey. Starting out every morning early and well equipped by praying, devotional time, and worship will help you navigate your day easier by being prepared and "on the lookout" for bad road conditions and how to handle them.

Growing up my dad had a "Holy Grail"-like collection of road maps that he used for decades throughout the United States. Road maps are a bit nostalgic now with the use of GPS and maps on the internet that give us audio instructions to our destination. With that kind of technology, there is not any reason we shouldn't use it to help us navigate spiritually. Bluetooth music can fill the car when driving. There are apps that can prompt us during our busy day to read a devotion, to help us pray, to connect us to other like-minded people, and to even read the Bible for us. A good start is important and will help us get to our destination−God.

Prayer:

Father, Set my feet on the right path. Let something that I do in my preparation and journey be pleasing to You. Thank You for this journey! In Jesus' name. Amen.

"You can catch more flies with honey than you can with vinegar."

"All you need to say is simply 'Yes' or 'No'; anything beyond this comes from the evil one." Matthew 5:37

In many open-air markets, instead of hearing what is being sold, you hear practically anything to get your attention. Good salesmen and game players quickly tell us what we want to hear. It is how con-artists snooker millions of people every year by telling them they have won a thousand dollars. I have accidentally signed myself up on several "free" subscriptions to receive mail faster, get discounts in the moment on my purchase, and overpaid for services after the "free" trial secretly ended. The whole world has secret ploys and deceptions up their sleeve. Any time I hear "includes a free magazine subscription" at a sales counter, I instantly crumple my face. No matter, your age you have to be "on the ball" to not be swindled.

Even though we like to hear good things that will benefit us, it damages the relationship once betrayal has set in. Saying things that are not open and honest about the whole truth makes others mistrust us. Sometimes the truth can be harsh, but people would rather hear it up front than feel deceived. The world occasionally "gives us lemons," and it is up to Christians to be kind, truth-speakers. Focusing on being truthful can be a challenge to some, but is the Christian aspect of being honest.

Prayer:

Dear God, thank You for being a source of truth away from the lies of the world. Help me speak truth always with kindness instead of being harsh. Give me the correct worlds that I may leave a meaningful impact for Your Kingdom. In Jesus' name. Amen.

"A chain is only as strong as its weakest link."

"How good and pleasant it is when God's people live together in unity!" Romans 12:15

One of my favorite things to recycle around the house is grocery bags. I almost use more than I receive each week at the store. I keep a supply of them by my cat's litter box making it easier to clean. I keep a supply in my kitchen cupboard that I use when making fresh dough (it keeps it from sticking to the cutting board.) I keep a few to line the collar of people's shirt when I cut or dye hair. I always put a few in our luggage when we travel in case, I need it for trash or to place a wet swimsuit inside. I use them to fill up the extra space in the bottom of gift baskets, and of course, I use them just as bags to carry things like fruit and vegetables from the garden.

At one time, when paper bags were more common, I even enjoyed making use from them. I would cut the paper and use it as a drop cloth when painting. Cut them in fine strips to line the bottom of gift baskets. I ALWAYS kept my freezer goods in them when traveling. I even wore a paper bag in Kindergarten as a vest for a play.

However, with all of these wonderful purposes for bags they have their weak points, too. Besides being harmful to nature, specifically the ocean, they don't always live up to their purpose. It is a horrible feeling when I am carrying in the groceries, and I can feel my bag start to break. It feels like I am slowly losing grip and then they all fall out on the ground, sometimes breaking a whole jar of pickles or breaking eggs and leaving me with a mess!

As Christians, we have an array of multi-talents. Just like the many uses of grocery bags, every person has a unique gift. It makes me so sad when I hear someone say, "I don't have a talent." Of course, you do! You just haven't discovered it yet. Every person is unique and can shine like a diamond.

We are all on a journey to do specific tasks and do the best that we can. When we see someone who is struggling and that their bag is "breaking," it is part of a Christian's duty to encourage and help them. If we see excelling, we are called to cheer them on.

Prayer:

Loving God, thank You for Your merciful love. May we be reminded to be merciful and love others in the same way You give to us. Help me look for all of the useful talents You created in me and to ask Christian friends when I know I need help. In Jesus' name. Amen.

"Time flies when you're having fun!"

"He would withdraw to desolate places and pray." Luke 5:16

One of my favorite things about holidays is that friends and family are off work, and we can spend time together. I love to fire up the grill, go swimming, watch fireworks, or even watch a movie together. When I close my eyes at night, I thank the Lord for the great day but also know that it went so quickly.

The more I activities I plan, the quicker the day seems to go by. Swimming and eating a hot dog suddenly can feel like a 7 minute speed-date. However, if we find time to all go sit on the porch and watch cars go by, listening to the homemade ice cream churn, I am under the impression that I got more quality time with my family. Sometimes less is more when planning our schedules with loved ones. Holidays are times most enjoyed when there is not a busy schedule. It becomes more meaningful when we add quiet time versus activities. Likewise, our devotion time with God is the same. Can we fully expect to have God restore us, give us peace and share His will in a 7 minute speed-date? Having a good relationship requires more time.

Prayer:

Dear Father, thank You for always being there when I need You. Forgive me for not always putting in the adequate time that is needed in our relationship. Help me set aside time so that our relationship is the best it can be. In Jesus' name. Amen.

"A rolling stone gathers no moss."

"When a stranger resides with you in your land, you shall not wrong him. The stranger who resides with you shall be to you as one of your citizens; you shall love him as yourself, for you were strangers in the land of Egypt." Leviticus 19:33-34

In my little town, it has always been frowned on to meet someone that is a "wanderer." I have grown up listening to my friends and family question why someone who is not related to anyone in our town would move here. Their curiosity was rooted in that they "must be up to no good" or some type of swindling.

Times and culture are changing. I find myself attracted to outsiders because they are new and interesting people, with new stories and experiences. However, being leery of "outsiders" is something I imagine was even more extraordinary 2,000 years ago. There were not any cars or airplanes, and moving to a new area would have likely made the new neighbors shut their doors and shutters.

When we encounter someone who is different than us, many of us still feel a bit guarded and nervous. However, it is the joy and acceptance of meeting new people that introduced us to Jesus. Jesus wandered across multiple regions, and had revolutionary ideas that were definitely brow-raising. We should definitely be on guard and "guard our heart" but not accepting a person because of their difference or because they are foreign might make you miss God's blessing.

Prayer:

God, Let my arms be open to receive those that come to visit and need a friend. Help me find the acceptance in the same way You accept me. In Jesus' name. Amen.

"A watched pot/kettle never boils."

"So do not fear, for I am with you; do not be dismayed, for I am your God. I will strengthen you and help you; I will uphold you with my righteous right hand." Isaiah 41:10

It can feel like insanity being stuck in traffic. Every Saturday, chances are if you take the interstate near my home, you will sit at a standstill for an hour or more. Whatever destination you were trying to get to is ruined (or heavily dampened) from sitting still, unable to move. That upsetting experience also equates to when our lives abruptly are stopped by life-altering events. Life feels like it is floating by gently and fun with the wind in our hair and things like a change in our relationships, health, finances and career can flip a switch and have us feeling out of control and in despair.

Hebrews 13:5 says, "I will never leave you, nor forsake you. During our hardest moments, it is important to remember that God never leaves us. Deuteronomy 31:8 tells us during those times not to be afraid and discouraged. The name "Emmanuel" comes from the Greek rendering of the Hebrew words "God with us" and where He is, He will bless and protect you like a good father does.

Life has many different experiences in store for us. Sometimes we would rather be a different place but no matter what the circumstances are, choose to pass the time singing praises to the Father, who will lift you up.

Prayer:

Lord, I ask You to help me get through the difficult hills in my life. May I be reminded that You are always with me. Shine blessings on my life and family. I love You and give You thanks. In Jesus' name. Amen.

"You reap what you sow."

"This is the day that the Lord has made; let us rejoice and be glad in it." Psalm 118:24

I find that most everything in life has a positive aspect if you search hard enough. During the worst historical events, many survivors get through the ordeal by looking for the positive parts of the situation. In "The Hiding Place" by Corrie ten Boom, she and her sister are in a Nazi concentration camp and on one occasion, pray thanking the Lord for lice and fleas. Due to the bugs, the SS guards did not come inside the barracks and bother them for fear of also getting bugs. Since the guards did not bother them, they were able to hold large prayer gatherings that were translated to many around the room. Although I have never lived through any experience like Corrie, I also try to find the positive in every situation. At the end of "The Hiding Place", Corrie paints part of her new house Spring Green so that everyone who visits can feel spring and the new life that comes with it. (I also painted a room in my home the same color to remind me that new life comes.)

Jesus promises us hope and new life. Isaiah 60:1 says, "Arise, shine, for your light has come, and the glory of the LORD has risen upon you. Whatever you are going through, no matter how big the issue seems, Jesus will prevail and help those who earnestly love and follow Him.

Prayer:

Father, Shine Your light on me, my heart, and path. No matter of the darkness that surrounds me, it is unimportant as long as I can see You. Keep my eyes on You. In my time of sorrow, I will look to the Heavens. Forgive those that have wounded me. Surround me with new hope as I look to the future. In Jesus' name. Amen.

"Beauty is in the eye of the beholder."

"Take my yoke upon you and learn from me, for I am gentle and humble in heart, and you will find rest for your souls." Matthew 11:29

Like all people, I like to feel beautiful. Regardless of body type, shape and size, dressing up and being seen does a lot for one's self-confidence. I remember one time in particular in my mid-twenties, I was waiting at a red-light and a car pulled up beside me. As we were waiting, I could see in my peripheral vision, he eased up about a foot to align with my car. This getting my attention, I looked over at him and saw an attractive man checking me out. He smiled, and I smiled back. His light changed, and he slowly drove off. I reached up to my rear-view mirror and bent it down, so I could see how attractive I looked. To my surprise, I had forgotten that I had dressed up for Crazy Hair Day for the church Vacation Bible School and had a dozen odds and ends tied into my hair. Of course, the man was going to stare, I had pieces of yarn tied in with paper clips, small sewing scissors and other random things I found in my desk earlier that day when I prepared my crazy hair.

Even though I realize now that the man wasn't interested in my "crazy" beauty, beauty fortunately does not have a standardized definition. One of the first things I noticed about my husband and fell in love with was a scar on his chin. It came from a horrible childhood accident when he fell through the floor of a horse carriage. To me, the scar is symbolic and a testament of his survival during a difficult childhood that he overcame; making him stronger and straightforward.

Within the interesting and different things about each of us, God assigns beauty to our story. Even though some people might be put off by yarned paper-clip hair or a scar, all of those things collectively tell a story about who we are. They are the curiosities that attract people and how God allows us to put "a shoe in the door" when we witness to people. Very few people (in my experience) have a talent of walking up to strangers and asking if they have a relationship with Jesus Christ. Most strangers run the other direction. However, when we have characteristics that attract people, in whatever form, it is a conversation starter to say, “I’m on my way to VBS. Do you have a church? Will you come?” or “I got this scar before I was a Christian and knew about the love of God. Do you know how much God loves you.”

What are your beautiful and unique characteristics? What makes you different? How can you use that to connect to people?

Prayer:

Dear Heavenly Father, thank You for making us all different and allowing us to use our differences (or similarities) to connect with other people. Help me identify what attracts people to me and to use that for good, to glorify Your kingdom. All praise and glory is Yours. In Jesus’ name. Amen.

"Don't put the cart before the horse."

"I have told you these things, so that in me you may have peace. In this world you will have trouble. But take heart! I have overcome the world." John 16:33

There have been many times in life when I was worried that I wouldn't live up to the time table that our culture assigns us. We are meant to have a certain job by a certain time, be married by a certain time, have children by a certain time, have so much money saved by a certain time, and retire by a certain time.

God's timing is immaculate. Even though you might have had plans to be a millionaire and feel that God didn't listen to your request when you prayed for that, He might have kept that lifestyle from you to keep your life simple, quiet, and humble, so that you can maintain peace and balance. Sometimes we haven't given consideration to how changes will impact our life, which ultimately changes us. Some of the most inspirational people of mankind lived a life less desirable and used their circumstance to change the world (think Rosa Parks).

If your life seems like it is headed to a destination you really don't want to travel to, it might be God delivering you from something awful or taking you to your biggest blessing (think Joseph and his coat of many colors.) Take a moment to breathe and thank God for this day and this moment. It will pass soon enough.

Prayer:

Lord, sometimes it is all we can do to hang on. Keep us on the right path for which we are meant to travel. Thank You for never leaving our side. We place our trust in You. In Jesus' name. Amen.

"Don't judge a book by its cover."

"You will receive power when the Holy Spirit comes on you; and you will be my witnesses in Jerusalem, and in all Judea and Samaria, and to the ends of the earth." Acts 1:8

As a child, I loved flying kites on our farm. The string that came with the kite was never long enough, so my father would tie multiple strings together until the kite was about 200 feet in the air. It was thrilling! However, one of my father's kite "rules" was that if I see the kite starting to fall over power lines, I had to let go of my string. I always felt sad when I let the kite go, but I knew that if I didn't it could potentially kill me.

Sin is very similar in that from a distance it can look appealing and fun. Even though it can be tempting to give in it is crucial to remember that at some point the sinner will feel owned by their sin. It takes over like in the classic fairytale "The Little Mermaid," the main character gives her voice away to be human. It might look tempting, but if evil is involved (even a little) it will not end well. Sin is like a giant whirlpool and once you get sucked in, it will keep pulling you down.

It is comforting to know that God offers us a lifeline and way out. To sustain our life, we have to name the sin and release it. We must ask God for His help. A change in life may not happen immediately depending on how much damage we have done, but rest assured that God will make a way for those who want a fighting chance and want to change.

Prayer:

God, You are my only hope to change. Forgive me of my sin. I want to change and live without the pain I am causing myself and others. Give me strength to change as I surround myself with Christian influence. Protect me and send Your Holy Spirit to guide me that You might use me as a living witness for Your goodness. In Jesus' name. Amen.

"That Ship Has Sailed."

"Truly, truly, I say to you, whoever hears my word and believes him who sent me has eternal life. He does not come into judgment, but has passed from death to life." John 5:24

In one of my favorite poems for funerals, "Gone From My Sight" Rev. Luther Beecher wrote about a beautiful ship on the horizon saying, "when someone at my side says: 'There! She's gone!' There are other eyes that are watching for her coming; and other voices ready to take up the glad shout: 'There she comes!'"

When someone leaves our life that has had great influence and invested time with us, it is inevitable that we feel a void in their absence. Our human brain might sometime waver in wondering where the person we love is and if we will come to know them again. There are so many human mysteries that surround death and our heart can grieve when we do not feel fully assured.

In death, the Bible says that our spirit returns to God in Heaven (Ecclesiastes 12:7).

On more than one occasion, I have prayed for God to hear my prayers, and He has always given His abundance and grace when asked. So when God gives us the promise that "whosoever believes in Him, shall not perish but have everlasting life (John 3:16) I know that God will fulfill my spirit and new life in Heaven with Him.

He is standing on the other side of the horizon, watching the ship come into His port.

Prayer:

God, Help us find peace and comfort in the Holy Bible that gives us a future and hope. In Jesus' name. Amen.

"Don't let the grass grow under one's feet."

I can do all things through him who strengthens me. Philippians 4:13

Recently, my family went swimming and fishing at the lake. I was out in the water with my baby and was surprised when my husband came up behind me and bit my back in the water. It hurt as he bit hard. I turned around to ask him "what was he thinking!?" And was surprised to see a gigantic black fish there instead!! I got out of the water quickly realizing that it had teeth! I saw my husband up on the shoreline and went to tell him about it and he laughed and reminded me that I had put hotdog weenies inside my swimsuit for convenience earlier when I was fishing. One was still in there on my back. I had NO IDEA fish had teeth like people! It hurt and felt just like a person! After I had time to calm down and research I am pretty sure it was a large mouth bass.

In our daily lives, our poor, unsavory actions may result in unsavory results. When we are not living up to the Godly lifestyle choices God wants for us and make bad choices we shouldn't be surprised when we are bitten and left with teeth marks in our back.

Whatever poor choices and sin you have been living with, now is always the best time to make a change. Even if change seems impossible, God will strengthen and help you if you seek Him.

Prayer:

God, Help me clarify what is important in life and live my life according to Your will. Help me recognize poor choices and know which path and action to take. In Jesus' name. Amen.

"Do not lock the stable door after the horse has bolted."

"For I the Lord thy God will hold thy right hand, saying unto thee, Fear not; I will help thee." Isaiah 41:13

Like every good Southerner, I have a few country hounds that live on the porch. They spent their youth growing up isolated on my family's farm, so when I moved to the middle of town, they both had culture shock. They like to bark and "carry on" when a squirrel is too close to their fence. (Living on the farm was open pasture and I do not think they have ever encountered a squirrel up until now.)

I do not always appreciate their built-in barking alarm and bought a white noise machine when my husband and I welcomed our baby home. Most of the time they are barking about something out of place, but on sleepless nights I don't always appreciate it. I roll over and block the sound out with my pillow.

A few years ago, they had running nights of barking scandal, and after waking up five nights in a row to tell them to "hush," I started ignoring them. The following Monday I came home to a ruckus of the dogs running around the yard. I saw that they had cornered a poor, defenseless groundhog! I called my husband, and after waiting an hour, he came to my (and the groundhog's) rescue. We boxed him up and delivered him beside a park lake. However, when I came home and began to survey the scene I saw that the groundhog had built an elaborate tunnel on the side of my yard, and the dogs had dug up what appeared to be a 30 foot long trench! There is no way that the dogs dug the entire trench up in one day, so they had been steadily working the whole week of barking to unveil him. The next two weeks we worked on putting the yard back together the way it was before, and it made me realize that ignoring their alarm left me to blame for allowing the situation to get out of hand.

When the world has a shock wave of things happen, many times we don't want to deal with it. We put those bad things on the side burner and deal with it when it's too late. The Holy Spirit usually prompts us multiple times to give attention to areas of our life. A groundhog and country dogs tearing the yard up is not as serious as other matters, but it is reminder that God wants us to address and confront areas of our lives that need correcting. "Sweeping the dirt under the rug" will only lead us to be haunted by it later on. Those hauntings can pile up and tower over our head until it comes crashing down.

God doesn't expect us to face our issues alone. He is always with us. His promise, "fear no evil, for I am with thee" lives on and secures our well-being. Whatever you are facing, face it and know that God is with you, always.

Prayer:

Dear Father, I lift my heart to You and ask You to help me in my life. Forgive me for not always being faithful and putting things in the order that they should be. Help me prioritize and give me strength to face things in my life. Surround me with Your presence that I might find strength in You. In Jesus' name. Amen.

"Don't try to walk before you can crawl."

"May the God of hope fill you with all joy and peace as you trust in him, so that you may overflow with hope by the power of the Holy Spirit." Romans 15:13

Perhaps one of the most adorable things our son did in his infancy was trying to walk before he could crawl. During "tummy time" he would extend his feet behind him and "kick-kick-kick!" It looked like one of those baby turtles trying to desperately make his way into the water, but he was stationary. Oddly enough, I have felt like that a few times in my life. Whether I was in a bad relationship or working for a bad employer, sometimes we find ourselves in an atmosphere that seems like no matter how hard we "kick-kick-kick," trying to make headway, nothing changes. During that time, we can start developing feelings of animosity and resentment while people don't seem to recognize our worth.

The beauty in the story of learning to crawl is that we eventually walk and even run. Those tiny sea turtles travel the world and can live to be 100 years old! In our vulnerability and most difficult times, it is important to remember that God's future holds things that our imagination can't even fathom. Keep your eye on the prize. Remember that you aren't just a tiny turtle, but created by a God with a "wondrous" vision for your life and future.

Prayer:

God, move us where Your will desires. Give us the courage to keep moving through the obstacles life throws at us. We fix our eyes on You. In Jesus' name. Amen.

"Don't make a mountain out of a mole hill."

"Jesus said to her, 'I am the resurrection and the life. He who believes in me will live, even though he dies." John 11:25

When I was about 9, I thought I would take the initiative of making myself a sandwich. I used a knife to slice open the lunch meat. Unfortunately, the knife went straight through the plastic and sliced open my finger. I gripped it firmly and calmly told my parents what had just happened. Upon unwrapping my finger, blood shot out across the bathroom. When my mother saw how bad it was she got loud, started lamenting and scolding me for using a knife. My father, calmly but firmly held my hand above my head to stop the blood flow, so he could clean and examine it better.

Life gets hectic and can take unexpected turns "at the drop of a hat." Anyone can shout, lament, and get upset about unwanted circumstances, but it rarely changes the situation. (It often makes it worse.) Confidence calms the storm (Mark 4:39-40). It is a natural human emotion to get upset in unwanted situations, but it is a divine difference that God equipped Christians with to have control over the response.

Jesus is "life-giving." That means that even though we might feel the world closing in around us when something bad happens, hope prevails through Jesus!

Prayer:

God, thank You for being the peace and calming our storm. Remind me that it is better to complete a task with a level head, not in fear and chaos, especially when I have You. Strengthen me when the world around me is failing. In Jesus' name. Amen.

"Fight fire with fire."

"So do not fear, for I am with you; do not be dismayed, for I am your God. I will strengthen you and help you; I will uphold you with my righteous right hand." Isaiah 41:10

Firefighting is one of the most admirable professions. Besides the pure bravery and quick critical thinking, firefighters rush in to dangerous situations to save lives. Some of their strategies in firefighting are "back burning" and "burning out" areas in which fire is used to deplete the area from all fuel and brush in order to "nip it in the bud." Many times, these techniques stop forest fires, but fire can sometimes jump over the line and continue burning.

People sometimes find themselves in a crisis situation. Whether it be court related, a serious health condition or financially bankrupt, the weight of the world can seem unbearable. It feels like our entire world is burning down, and we are helpless to it. In those desperate times is when many people look to God for help. In I Peter 5:10, the Bible says, "And the God of all grace, who called you to his eternal glory in Christ, after you have suffered a little while, will himself restore you and make you strong, firm and steadfast."

During our trials, God is greater than the fire that fights fire, because He is infallible. Wildfires never jump over His "burnout" areas because He is the Creator and always in control. When you feel lost in the fire, look to God and ask Him to deliver you from your crisis. He is merciful and will see you through to a better life.

Prayer:

Dear Almighty Father, Help me to keep my eyes on You when I am afraid. See me through my crises. I humbly ask You to stomp out the fires in my life but know that You have control in everything. I place my trust in You. In Jesus' name. Amen.

JULY 1

"Put your best foot forward."

"I will instruct you and teach you in the way you should go; I will counsel you with my eye upon you." Psalm 32:8

Occasionally, I lose signal on my phone. Most of the time, it is not something that bothers me. It annoys my husband that his favorite song (that is streaming) is interrupted. We obviously cannot check social media or ask Google a random trivia question which disrupts life somewhat. The only thing that I find upsetting about losing signal is when we are traveling and I am using navigation. I very rarely am paying attention to what road number I am on, much less the next step I am supposed to take. I just relax and drive until it tells me to "turn left in 1000 feet."

Navigating life feels very similarly. We are on cruise control and enjoying every day until something devastating happens. When something happens that upsets our normal daily living it can make us feel desperate and scared in that we are lost; uncertain of the next step to take.

In whatever occurrence that has upset your daily life, you are not stranded without GPS. God blesses us with many lighthouses when we are feeling lost, confused, and scared. The Bible is the go-to guide on which direction to turn. He places people in our lives to ask for direction. It is important to know which people to ask for help. They are marked by the "fruits of the Spirit" with: love, kindness, gentleness, joy, peace, self-control, generosity, faithfulness and patience.

Prayer:

God, Quiet my heart and own ambitions. I am listening. Teach and humble me in how to respond to the conditions of my life. Affix my eyes to the future so that I might gain momentum in my stride ahead. In Jesus' name. Amen.

"Stop and smell the roses."

"In his hand are the depths of the earth, and the mountain peaks belong to him. The sea is his, for he made it, and his hands formed the dry land." Psalm 95:4-5

God gives us so many things every day that He wants us to stop and notice. The South is full of God's masterpieces. Besides the obvious sunsets and smell of honeysuckle, there are beautiful pleasures in listening to the Whippoorwills and frogs chirp, watching a calf being born and sitting on the porch.

God's love and creation is vast. He is wooing you. He displays all of this in the sunset, a whimsical spread of imaginary colors because He wants your attention. What would you do to win the person you loved? Would you fine tune the beat of the universe for their delight? God is serenading us each day with the delicate way the leaves dance when the wind blows. He flexes His muscles through the thunder of the land, so you will know His power. He sets stars in the heavens each night to see your eyes light up. He comes and sits outside of your door each day and waits for you to wake each morning. He watches you and whispers things while you are sleeping. You are in His eye.

Sin and malice of the world have a way of distracting us, even disorienting us. Set your eyes on God and enjoy the beauty of His love.

Prayer:

God, thank You for the beauty you give us each day. Set my eyes on what You want me to see instead of the "waves" of life. Help me feel Your steady presence around me and in Your creations, reminding me that You are the Almighty, above all and everything. In Jesus' name. Amen.

"If you can't stand the heat, get out of the kitchen."

"Be wise in the way you act toward outsiders; make the most of every opportunity. Let your conversation be always full of grace, seasoned with salt, so that you may know how to answer everyone." Colossians 4:5-6

Summers in the South are nothing to play with. The moisture from the air mixed with the sun makes the most ghastly humid wave that makes everything in the South 1/3 pound heavier than it actually is. My sister recently told me that she shops for clothes that she doesn't have to iron, "because it's too hot to iron in Eufaula." However, my mother has always made me feel partly grateful for humidity by telling us that the moist air keeps us from drying out and getting wrinkles as we age.

During the summer months, I make our family's meal calendar according to the weather. If it is very hot and humid, I don't plan to heat the house up any more and will usually make something in the slow cooker. The kitchen being too hot for comfort is a sure sign that I don't belong in there.

Have you ever been in a similar situation during a conversation? Around certain people or actions, you might start to feel your blood boiling. When it starts you can feel it coming like a volcano burning inside of you. Those are warning lights that you are about to blow and a good sign that you need step away. Some people enjoy "getting rise" out of others that they know will be triggered during the conversation. In Colossians, it states that we are always to respond in grace. God expects more from us. Pray now for the strength to leave and walk away from the future encounters that will come one day.

Prayer:

God, Some people lure us into their conversation with ploys to argue. May I have Your wisdom to realize it in the moment. May everything that comes out of my mouth be pleasing to You. In Jesus' name. Amen.

"The Truth will set you free." John 8:32

"Keep your lives free from the love of money and be content with what you have, because God has said, 'Never will I leave you; never will I forsake you.'" Hebrews 13:5

Today is a day to remember the liberties, that "United" we share. Although backgrounds, cultures, and opinions vary widely across the country, we all share the common denominator that we live in the same country where people still have the right to "life, liberty and the pursuit of happiness" – all things not to be taken for granted.

Freedom comes at the precious price of life. It is a gift to you. Also a gift is the precious freedom that God offered humanity when Jesus gave His life for us. In the same way that man can denounce or claim his country, people can deny or accept Jesus as their Savior. It is a gift that must be claimed in order to be received.

Many people that are living a life without God do not know how to begin a relationship with Him. Confessing your sins to God, asking God to come into your heart and life, and believing that Jesus died for your sins is all that is necessary in becoming a Christian. Whatever life or sin that you have been living can be instantly cleaned, and you will receive liberation from sin.

Prayer:

Dear God, I'm sorry for all the sinful things I have done. I ask You to forgive me and come into my heart. I accept Jesus as my Savior. Free me from the sin and misery that surrounds me, that today I will have freedom in You. In Jesus' name. Amen.

"That's worth its weight in gold.

"These trials have come so that the proven genuineness of your faith — of greater worth than gold, which perishes even though refined by fire — may result in praise, glory and honor when Jesus Christ is revealed." I Peter 1:7

One of the most beautiful things about this planet (in my humble opinion) is the color my neighborhood changes right before sunrise and right before sunset. Everything around us turns the loveliest shades of blue, casting peace over everything. At sunset, everything turns yellow and gold, like a vision into Heaven itself.

As a photographer, I have tried several times to capture the magnitude of EVERYTHING being cast in those two shades, but it is nearly impossible because a camera will only capture so much.

I love to see the sunlight hit the grass at the perfect angle. God loves us so much that He even has turned the blades of grass into gold solely for our pleasure. I chase it with my camera trying to savor everything until it dies right there before my eyes. It feels like death losing something you love. Seasons come and go and nothing ever will stay the same but I know everything beautiful has changed me. It has changed my perception. I am stronger now. I know that grass can be gold. I know more beauty will come again tomorrow. It will be different and some something new but again filled with delight. For now, be grateful for the moment in which God has placed you.

Prayer:

God, thank You for the way Your love changes us. I am grateful and will praise You in the morning and praise you in the evening. In Jesus' name. Amen.

"Take your mind off things."

"I will say to the Lord, 'My refuge and my fortress, My God, in whom I trust!'" Psalm 91:2

The summer in the South is not for the faint of heart! It feels awful and at times, I have even found comparing myself to Moses wandering the desert in Wal-Mart's parking lot.

Last summer, the air conditioning in my car started to go out, and it made me feel a bit desperate until I took it to be repaired. However, to my amusement, I noticed that every time I drove in a shady area, the temperature dropped noticeably by a few degrees. Roads that were in valleys and under a tree canopy even felt nice riding with the windows down.

Trees in their great, strong stature have the ability to be a game changer on hot days. The tree canopies covering the roads are the only thing that kept me going until I was able to have my air conditioner repaired.

God's love is much like the trees. It is strong and being in His presence has the ability to shield us from anything harmful. It is consoling and an enjoyable experience that we long for, especially when we are feeling "the heat" of everyday life.

If you are in need of refuge from life's problems, look for God. You can find him wherever you are (not just forests.) Call on Him and He will provide relief and shelter.

Prayer:

Father, I lay the issues in my life at Your feet and ask You to protect me. Help me navigate through difficult times. Give me discernment in the areas I need it. Restore my body, mind, and soul. In Jesus' name. Amen.

"Sitting around like the village idiot"

"Then God said, 'Let the earth sprout vegetation, plants yielding seed, and fruit trees on the earth bearing fruit after their kind with seed in them;' and it was so. The earth brought forth vegetation, plants yielding seed after their kind, and trees bearing fruit with seed in them, after their kind; and God saw that it was good." Genesis 1:11-12

There is so much to admire in the great outdoors. Each leaf is its own masterpiece. Only an inch long, so tiny, and in a world full of trillions of leaves, look at how much attention nature gave to just this one leaf! Consider its perfection and individualism.

Shucking corn for the end of summer's harvest is a great time to bask and praise God for His goodness. It is amazing that under the many layers of leaves and silky hair, there is a product from heaven that sustains life on our planet. Each ear of corn wrapped up like a gift for a person.

It is not just leaves and the corn, but all of nature. The way water cleans and replenishes life. The precious soil and rain that store all of the nutrients you need to survive. Every part of the eco-system is a masterpiece; so large that we cannot foresee the way every chess piece will come into play. In the same way, God loves and created you. These gifts from God are meant to inspire you to be the best you – a glorified masterpiece and live for the Lord. Thank God for His beautiful creation.

Prayer:

Father, how wonderful You are! I pray for those who do not know the joy of knowing You. I pray for those sitting around "like the village idiot" and becoming blind to the blessings of the day. Put me in their path to spark their interests to the joys of Your abundant blessings. In Jesus' name, Amen.

"There are enough of God's blessings to go around."

"I will open the windows of heaven for you. I will pour out a blessing so great you won't have enough room to take it in!" Malachi 3:10

Reasons for jealousy are not well-defined. It is only fair to say that jealousy stems from the devil, and people allow it to creep into their life when they see something they wish they had. Whatever the "something" is, it might not even be that obvious to the other person (an outgoing personality, a great singing voice, a new pair of shoes, etc.).

I once knew a woman who owned a clothing store, and when she found out that another clothing store was moving in next door, she and her husband started parking their vehicles in front of the other woman's display windows. She didn't advertise that she was sabotaging the new owner, but it was obvious to the town's residents.

Jealousy is a disease that becomes obvious to the others around you. Everyone needs love and encouragement, even the person you don't like. Always try to encourage the person beside you in a positive, loving way. Don't talk about them. Don't keep them from success because of your own ambitions. Help push them ahead. You will be rewarded for that and the riches are much greater than the gain of your own intentions.

Prayer:

Father, thank You for the gift of other people. Forgive me for not always loving my neighbor as I should. Help me see ways I can bless others, especially those I consider my enemy. In Jesus' name. Amen.

"Let your hair down."

"Jesus said, 'By this all people will know that you are my disciples, if you have love for one another." John 13:35

What gets you all tied up in knots? Many times it is the actions of others that we claim brings out our worst side. "Letting your hair down" can be a catchy phrase meaning to "relax and enjoy the day," but enjoying the day has many more factors to it than just taking a nice drive with the dog. Living a life with your hair down, is partly dependent on knowing how to love others. I once knew a real-life "Jethro" from the Beverly Hillbillies. Everything that came out of his mouth sounds like something from the "holler'." I'm not sure I ever met anyone who made me feel as uncomfortable as he did. He was loud and uncouth. He was impossible to dodge. However, God blessed him with a heart of gold and love for others. Most every day, he nearly worked himself to death helping others in doing handy work.

"Letting your hair down" can mean finding the hate and resentment you have held onto about a certain issue or person and replacing it with love. That is not always as easy as it seems. Some people "are real pieces of work" but God has a radical love that can change us and help us evolve. The secret ingredient being our willingness to let Him.

Prayer:

Sweet Lord, teach me Your radical ways of loving others. Knowing that You were being set up to die, You knelt at the feet of Judas and served him. Washing his feet, you placed Yourself in humility and servitude. Help me bend my knee to others, so that the unloved and lost might know Your radical love. Forgive me, Father. May Your love radically change the world and my perception of others. In Jesus' name. Amen.

"Reduce, re-use, and recycle."

"The point is this: whoever sows sparingly will also reap sparingly, and whoever sows bountifully will also reap bountifully. Each one must give as he has decided in his heart, not reluctantly or under compulsion, for God loves a cheerful giver." II Corinthians 9:6-7

I love a good second-hand store. I recently acquired a large 40x30 framed print of a shack. The shack looked unwelcoming and maybe even haunted. My first impression was "why would anyone want to hang a picture of a haunted house in their home?" However, its size and the wonderful way it was matted made it exceptional. I bought it for a few dollars and took it home. After a week of looking at the shack, I decided that a life-size portrait of my baby would be a perfect replacement. I could never get tired of looking at him. I ordered a 40x30 poster of my baby in his Easter outfit, and he now is the focal point of my living room.

What do you want to see as the focal point of your life? Perhaps such a vision seems so distant that it does not seem possible. If you find yourself unable to dream or staring at your empty hands, look around you. God's blessings abound! If your dream seems impossible, ask God to make it possible. God asks us to be good stewards of all that He gives to us. It is ideal to have a goal and pray about it. God will send you every resource that you need. What do you have accessible to you right now? How can you transform it into a blessing?

Prayer:

Good Father, thank You for everything good that You bless us with. Help me to see and understand Your plans and how I may play my part in Your will for the future. In Jesus' name. Amen.

Guard your heart.

"Above all else, guard your heart, for it is the wellspring of life" Proverbs 4:23

In books like "The Outsiders" and movie, "Grease" there are a few "tough guy" characters that don't seem to be phased by love and are cold to the concept. In the 1990s, a slew of songs by rappers like Eminem made it trendy to be a "tough guy" again. That tough guy (and gal) generation spawned broken relationships and children that did not know their father/mother, along with the issue of substance abuse. It is fair to say that the "tough guy" act breaks the individual and everyone around them.

At the same time, God made several points to warn His children to guard your heart. The devil is a hungry lion that is eager to pounce (1 Peter 5:8), so every person should be aware of what he is entering and who he entertains. With that knowledge it is hard to know who to let in to your life and who to have reservations about. Do you trust them or don't you?

The most important thing to remember is that the Lord is your shepherd and comfort. He is going to restore all. If you know you are entering a possibly dangerous relationship or engaging with the enemy–pray yourself up! Pray every day for God to help you with discernment and protection.

Discernment is a spiritual gift from God, and you can pray for God to bless you with it. God calls all of us to love and help everyone, but to have good discernment in every decision.

Prayer:

God, Help me know good from evil, the truth from lies, and when someone is truly in need. Protect me from the malice and evil that surrounds money. Thank You for giving me the opportunity to love and serve others in Your name. In Jesus' name. Amen.

"Count your blessings."

"Every good gift and every perfect gift is from above, coming down from the Father of lights with whom there is no variation or shadow due to change." James 1:17

Every morning at 5:30 a.m., I walk with my dogs down our hallway. I am still half asleep and there is barely enough light on to navigate, but to the dogs it is an exciting time, and they are on "full alert." Even though they have been outside many mornings before this one, this is a new opportunity to be outside again with me.

As we round the corner into the hallway, my Labrador begins to dance a psycho-social ballet, complete with mid-air turns. (He might have some Boxer in him that helps him accomplish this.) He dances and turns all the way to the door. I ask him to sit and calm down, so I can put his leash on. He does mini-jumps as I am touching him. When I open the door, he stands at an eager salute and bumps the screen door with his nose, as if to say "open!" However, before the glass door is open he can already see the entire majestic splendor that waits on the other side: a golden sunrise, chipmunks, squirrels, a yard, and fresh smells! Before opening the door, we just stand there for 30 seconds soaking in the things he appreciates.

Have you stood back and evaluated the goodness in your life? Do you watch the golden sun rise? Before you go play or go to work today, count your blessings.

Prayer:

Use this prayer time to count your blessings and thank God for the many things we don't always thank Him for.

"See no evil, hear no evil, speak no evil."

"Consider it pure joy, my brothers, whenever you face trials of many kinds." James 1:2

One of my favorite knickknacks in my Grandma's house was a trio of monkeys that sat on top of the T.V. set. To a child they appeared to be like tempting toys waiting to be played with. They showed the actions "See no evil, hear no evil, speak no evil." Those little monkeys surrounded by quilts, soap operas, and wafts of country fried steak in the air, became an image I associated with good country living and old-fashioned Americana. Years later, I discovered that the monkey's image actually originated from Japan. Although I felt sad not being able to claim the cute monkeys as "Americana" anymore, they are still a powerful image that resonate with people. They are reminders to live a clean Godly life.

Good ideas are sometimes thought up by other people, and not always people we like. Given Japan's tumultuous history with the United States, I am not sure that my grandmother, who was in her prime in the 1940's, would have kept the monkeys if she knew they were Japanese, which is a shame.

Sometimes we shut people out because they have said or done something in the past that deeply hurts or offends us. We are meant to learn from one another. God has greater purpose for us. If we can manage to work together, we bring endless talents, concepts, and resources to work together for God.

Prayer:

Father, Help me see past people's differences. Help me forgive those that have wounded me. Help me approach others with love and a humble heart to form a Christian pact to work together for the good of Your Kingdom. In Jesus' name. Amen.

"Do not bite the hand that feeds you."

"We all, like sheep, have gone astray, each of us has turned to his own way; and the LORD has laid on him the iniquity of us all." Isaiah 53:6

Anyone who knows me will attest that I love nature. My happy place is in a forest. I feel like sightings with wildlife is a spiritual encounter. It takes a person to silence themselves and listen to hear the gentle footsteps of an animal. With that love, I am passionate about saving wildlife. I have put many a baby bird in shoeboxes and moved many a turtle to the side of the road.

On one occasion, I was driving down Highway 22, a fast-paced, curvy, two-lane road that is frequented by 18-wheelers. I had my mother with me, who I might add is a nervous passenger. Suddenly, we came upon a massive turtle in the road. It was larger than any turtle I have ever seen in the wild. His shell was about 18 inches long. I threw the car into park in the middle of the road and jumped out quickly to move him to the side. (My mother immediately started yelling that we were going to get ran over.) As I approached him and reached down to grab the sides of his shell. CHOMP!! He completely turned around to face me! This was not an ordinary, slow-paced turtle. He was ninja-fast! Although his bite missed my hand he was determined to continue fighting. I quickly danced around behind him to grab him and CHOMP! Again... he was so fast I could not touch him. He was just as fast as I was, and furthermore didn't want to be saved. (We must have looked like country fools out in the middle of a highway brawling with a turtle!) At that point, the traffic began to accumulate on the busy road, and I returned to the car to satisfy my mother. However, I planned to turn around up the road and return for him. After all, even though he was mean as a snake, I could not let such an old, magnificent creature be killed by a car. When I finally made it back to that part in the road, sadly, someone had hit him. He literally was "biting the hand" trying to help him.

It seems ridiculous that creatures in nature often refuse human help. It is part of their nature to resist. Perhaps, they have even experienced abuse that has made them afraid of people. People are the same way. Frequently, when God offers us a way out from a bad situation, peace, restoration… many will turn and run the other way because it is not on our terms. Rejecting God's help and love can only have one ending … death.

Prayer:

Dear Heavenly Father, Thank You for being our father and giving us a way out. Forgive us for not always trusting you. We want and need someone to take away our sin and restore us. Raise us up! In Jesus' name. Amen.

"Do not keep a dog and bark yourself."

"Two are better than one because they have a good return for their labor: If either of them falls down, one can help the other up. But pity anyone who falls and has no one to help them up. Also, if two lie down together, they will keep warm. But how can one keep warm alone?" Ecclesiastes 4:9-12

There is nothing worse than being asked to do something and then told how to do it, step by step. In order to help you really need to get your hands dirty with some good elbow grease. When I encounter people that are "telling me how to" fix a project, I find that redirecting their unsolicited advice can actually help when I tell them what I need in order to complete the task. That might come in the form of asking them to hold the flashlight or go to the store to buy new batteries depending on what the project is. People like to be involved and help in resolutions. They want to play a part.

Many times, I find this scenario to also be true when people attending churches are looking to help and be part of the movement. Some attenders are happy sitting on their pew until Jesus returns, but the majority of people need and want to help. If you are part of a church group or small group and want to see it grow, instead of standing over them supervising them, ask them to help in various ways. Jesus knew that making disciples was the way to carry His message across the centuries. While He was the most important figure in the storyline, disciples came beside Him and carried His message to our homes.

Prayer:

Dear Lord, Thank you for the talents and gifts of all people. May we build something worthy of Your praise and be the disciples that carry the Lord's message into the future. In Jesus' name. Amen.

"Give him an inch, and he will take a mile."

"Now to him who is able to do immeasurably more than all we ask or imagine, according to his power that is at work within us, to him be glory in the church and in Christ Jesus throughout all generations, for ever and ever! Amen." Ephesians 3:20-21

Most people have met a swindler or two that tries to "pull the wool over your eyes," given the chance. It makes for a peculiar and uncomfortable situation. In my own life, giving the person what they are requesting usually equates to "a short ride up the road" becoming an all day journey, loaning "a few dollars" becomes giving them all the cash you have, and letting them "spend the night" turns into a month (or summer)! In my early 20s, I wasn't familiar with dealing with people of the like.

It is hard to know when helping is actually enabling and hurting.

When you give someone in need "an inch and he will take a mile" giving them something for sustainability will last longer – like God's Holy Word.

Many times people that have hit rock bottom are feeling desperate, alone, and afraid. The Bible does say to help those in need, but it is equally important to equip the person with spiritual food so that they can find hope, Christian unity, and peace. Those three things are not frequently found in this drama-filled, chaotic, evil world. Sharing the message of God's word is everlasting and universal.

Prayer:

Father, Help me navigate this manipulating world while also helping those in need. Protect me, guide me, and give me discernment. Help me be prepared by knowing which verses to share, and which parts of my own story to share with them for the most meaningful experience. In Jesus' name. Amen.

"If at first you do not succeed, try, try again."

"Let us not become weary in doing good, for at the proper time we will reap a harvest if we do not give up." James 1:12

With the population growing, food shortages, and world problems on the rise it makes people feel inadequate and helpless in preventing disaster and knowing how to help. Although small, we as individuals are important and can make a difference. In the Bible, God used small details to make the stories complete. In addition to the small "unimportant" people that God deliberately chose, each character was resilient in finishing God's mission. He chose housewives, mothers, fathers, laborers, slaves, prostitutes, and prisoners. They all finished their task no matter how horrible or impossible it seemed.

When I think of the long suffering that many people in the Bible carried with them (Joseph, Noah, Moses, Job, Mary, Paul and especially Jesus), the memory of them has lived through the centuries because of their resilience and devotion to God. Whatever you are going through, hang on. God will see you through it and you will be rewarded for your faith and devotion. Meanwhile, if you see someone beside you suffering, reach out to bless and pray for them.

Prayer:

Father, I pray that You give me glimmers of ways that I may be useful. Strengthen me daily in my walk. May You continue to be the fuel that feeds my desire. In Jesus' name. Amen.

"Keep your friends close and your enemies closer.

"But to you who are listening I say: Love your enemies, do good to those who hate you, bless those who curse you, pray for those who mistreat you. If someone slaps you on one cheek, turn to them the other also. If someone takes your coat, do not withhold your shirt from them. Give to everyone who asks you, and if anyone takes what belongs to you, do not demand it back." Luke 6:27-30

For me, the most difficult request of Jesus is to love our enemies. I try to convince myself that I am doing my enemies a favor by not talking to them or staying away. When I think of my enemies, people that have spoken ill of me to others, belittled, or made my life harder in some way, it is difficult to know how to "do good to those who hate you."

When I was a child, my father only gave me and my sister "one fair warning" when we misbehaved. He would tell us once to clean our room, be home by a certain time, or to not say certain words. After our "one fair warning," if we chose to do the action again, we were punished for it. Perhaps, part of the reason we don't speak to those who have offended us is because we feel we have given them their "one fair warning."

Fortunately for us, God is a loving and forgiving God. When we make offences against Him, He is not counting. In Luke 6:27-30, our Father is saying to make action and bless your enemies. Not knowing where to start, begins with praying to God for His guidance on ways and reasons to approach the enemy.

Prayer:

Father, Forgive me of my hate and lack of action towards others. May I pray for them as many times as I pray for my own family. Help me in knowing the needs and ways to bless them and their household. Open my eyes so that I might see and understand the reasoning behind their behavior. Bless them richly. In Jesus' name. Amen.

"Look before you leap."

"The plans of the diligent lead surely to advantage, but everyone who is hasty comes surely to poverty." Proverbs 21:5

As a teenager, my friends and I used to frequent the local university and hang out there. A hallmark of the University of Montevallo's campus are the lovely, red-brick streets around campus. Once during a heavy thunderstorm, we decided not to wait for the rain to pass and ran out of the library. As soon as my feet touched the red brick, I slid into a GIGANTIC puddle that formed over the bricks. I was drenched and left to drive home soaking wet. On the way home, I pulled over on the side of the road to let some of the heavy rain pass. When the rain subsided, I tried pulling back on the road, but my car was stuck in the mud! It took everyone, standing in the rain, being covered in mud to free my car. We looked like muddy drowned rats when we arrived home.

Sometimes life presents choices and you are not sure if you should wait a while or run out in the rain and "go for it!" Only you can make the decision for yourself and life. However, being wise and looking to God for guidance will keep you from being so hasty. For each of us, the devil uses our failures and insecurities into believing we are inadequate and incapable. The first part of realizing your dream is to remember that with God all things are possible. The second part is to devote meaningful time with God in helping you see and understand His will. Decisions made in haste make waste.

Prayer:

Guide me, Lord, in everything I do. Help me be mindful in all angles of how my decisions will affect me and others. Help me know the steps to take. May I be a good steward of Your blessings and use them to bless others. In Jesus' name. Amen.

"Misery loves company."

"A miserable heart means a miserable life; a cheerful heart fills the day with song." Proverbs 15:15

In perhaps one of my favorite movies of all time, "Pollyanna," the main character, always finds the good in every situation by playing what she called the "Glad Game". The Glad Game is not as easy as it sounds because besides the obvious bad events that hurt our lives, there are also "sour pusses" that never seem to be glad about anything.

Finding the "silver lining" can be difficult in tragedies. When my father was diagnosed terminally ill, he came to live at my house to live out the rest of his days. At the same time, I was taking nursing classes in Selma and studying became too much for me emotionally. I never finished my last semester. Although that moment seemed like "rock bottom" to me, there were many daily blessings that I witnessed in taking care of him. The most notable blessing was that my training from nursing gave me the knowledge in how to care for my passing father. Rotating him in the bed kept him from having bed sores. I was able to change his bed sheets regularly while he was lying in it. It helped me in administering his medicines, understanding what was happening to him, and how I could help.

During that miserable era of my life, the answer to the Glad Game was that God equipped me for it. The answer to every Glad Game is that God always equips all of us, no matter what we are facing. Was that time difficult for me? Did I cry? Did I plead with God? Yes, of course, but we can be glad in every situation because God never leaves us.

Prayer:

Blessed Father, *I will lift up mine eyes unto the hills, from whence cometh my help. My help comes from You, which made heaven and earth.(Psalm 121:1)* Be with me in everything. Save me from added negativity. Give me peace and restore me. In Jesus' name. Amen.

"Necessity is the mother of invention."

"The jar of flour was not exhausted and the jug of oil did not run dry, according to the word that the LORD had spoken through Elijah." 1 Kings 17:16

I remember my grandmother telling me stories of the Depression and the many ways her family thrifted in order to stay alive. They ate sweet potatoes every day because it was the only food available, which led to my grandfather never eating sweet potatoes again once the Depression ended. People from that generation had to be creative in order to maintain their lives. Practically everyone from that generation became thrifty for the rest of their lives for fear that they were being wasteful and knew "how to stretch a dollar".

I'll never forget my first encounter when meeting a certain woman in my community. I explained that we were actually related by marriage and she responded, "yes, I remember your grandmother. I went by her house once and she was out in her yard walking a dog tied to a brassiere." In the moment I felt absolutely mortified, but later came to understand that it wasn't my grandmother's dog. She didn't have a dog leash and the dog needed to go outside. She was also my thrifting Grandmother that made every situation work.

God instills creativity in us when we need it most. Even though the economy may wax and wane, God's provision and presence never does. It is our responsibility to look at the resources He has given us, be thankful for them, and be a good steward.

Prayer:

God, open our eyes to being good stewards of all that You give us. Help us see the tools You place in our hand and know how to use them. Take away any pride that I harbor that keeps me from using the resources You give. May my work be fruitful and pleasing to You. In Jesus' name. Amen.

"Hindsight is always twenty-twenty."

"Neither height nor depth, nor anything else in all creation, will be able to separate us from the love of God that is in Christ Jesus our Lord." Romans 8:39

I have made my fair share of mistakes in life. Some of them have included: not always knowing the best thing to say during a conversation, trying to remove baby clothing by pulling the entire outfit off around his legs before I knew there were stride snap buttons, and the time I decided to haul a curio-cabinet in the passenger seat of a Miata.

The perfect solutions always seem to unveil themselves after the situations have come to a close. For many things, we don't get the opportunity to do things over if we mess up.

One thing that we, as Christians, will never be sad for is making the "right" moral decision. Even if there is some kind of annoyance like inviting the black sheep of the family to your holiday party, it is in the best Christian decision to include everyone that would benefit from holiday celebrations.

Making decisions can be difficult, and life constantly has crossroads that point in all directions. Many times no one is there to point to the correct path other than the Holy Spirit and the Bible. Praying for the Holy Spirit to guide your moral compass is second to none in combating stressful decision requiring immediate attention. At the end of the day, even if we feel we didn't make the right decision, God is there to love and comfort us. He wants us to draw closer to Him, which includes when we feel we have errors.

Prayer:

God, thank You for always loving and accepting us. Holy Spirit, come; guide and protect me. Use me and my life to show others the unconditional love that You give, even when we don't feel deserving. In Jesus' name. Amen.

"One man's trash is another man's treasure."

"My God will meet all your needs according to his glorious riches in Christ Jesus." Philippians 4:19

While some might find "dumpster diving" cringe-worthy, I absolutely love it! I have not ever been inside of a dumpster, but I love seeing "roadside treasures" put out beside the trash. Some of my favorite finds include a high-powered saw that needed a new cord, a bed frame from the 1800s and two riding lawn movers! When I had my small, two-seater Miata that didn't stop me either. Even though there was just enough room for one person, I found two wicker loveseats and hauled them home; standing one straight up in the passenger side and the other tied onto the trunk. It gives me satisfaction knowing that I find valuable things I love that someone threw away.

God loves us in the same way as finding a treasure that hasn't always been loved and appreciated. Sometimes you can visibly see when people have not been loved or have even been abused. Someone equivalently "sat them on the curb beside the trash" and it shows. They don't know love because they haven't ever been shown it. With God's help, every person has the opportunity at a second life. It doesn't matter where that person has been or what they have been through, God has the power to transform us and give us new life, new hope, happiness and security. His ability is not limited to the size of a Miata, because He is all-powerful. Trust in Him to recreate your future.

Prayer:

Dear Father, thank You for loving me when I see myself as unlovable. Thank You for fixing and creating something new in me. My life is Yours to recreate. May I be patient while Your masterplans are drawn and Your actions are in the works. Give me peace in knowing that I am finally in Your hands. In Jesus' name. Amen.

"Practice makes perfect."

"Do you not know that your body is a temple of the Holy Spirit, who is in you, whom you have received from God? You are not your own." 1 Corinthians 6:19

One of my favorite memories as a kid was going to church camp in Springville, Alabama. The campground overlooked a beautiful 30-acre lake that was the perfect atmosphere to clear your head (yes, even a kid clears their head)!

During that summer, I'm not sure I ever felt more encompassed as a child than I did with strong leadership and surrounded by prayer and praise. It was a great experience that stuck with me throughout my life. I even learned how to skip rocks on the lake. Living in that environment, surrounded by Christians, always praising, always praying was great practice for life.

All of that real, living in the moment, intentional worship that happens throughout the day by people that are experiencing real pain is a moving experience. It is channeling God's presence; calling Him and the embodiment of the Holy Spirit to fill the room. It is life-changing and unforgettable.

If we want that for our daily lives (and not just church camp), we have to actively practice worshiping Him and living a life always praising and always praying. We have to share our pain together and our life experiences. We have to create that same environment if we want to feel and see a revival in our lives.

Prayer:

Dear Holy Spirit, Come! Fill this space and our lives. Set our hearts on fire to lift the King high! Break the evil that surrounds our lives as we cry out, Holy is our Lord! In Jesus' name. Amen.

"Put your money where your mouth is."

"This is how we know what love is: Jesus Christ laid down his life for us. And we ought to lay down our lives for our brothers." 1 John 3:16

Big talkers and big spenders always seem to know how to live perfectly. Anytime a big decision in life is made there are always a handful of people that are first to tell you how to fix your life, that your mate is not the right fit for you, that your job should be paying you more, how to raise a child, and what your next financial move should be. One of the simplest decisions to understand and hardest to apply to our life is how to be a Christian. We find evidence of this all over the internet where you can read comments of Christians who are judging others.

Signing up to be a Christian is more than memorizing the Bible and going to church. It can be difficult at times. Even the greatest of people have a hard time with one of God's great commandments–"Love others as you love yourself." (Leviticus 19:18) I can think of two dozen incidents off the top of my head where people (including myself) lacked love and grace while they were in the church building. Why is it so hard to just get along with others?

People are imperfect, including you and me. In our imperfection, we can behave badly, selfishly, and respond without regard to the implications another person may take away from our words. In our church, work, personal lives, and neighborhoods – we forget that everyone should be getting the same treatment that we give ourselves–Love.

Prayer:

Dear God, We have not done your will. We have not loved others as ourselves and have not helped those in need. Forgive us. May we strive to do better and be the love the world so desperately needs. In Jesus' name. Amen.

"The left hand doesn't know what the right hand is doing."

"How good and pleasant it is when brothers live together in unity!" Psalm 133:1

In perhaps one of the most comical acts of summer, my husband and I went camping. I loaded our vehicle down with everything, maybe too much, but I was sure that I had everything – except an air pump and the instructions to put up the tent. My husband and I are a great team, but we were practically to our breaking point of throwing it all back in the car and driving home (or even leaving it behind). We eventually worked together as a team and assembled the tent. I have never been so proud! Trying to blow up the air mattress without a pump was another story. Fortunately, my husband had the great idea to stop the maintenance men who were blowing leaves off of the driveway and borrow their blower to inflate the mattress. Worked like a charm!

Remembering that camping trip is hilarious now, but at the time I thought we were going to lose our cool. We both had different ideas of how to solve the problems, but none of our ideas were working. Only when we came together could we understand the answer. Meanwhile, I am sure we gave other campers nearby the perfect example of how NOT to act when doing a project together.

God places us all here for a reason and to work in unity together. When we respond to one another with short-tempers and anger it repels others. Who wants to be part of the Angry/Short-temper Club? No one.

Prayer:

Heavenly Father, forgive me for my outward anger towards others. Help us put our cynicism aside for the benefit of Your Kingdom. In Jesus' name. Amen.

"The pen is mightier than the sword."

"Peace I leave with you; my peace I give you. I do not give to you as the world gives. Do not let your hearts be troubled and do not be afraid." John 14:27

Words are a powerful tool and weapon. Words have the power to unite countries, help people heal, inspire, give life-saving instruction and live on throughout time. Even much of Christianity is bound in gratitude to the written Bible.

Unlike basic elementary name calling, literature is something that lives on after a person's death. In a hundred years, it is likely that we will all be remembered by things we wrote on social media and in emails, revealing who we were, our interests, and shortcomings. What we write is a testament to our belief in God and how well we live as Christians. We are leaving our personal thumbprint in time every time we send an email, take a photo, or send a mean message to someone. Likewise what we leave behind in our online communication uplifting others and scripture will also be remembered, and will be delivered to a time where people are more likely to be living without God.

Prayer:

Heavenly Father, help us remember that every action we make is either for You or against You. In Jesus' name. Amen.

"Cold hands, warm heart"

"For the word of God is living and active. Sharper than any double-edged sword, it penetrates even to dividing soul and spirit, joints and marrow; it judges the thoughts and attitudes of the heart." Hebrews 4:12

When I think of the ideal Christian, I think of someone smiling, friendly, and a great personality that reaches out to everyone, but God plans and designs people uniquely. People come with all types of different personalities.

When I started dating my (now) husband, he played drums for a Sunday morning worship band. I wasn't sure exactly what kind of person he was because he always kept a very blank look on his face. I can never tell if he is angry or happy until he opens his mouth. It turned out that he is kind and giving, but you would never know that seeing his stoic face. My mother who is always worried about getting robbed or mugged in big cities always feels safe with him because he looks like he will bop you on the head. Recently, I also watched the movie, "Lean on Me" about the true story of Principal Joe Louis Clark who reformed high-crime Eastside High School in New Jersey. In the movie, Clark is portrayed as a direct, hard, no-nonsense leader that weeded out drugs and violence that plagued students that wanted to succeed. His stoic face helped him make progress in schools.

Regardless of who I think "fits the bill" in being the ideal Christian face, God uses people in every setting to reach all types of people. In whatever aspect of your life that you struggle to get along with someone, God needs them, and has given them an assignment. It is not up to us to approve who God has set on the path.

Prayer:

Lord, Please bless the people in my life that I can't see eye to eye with. Bless their ministry and mission that You have appointed them to. May they know that I am an ally and not an enemy. Prompt me in identifying ways to help and bless them. In Jesus' name. Amen.

"When life gives you lemons, make lemonade."

"Greater love has no one than this, that he lay down his life for his friends." John 15:13

Have you ever been out to lunch with someone that said, "we have been here for five minutes and they haven't even taken our drink order, yet." Life is fast-paced, and more so for Americans, but sometimes we become obsessed with time to the point of it stealing our joy. Voicing this lack of patience as a Christian only makes everyone at the table miserable, as we obviously cannot change the situation.

On a different occasion, I was once waiting to have my picture taken. Everyone in the waiting area was waiting for their name to be called. We had waited at least 40 minutes and felt miserable because of it. Suddenly, one of the women went to the blackboard and drew spaces for letters, and we took turns guessing the letters and what the mystery phrase could be. It became a fun game show. I was grateful to her.

Even though it might seem silly, all of life is that game show. Every day and circumstance can either be a miserable wait or an engaging pleasantry.

Our response to less than ideal situations reflects how we are perceived as Christians. Let your witness shine for Christ. Always be vigilant and in control of your actions and words. Other's acceptance of Christ might depend on it.

Prayer:

Dear Heavenly Father, Open my eyes that I might always be conscious of how I might be a better witness. I want to always live in Your light and as a good example of the love You have given me. May my actions and words reflect that. In Jesus' name. Amen.

"To the victor go the spoils."

"He has showed you, O man, what is good. And what does the LORD require of you? To act justly and to love mercy and to walk humbly with your God." Micah 6:8

People like to win. Not only do they like to win, but they enjoy surrounding themselves with other winners. Salespeople run their entire life and image on positivity and "fake it until you make it" because people are so highly drawn to winning.

People would much rather be around positivity than negativity, however that is not all there is to life. Much of the Bible includes negativity and what has made it so widely popular over the centuries is people also endure hard times. The Bible shows us how multiple people endured difficult times and how they prevailed. A former church pastor encouraged all congregants to get involved in the church's substance recovery program because we are all broken in some way, and the program focused on healing with Jesus and living a better life.

"The victor" might get "the spoils", but even winners are weighed down with the stress of daily life. The person you idolize that seemingly has a perfect life, has stress and parts of their life that weigh them down. The great news is that no matter whether we deem ourselves the "winner" or "loser" God has a promising future for those that love Him.

He requires us to act justly, to love mercy and to walk humbly with Him no matter what situation we find ourselves in. In the end, how we respond to His call will determine the "spoils" He gives us.

Prayer:

Dear Heavenly Father, May I live a life true and honest; that others may see the provision You bless me with despite desperate times. Help me to see people for who they are instead of what they have and always be willing to share Your Word with everyone. In Jesus' name. Amen.

"Well done is better than well said."

"Consequently, faith comes from hearing the message, and the message is heard through the word of Christ." Romans 10:17

When I think back to the people in my life that have passed away over the years, the things that I loved most (and miss most) about them are gifts from God. I love how my grandmother always had a fresh bed made for me with sheets that smelled like sunshine. I love the sincerity and integrity that my father spoke with. My uncle was blessed in becoming your personal chef and would cook to your preference. I love that my Cousin Julie was always looking for acts of service to bless people with. All of these actions and words were solid and affirming to receive. You could feel the love of God through the energy and effort that they gave.

I am so grateful that Jesus lived out the actions and words that He gave. Christianity would have turned out very differently if Jesus would have said "love everyone" but turned around and lied, cheated, and stole. Sharing the Gospel is more than telling someone about God and a better way of life, it is showing. You have to "walk the walk, if you talk the talk." Thank God, we as Christians, know the actions to make by living out the word of Christ and sharing that with the world.

Prayer:

Father, thank You for the blessing of good people that you have placed in our life. We are blessed that we have shared in their life and are benefited from having known them. Show us all the ways that we can pass that same love on to others. In everything we do, may You be exalted. In Jesus' name. Amen.

"A friend to everyone is a friend to no one."

"Blessed is the man who perseveres under trial, because when he has stood the test, he will receive the crown of life that God has promised to those who love him." James 1:12

In my younger years, I tried to be friends with everyone. While I still do initially try to be friends with everyone, sometimes others don't want friendship. In my older years I have come to realize that some people, especially those that live toxic, dangerous lifestyles, need to be left alone. Of my old high school friends, half have died from drug over-doses, and most continued to use drugs after seeing our friends drop off like flies.

At the time, it wouldn't have been "nice" or "friendly" to tell them "drugs are going to kill you if you keep using them." Even though we live in a "tolerance is cool" culture of accepting everyone's individual choice lifestyle, it is dangerous, and it is not being a friend. There are many other lifestyles that live on the line and are dangerous, and it can feel like stepping on toes to try and speak truth about concerns and dangers but saying nothing is dangerous and wrong.

Breaking bad habits and changing your lifestyle is not easy. It usually requires that a person selects completely new friends and sometimes even relocates. As a friend, you might even ask, "What do you need in order to change your life around, and stop doing these bad habits?" At the end of the day, it is entirely up to the other person and out of our control. God gives us all free will and unfortunately sometimes people choose self-destruction. However, we do not have to chain ourselves to the problem.

Prayer:

Heavenly Father, Free us for joyful obedience! Cleanse us and help us see a better way of life instead of drowning in sin. Help our loved ones see a better way of living with You, but if not, give us peace, as we walk away for our own self-preservation. In Jesus' name. Amen.

"All that glistens is not gold."

"Be sober-minded; be watchful. Your adversary the devil prowls around like a roaring lion, seeking someone to devour." I Peter 5:8

Growing up in Chilton County, Alabama, I remember hearing stories of huge golden nuggets that were once found in a now defunct gold mine in the south of town. Such stories filled my imagination with finding my own golden treasure in our small creek. I never did find one, but what I did find was an abundance of Pyrite, also known as "Fool's Gold." There were endless buckets of huge rocks that glistened brilliantly, so much so that if there was a true piece of gold in the mix, I would have thrown it out thinking it was just another shiny rock.

The whole world can be deceiving in a similar way, in that you need to be sure of what you are looking at. Trickery follows every profession and it is important to keep a level head when doing anything with finances so you aren't labeled the "fool." If the dog bites you once, it's his fault. If he bites you again, it's your own fault. God gives us tools for weeding out bad actions and having discernment.

The Bible is the world's moral compass to know right from wrong. From the Ten Commandments to one of Jesus' greatest commandments, "love others as you love yourself," the teachings help us with every crossroad we experience in life. (No other book is so anointed!) When faced with a difficult decision, a Bible study is in order.

Prayer:

Father, thank You for Your provision. Help me know what the right decisions and actions are. Help me in discerning the best choice for my life. Help me identify and weed out any evil that will take away from my blessing. In Jesus' name, Amen.

"Fretting cares makes grey hair."

"For I am convinced that neither death nor life, neither angels nor demons, neither the present nor the future, nor any powers, neither height nor depth, nor anything else in all creation, will be able to separate us from the love of God that is in Christ Jesus our Lord." Romans 8:38-39

I am always interested in hearing people's accounts of strange occurrences. One example in my own life is when a friend and I were driving in Mentone, Alabama. We had been carpooling and I was taking her back to her car parked on the top of the mountain. Suddenly, we came into a dense fog. It was like driving into a wall as I could no longer see anything other than a white screen. I wasn't sure that I was even still on the dirt road and continuously opened my car door to check the ground. It was about 8 p.m., and the darkness mixed with the fog created the feeling of disorientation. It was a necessity to keep driving because otherwise we would be stranded and become vulnerable, but it was a great risk to continue driving blindly into a void. Both of us stared with wide eyes trying to make out any visual guide such as the side of the road. At which point, I did the only thing I knew how to do that would help us–I prayed aloud.

During my prayer, I made sure I included all of the things that I knew. We were both scared and felt like we were driving in the belly of evil, so I rebuked those things. I spoke to it and said that God was our Victor. I prayed for angels to surround and protect us. I prayed for the fog to clear, so that we may at least see the side of the road. Eventually, it cleared just enough so that we could at least see where she parked. We began to descend the mountain, and even though it was a sparsely populated area, God sent a vehicle to follow their taillights to lead us down the mountain.

Whatever fear you are living with today, God is much bigger. It doesn't matter if it is a billion dollar corporation against you, fighting an illness or you can feel evil surrounding you–Jesus Christ loves you and defeated death. Call out for His help, and He will be with you.

Prayer:

Dear God, In the midst of my fear, uncertainty, and fog lead me to a safe place. Send Your angels to comfort and save me. Protect me, Lord. Make a safe path and send people to guide me. I know that in everything You are always with me and will never let go. May I be reminded of the children's song, "This Little Light of Mine", and that we always have you to "shine, shine, shine," even in the midst of darkness. In Jesus' name, Amen.

"Never let the sun go down on your anger."

"Don't sin by letting anger control you. Don't let the sun go down while you are still angry." Ephesians 4:26

Growing up, my uncle was a fun guy. He was the "fun uncle" that would get you in trouble and apologize to your parents afterward. However, he also had a drinking problem that would turn him into a monster. Once when I was a teenager and visiting my grandmother, he drove into her driveway like a mad man and hit my car. When I came out to see the damage, he was angry, drunk and directed his anger at me. He shortly thereafter left my grandmother's house, and we never saw him again. He died in a drunk-driving crash and accidentally ran off the side of a country bridge.

Although most memories of him are fun-filled and hilarious, our angry words left a dent in our relationship. He was haunted and possessed with a demon that sometime controlled who he was. It can be difficult to love and reason with someone like that. You can't control the actions of a person. You can only control who you are and your own response. For that, I am sorry that I left him with my angry words. God calls us to be wise, prayerful, loving, gentle–anything else is destructive.

When confronted with anger, respond with love. It is not expected. It will leave a lasting impression (if only on you).

Prayer:

Dear Heavenly Father, The world is hungry for the love, peace and restoration that only You can give. God, forgive me of my anger towards others and restore my soul. Soften my heart and close my mouth when I have only negative, hateful things to say. Give me Your wisdom on how to respond. Strengthen me when I need it most. In Jesus' name. Amen.

"If you pay peanuts, you get monkeys."
(If you don't invest time into God's word you are going to feel lost.)

"Through these he has given us his very great and precious promises, so that through them you may participate in the divine nature and escape the corruption in the world caused by evil desires." 2 Peter 1:4

As a child, I had a wonderful Children's Minister. Sister Kelly spent a good portion of her life creating Bible stories and props to bring the Bible to life. Throughout the year, she collected various toys and nicer quality yard sale items to have in her annual Christmas Store for children. Children who earned points during Bible Jeopardy could purchase Christmas presents for their family members. It was the only way a poor, twelve-year-old girl like me could afford Christmas presents.

Thirty years later, my mother still has an indigo blue crystal candy dish that I gave her for learning those lessons. Besides the joy that came from Bible Jeopardy and the Christmas Store, learning those lessons helped set the foundation of my life. If a person doesn't invest in the time to get to know God, where can he/she look when they are lost? Even when people grow up without knowing God, thankfully, their background does not keep them from being able to have a relationship with Him which sets our compass in life.

Prayer:

Father, thank You for Your gift of the Bible and the price You paid with the precious blood of Jesus Christ. May we always seek Your will when looking for direction for our life. In Jesus' name. Amen.

AUGUST 6

"Learn a language, and you will avoid a war."

"He who answers before listening- that is his folly and his shame." Proverbs 18:13

For me and my husband, the expression "opposites attract" is valid. Where he values new purchases, I love everything antique. Restoring our home was a bit of a challenge. I refinished the hardwood floors in three rooms, and he thinks that covering a rustic 125-year-old hardwood floor with plush modern carpet is a better move. Our work ethic is also totally different. I do not want to call myself "lazy", but my husband works circles around me and works until he is about to fall out from exhaustion. I once envisioned sharing a vegetable garden with him. However, after he planted 100 tomato plants, I knew he was crazy and we were not the same.

In the moments of differences and strife, things can get heated quickly over the "correct" way to do things if we don't diffuse disagreements quickly. However, my husband and I know each other well enough to understand why we have our certain preferences. I know ahead of time that he prefers "new" over something "old," because he never had anything new growing up. I know he will work from sunrise to sunset because he once nearly starved not being able to find work. Putting aside strife during differences builds a new bridge that allows you to see every possible angle. Not only does it make you stronger and creates relationships but God uses it to build His Kingdom to a new group of people.

Prayer:

God, help us hold on to people with love so that we may work together. Help us genuinely listen to the other side and try to understand from their perspective the reason they make their decisions. In Jesus' name. Amen.

"Love is blind."

It is as if the dew of Hermon were falling on Mount Zion. For there the LORD bestows his blessing, even life forevermore. Psalm 133:3

Once during my teenage years, a friend and I were outside on her porch and happened to see a shooting star. We both saw it at the same time and both made a wish, but seconds later a second shooting star fell, then a third, fourth and a fifth! We did not know it at the time, but it was the Perseids meteor shower that happens every August. I made a point to remember that it happens every year during my father's birthday, so that I would never miss it. For twenty something years, I have watched the Perseids. It always bedazzles and gives a great performance. In the years after my father passed, the Perseids were the best way to remember him. It felt like a special show he sent from Heaven. Years later, my son was born on my father's birthday, and so I have a new Perseids baby and the best fireworks nature could make.

There are so many inspiring, beautiful, and unimaginable ways that God tries to capture our attention; ways that He continuously pours love into our life and creates things that we might not even be observant of because we are not paying attention. God is God and is the beginning and the end. His love can be reimagined into ways that we need and cannot find elsewhere. He created the stars for your joy, for your love, to see your eyes shine bright when you see them.

Prayer:
God, Thank You for the Perseids and all of the endless ways You show us love. Show me the ways I can serve You. In Jesus' name. Amen.

"Loose lips sink ships."

"Let us then approach the throne of grace with confidence, so that we may receive mercy and find grace to help us in our time of need." Hebrews 4:16

The old house that I live in was built in the late 1800s. These old houses, even though they are old are solid as a rock because they were constructed with special detail. I once had a long window frame removed from the side of the house to install a French door and it took the construction guys longer to take out the window frame, because it was placed into the wall piece by piece in a specific order, without nails (like a puzzle). The old house is solid and can withstand storms.

Even in modern homes, when a tornado comes around, most everyone wants to be in a brick home or underground because of their durability. Likewise, how we build our life depends on how well it will stand through tough weather. Being an honest, genuine person invested in reading God's word regularly will withstand a storm longer than someone who "burns a candle at both ends," gossips, and loves "to keep the pot stirred." When we speak badly about others, it is often with the intention of making someone else look bad, but it says more about the gossiper's character and weakens their "frame."

Building your life in a way that will survive storms includes "tongue and groove boards" and "bricks." That translates as a Christian to being caught up and current on Bible-reading, prayer, and adoration.

Prayer:

Dear Father God, shield me from the storms of wickedness. May I be intentional about taking preventative action to guard my heart and build up the faith of my family. In Jesus' name. Amen.

"Jack of all trades, master of none."

"Delight yourself in the LORD and he will give you the desires of your heart." Psalm 37:4

We all have many talents. However, even in the areas we excel in there is always room for improvement. I can "throw down" in the kitchen and cook a wide-range of multi-cultured cuisine, but even in the kitchen there are things that I have not mastered. I have never been able to successful make a Louisiana roux, and I have ruined divinity candy more times than not. Whatever we spend our time doing, we always need to be mindful of ways to improve.

For many people, including myself, when we identify what our faults are, many people degrade themselves. As an artist, I frequently invite friends and family over to my house to join me in painting, and I have heard too many times, "I will come but I am not creative." For whatever we need to do, are asked to do, are called by God to do–He will supply us with the aptitude. In the Bible, the small, young David was hardly a fair opponent to fight Mighty Goliath, but he stepped up, and God equipped him. Whatever seems impossible and whatever the areas you feel inadequate in, God can and will enable you to accomplish your goal through prayer in order to glorify the Kingdom.

Prayer:

Dear Father God, I frequently feel inadequate when I ___________. You are mighty and the life source of the universe. Bless me with the ability to accomplish my task. Show me new ways that I might accomplish this and put the gift to a Godly, good use. In Jesus' name. Amen.

"Know which side one's bread is buttered on."

"The saying is trustworthy, for if we have died with Him, we will also live with Him; if we endure, we will also reign with Him; if we deny Him, He also will deny us." II Timothy 2:11-12

Newer generations of young people do not seem to stop and pray before long car rides or especially at meals when they are with friends for fear of stopping the flow of conversation. I have also noticed certain celebrity pastors do not display crosses during their T.V. programs. They only preach about being blessed and healed when money is involved and refuse to teach certain aspects of God's word because it sounds "too negative."

God will not bless those that are afraid to step forward in His name. Matthew 10:32-33, says, "Everyone who acknowledges Me before men, I also will acknowledge before My Father who is in heaven, but whoever denies Me before men, I also will deny before My Father who is in heaven." If "Christians" are blatantly not giving God the reverence and honor He deserves in order to look "cool," there will be consequences. If it appears those people already have a blessed, abundant life, it might be that God is not the one blessing them. Their rewards will be short lived.

Prayer:

God, let me always be eager to stand up and defend You and what it right. At every opportunity, let others see that You are the reason for everything good in my life. If I may be an outlet to others coming to know you, I happily accept being made fun of and labeled as a "Christian." Mold me into the Godly person you want me to be so that others may see the fulfillment of what a blessed life is. In Jesus' name. Amen.

"Don't shoot the messenger."

"I must keep going today and tomorrow and the next day—for surely no prophet can die outside Jerusalem!" Luke 13:33

"Salvation is found in no one else, for there is no other name under heaven given to men by which we must be saved." Acts 4:12

For most of us, if we found out that we might possibly die, we would walk the other direction for self-preservation. Jesus knew that his mission was important and life-changing. When He felt the disciples needed to know, he gave the news "head on" because it was a destiny that had to happen.

I remember when one of my beloved friends told me that she was dying of cancer, I didn't want to listen to her and tried to redirect the topic. She had been battling radiation, chemotherapy and surgeries for a while. When she told me during our lunch together, "I am dying," I responded with an upbeat smile, "No, you are not! You will get better. You are just in a bad slump with this round of chemo treatment." She said, "No. I am dying, Elisabeth. The numbers are not getting better."
I didn't know what to say and listened in silence. She died at the age of 47. Six years after her death, I still don't know what I should have said to her telling me that awful news. The pain I feel for losing her still hurts.

No one ever wants to be the bearer of bad news. Bad news can bring feelings of anger or sorrow and those are emotions no one wants to evoke. In the past, kings and queens have put people to death for being the bearer of bad news. Important news can change the direction of our future. However unpopular of a topic, Jesus knew that He was confronting death when He spoke to the disciples. Jesus didn't "beat around the bush." He accepted that fate head on. As He entered Jerusalem He said, "I must keep going today and tomorrow and the next day—for surely no prophet can die outside Jerusalem!" (Luke 13:33)

Whatever obstacle or dreaded fate you are up against, the Almighty Power of God is with you. Bad news that you have been dealt might be causing you pain. Jesus and my friend, both experienced pain in their journey. However, both of them knew that God was King and in knowing that, it gave them power to keep going every day toward a new victory. May God give you strength where you lack it.

Prayer:

Dear God, thank You for the hope You give for tomorrow. I pray for those hurting and in need of Your strength. I pray for those that also have received bad news and don't know how to deal with it. Give them the strength that Jesus and my friend had that they "must keep going today, tomorrow and the next day." Help them have courage and to be brave in the arms of God, who will carry us all when we can't go any further. In Jesus' name. Amen.

"Many a true word is spoken in jest."

"You will keep in perfect peace him whose mind is steadfast, because he trusts in you." Isaiah 26:3

Some of my friends from Czechia (a portion of the former Czechoslovakia) nicknamed me several years back "Lizinko", which is the equivalent of "Tiny Elisabeth." I am not tiny, nor have I ever been. In fact, I have always been overweight. Their naming me that was a jest in calling me "hefty." In turn, I have always called my friend, Petra the "Machine" because she runs five miles a day, works, cleans, cooks, raises 3 boys and still has energy to be life of the party. We have always taken the nicknames "with a grain of salt" and are still the greatest of friends.

In my opinion, one of the greatest gifts a preacher can have is the ability to jest in truth of what needs to be said to the congregation. Life is full of temptation, and it is a wonderful ability for a person to say "you have had too much cake" with a smile and not be hated for it.

Somewhere in time, the ability to tell people the loving truth on important matters was lost (with emphasis on "loving"). You can tell the difference between someone being hateful and sly and when someone you love is pointing out what is a truth and lovingly trying to bring light to it.

Prayerfully ask God to guard and guide your words when speaking on important and sensitive issues.

Prayer:

Lord, may I always prayerfully petition You on how to approach those I love about matters that I feel are important. Let our communication be full of light, in love, and heartfelt. In Jesus' name. Amen.

"Many hands make light work."

"He himself bore our sins in his body on the tree, so that we might die to sins and live for righteousness; by his wounds you have been healed." 1 Peter 2:24

There haven't been many "oh no, what have we done?!" moments in my life, but one of those said times, was when Bro. Rob West ordered an 18-wheeler truck load of sweet potatoes to be delivered to the church parking lot on a Saturday! The size of the pile was comparable to a mobile home being delivered and took up a quarter of the parking lot. The "oh no" moment was trying to imagine where cars were going to park the following day for church services.

The sweet potato delivery comes from a wonderful program in which potatoes are gleaned from the fields and given to the hungry. It was a task that God was surely behind, even if it did take away the church parking. Twenty thousand pounds of a potato mountain would surely take days (if not a week) to sort through. However, it was an equal blessing to witness 50+ volunteers show up at the same moment and begin bagging potatoes, putting them into cars, and driving them out to various low-income communities within the county. It was a wonderful moment in my Christian life when I received the message that when God is involved, there are not any "oh no" moments.

Allow whatever "situation" you are in to be seen as something that God see's and can use as a "blessing!

Prayer:

Dear Loving Father, help me to always put my faith and trust in You. Even when there is a 20,000 pound problem we are facing, You are "in it to win it". Your blessings and the fruits of Your blessings are so big that we can't always see how the outcome will turn out, but give us assurance that You are bigger than any challenge we face. In Jesus' name. Amen.

"Work smarter, not harder."

"Do not let this Book of the Law depart from your mouth; meditate on it day and night, so that you may be careful to do everything written in it. Then you will be prosperous and successful." Joshua 1:8

The first time I heard the expression, "work smarter, not harder" was from a preschool director who lined all of my decorative paper cut-outs for the laminator. I was trying to laminate them one at a time, and she said "work smarter, not harder" and in one quick sweep, memorialized my craft in one sheet of plastic.

Wouldn't it be wonderful if during every difficult task in life, a "smarter" helper came and showed you an easier way to complete the task? I have a small chandelier in my foyer, and I know the day that I read how to clean the crystals using glass cleaner and white gloves changed my life (instead of taking the 50 pieces off and washing them in the sink). People can give us great ideas and "life hacks." I am grateful for the various gifted people that are kind enough to share their ideas on making life easier.

God has placed wonderful and talented people in our path to learn from them. It is "working harder" most of the time to try it our own way. When people come together to do good things, it is a powerful movement. Whatever you trying to accomplish spiritually you are more likely to succeed when you come together with other Christians who can motivate and help you.

Prayer:

Thank You, God for other people, especially Christians that can move, motivate, help, and teach us. Help us look for Your signs on which paths to take. Thank you for the teachers and mentors that help guide and improve our technique. In Jesus' name. Amen.

AUGUST 15

"If it's not broken, don't fix it."

"Everything you do in your journey of self-improvement, including serving others in love, matters to God. He wants you to be diligent in meeting others' needs as well as managing your own. God doesn't want you only focusing on yourself but growing in Christlikeness as you give back to others." Hebrews 6:10-11

One of my father's favorite pass times was Hot-Roding. He owned a 1976 burgundy Chevrolet Vega with a 350 motor. When he cranked the car and "gave it the gas" it sounded like a portal to another dimension being opened. There is nothing comparable to the chuckle of the motor, seeing the car jump "ready to go" and "hitting it" on a burnout. After the restoration and rebuilding cost, there was always something he wanted to add to the car to make it better. It was not "broken" per say, but as any collector continues to add to their surplus, he continued to add to the car's amenities and features.

Christians everywhere get into a comfortable safety zone once we are "rebuilt and restored," but the truth is that we, too, are in constant need of being worked on and adding on to our features. Millions of Christians feel restored and sit comfortably in a church every week, which is the equivalent of a garage. You can get tune-ups there and get some work done, but the real fruit of being a Christian is out in the streets, helping the poor, hungry, and spiritually hungry.

Prayer:

Heavenly Father, Help me know what features I need to work on in my relationship with You. Set a fire in my soul to take my Christian relationship "out for a spin," so that others might see and come to know You. Use me. In Jesus' name. Amen.

"Comparisons are odious."

"Don't urge me to leave you or turn back from you. Where you go I go, and where you stay I will stay." Ruth 1:16-17

One of the best duos is my son and our family cat. I never wanted a cat, especially with an infant, and had reservations about fostering the cat. My husband brought him home at four weeks old from a construction site where he had been abandoned. It was an emergency setting. He needed to be bottle fed and cleaned every two hours, and someone to care for him immediately. While already caring for an infant, caring for a newborn kitten was pushing my capabilities to the brim. I also constantly worried about cross contamination with the kitten and giving my baby a disease. However, they both started to grow up and mature together. They are both curious and explore the world together. They play with toys together and where one is, the other will go. The cat even ran to use his body as a barrier to keep my son from walking off the porch. I was close enough to grab my son, but I still appreciated the cat's protection and thoughtfulness. My son's second word wound up being "cat" and he is part of our family forever.

Sometimes the best duos are not what you expect to see. God has a great way of pairing us up with what we need instead of what we want or what we anticipated. All that is required in the pairing is the human willingness to participate in God's plan.

Have you ever been paired in an atypical situation and feel a bit confused by it? Ask God for guidance and to help you see the endless possibilities in the new opportunity.

Prayer:

This is the day the Lord has made! God of the ages, I seek Your wisdom and love. I know You have blessed me and everything good I have is because of You. Help me in connecting with the people You have placed in my path. In Jesus' name. Amen.

"The proof of the pudding is in the eating."

"I am the true vine, and my Father is the gardener. He cuts off every branch in me that bears no fruit, while every branch that does bear fruit he prunes so that it will be even more fruitful. John 15: 1-2

Oh, there is so much happiness and glory to share within the Christian church family! Some of my best relationships and best memories have been made in churches. Lessons that I did not learn in other places of my life were learned surrounded by congregants. I have learned how to make holidays bows at Christmastime, how to respond to hatefulness and when not to respond and of course, some of the South's best recipes – all within the church! There are many other joys that I found there. It is happiness to see someone who has suffered set free! With so much misery and evil found in the world, it is a also wonderful to see thousands singing praise to Heaven.

In the midst of such a wonderful place, church families are not error-free. We are, after all, living in a sinful world and sin has the capability to creep into any place or group of people. For that reason, it is all too easy to find stories about people leaving churches because of adultery, abuse, embezzlement, or hatefulness within the church. Christians are held to a high standard because their actions can mean someone's fate in eternity.

The old saying "the proof is in the pudding" is ever-so-true for churches. If your church is not conveying the love of Jesus, it is not going to taste as sweet. In fact, it will turn sour. If you don't go to church, you are missing the world's best library of love, friendship, and thanksgiving.

Prayer:

Heavenly Father, thank You for the church, that such a marvelous witness and love can come together in unity and praise You. May we be awake in knowing how our actions affect others and knowingly claim responsibility for other people's future when we engage with them. In Jesus' name. Amen.

"Nothing ventured, nothing gained."

"For I know the plans I have for you, declares the LORD, plans for welfare and not for evil, to give you a future and a hope." Jeremiah 29:11

Life frequently gives us a game of chance in many different ways. Many people have the opportunity at least once in their life to sell everything and buy some large investment that may greatly change their financial freedom for the better. Some people also play this chance with gambling, while others may get their kicks from living a life on the edge with adrenaline (like sky-diving, bungee-jumping or auto-racing.) In all of these activities, there is always a common risk for becoming hurt. Becoming hurt can scare us because it makes us vulnerable, but, at the same time, it is what drives the passion. Many people look at love as that same risk. Loving others is a game of chance that we play that can break our hearts. With the loves I have lost along the way, I can attest that it is painful, possibly the greatest pain, but still worth the risk.

Whereas other games of chance are deal breakers if you don't succeed, taking a chance on love is different because even if you walk away alone, in the end, you know that your heart is capable of love. Love is a powerful asset. Love has the power to motivate the disabled. Love has initiated war and stopped war.

Several years ago, my husband, knowing that I love history, took me to Atlanta to see the opera "Silent Night." It accounts the true story from World War I, when soldiers in the trenches decided to stop fighting on Christmas day in 1914 and instead sang and celebrated Christmas together. What a humbling moment to witness the Holy Spirit cover a bloody battlefield and the Spirit of God be felt by each man.

The love of God is ever present and ready to be received. Take a chance on love.

Prayer:

Spirit of the Living God, fall afresh on me. Open my heart to receive others that I might be the difference in this world. In a world full of rife, let me be strong enough to always take a chance on love, because You ARE love. In Jesus' name. Amen.

"Those who know many languages live as many lives as the languages they know." - Czech proverb

"We who are strong ought to bear with the failings of the weak and not to please ourselves. Each of us should please our neighbors for their good, to build them up. For even Christ did not please himself but, as it is written: "The insults of those who insult you have fallen on me." Accept one another, then, just as Christ accepted you, in order to bring praise to God." Romans 15:1-3,7

Anyone who has devoted time to Christian missions will tell you that the secret to good missions is to get involved in the people's lives. As a young teenage missionary, I thought that the "mission" was to build a basketball court. In such a brief time, it can be difficult to get to know someone, especially with a language barrier. As a person sharing the love of Jesus, there cannot be any emotional "walls up" if you wish to make a connection with the people you are visiting. Once in Ecuador, we ate Guinea Pig "with a smile" because it is what was offered for lunch, and the humble people offering it did not have much more to offer. In that moment, it was me that was receiving the "mission" – the opportunity to see the love and humility of Jesus in that the family chose to give me everything they had.

When you humble yourself in a Christian manner to live with a people, become like people in the way they eat, work, and play, you can see life from their perspective. You become one of them and understand the path that their life must take in order to know Jesus. The message of Jesus, very rarely is received by gifting someone a basketball court.

Prayer:

God, humble me that I should speak and show love to those in the community and world who need and want to see it most. In Jesus' name. Amen.

"Truth is stranger than fiction."

"Whatever you do, work at it with all your heart, as working for the Lord, not for men." Col 3:23

When my sister got married in Eufaula, Alabama I couldn't wait to drive into town and see the beautiful, historic homes that the main street boasts. From Montgomery, the road to Eufaula is all scenic backroads full of old barns and countryside (my favorite). However, on the last hour of the journey on Hwy. 82, the road is very isolated. My mother and I drove alongside the road at dusk in mid-March, and without exaggeration, we easily passed 1,000 deer. There were Daddy deer, Mama deer, Baby deer, cousins, local resident deer, political deer, deer without a cause−there were so many of them it would have been impossible to count them all! Fortunately, they were not afraid of my car. I was afraid they would run out and trample my windshield, but they seemed happy eating on the sides of the roadway and at times, even socializing in the middle of the road.

There are so many accounts in the Bible that people try to disprove. People get downright viscous trying to come up with the scientific reasoning of events instead of letting it be a "miracle" that God has created. There is always a TV show trying to explain how Moses parting the Red Sea was a natural "tide" occurrence or how God turning the River Nile into blood was really an organism in the water. Some people don't want to believe how big God is and that His power is infinite. If He can create 1,000 deer to come together for an evening social, He can call two of every animal onto Noah's ship. Seeing the way the world works is a testament to how powerful God is. When an extraordinary God calls nature into power and action, it is breathtaking and leaves you speechless.

Prayer:

God, forgive us for doubting the magnitude of Your majestic hand. Thank you for blessing us with the witness of seeing Your miracles. Place me with people that I might share the wonder and depth of Your love. In Jesus' name. Amen.

"Two wrongs do not make a right."

"Jesus replied, 'Love the Lord your God with all your heart and with all your soul and with all your mind.'" Matthew 22:37

I will never forget twenty years ago, my dad helping me install a surround sound in my living room. Technology was not the same as it is today. Wireless surround sound did not exist and everything had to be wired to the T.V. set. Whether right or wrong I couldn't say, but he insisted that we make a tiny incision in the carpet and stuff the surround sound wiring in the slit. Taking a long metal pipe, we shoved the wire underneath the carpet until the wire reached the desired location. The wiring ran across the living room, under the carpet and none of it was visible–mission accomplished! However, during the process, a piece of the carpet padding snagged and made a tiny mountain of padding on the side of the room. I lived in that house for 15 years and never fixed the mountain of carpet padding. Knowing how to fix it was not in my wheelhouse. When I had company over, I put a small table on the top of it. No one ever noticed it, but it always bothered me that it was unresolved.

Similarly, when we argue with others with vengeance, it does the same thing to our soul. Someone we know says something hurtful or wrong to us and we respond by lashing back out at them, like the world's most hideous ping pong match. Once words have been unleashed, there is not any way to "take it back" because it has already been said. Taking poor vengeful actions with others does the same thing. It just continues to gnaw at your heart and mind. It is exhausting and stressful. Even though we like to think that "we got the last laugh," nothing about the experience is life-giving–like the carpet padding mountain, it just sits there in our life, looking hideous.

The only thing to do when confronted with a wrong, is to rip the padding up and start again, making it right. When we say or do something vengeful to someone, we need to make amends with them. Placing a table over it, just won't do. Usually in the moment of the disagreement neither party has the humble, gentle heart needed for discussion, which can take time. Pray and ask God for His help in fixing the relationships that were broken.

Prayer:

Dear Father, thank You for being love when I need it most. I have been hurt and in return, given hurt. Forgive me for my quick return on hate. I don't want that for my life. Help me repair what is broken. Give me the words when I reach out and respond to other people. Help me understand their hateful words are a reflection of the way they have been hurt in this world. Regardless of their response let them see love and hope in my response. May Your kingdom be blessed and receive the glory. In Jesus' name. Amen.

"What goes up must come down."

"It is like precious oil poured on the head, running down on the beard, running down on Aaron's beard, down upon the collar of his robes." Psalm 133:2

As a young teen, my friend Faith spent the night at my house. We were excited. In the early 1990s, there was not much entertainment for two girls to enjoy in our small town, so sadly, we made prank phone calls. I had my own phone in my bedroom. It was one of the clear ones that you could see the insides of–very trendy! We called a random number and asked them if their refrigerator was running and hung up. We both giggled. However, seconds after I hung up, the phone rang back. It was the person we prank called! Both, Faith and I dared not answer the phone and froze "like deer in headlights." In the same moment, I could hear my mother walking to her bedroom to answer the phone. (We shared a phone line.) Oh no! A few minutes later there was a knock on the door. I was scared to death. Mother, with an expressionless face said, "You girls need to stop calling prank-calling people. Do you understand me?" I'm not sure that I was ever more afraid of my mother's seriousness. I asked her how the person knew our number, and she explained the *69 service (new in those days).

Years later I heard the expression, "play stupid games, win stupid prizes." Every day people deliberately make poor choices. We should all be mindful that the world is full of consequences. Whatever we are willing to gamble could make or break us. More importantly, gambling with our relationship with God will end in suffering and death.

Prayer:

Dear Father, help me to always be mindful of the actions, words and choices I make. I pray for Your guidance in consideration and respect for others and good discernment in everything I do. In Jesus' name. Amen.

"What the eye does not see, the heart does not grieve over."

"Behold I make all things new." Revelation 21:5

In my younger years, my father gave me two pet cows. They were born on our farm and their sole purpose in life was to keep the grass cut. They both lived on the farm for 25+ years. Despite both of them obviously being outdoor pets, they were both domesticated. They would follow me around the farm, alert me to any kind of intruder that was near, and if I sat down in a field, they would lie down, too.

In their younger years, "Bessie" my beautiful, black Angus became pregnant, and we became excited at the idea of "a new family member." On the day Bessie went into labor, my father went to the barn to try to help and after many hours returned with a sad face. Her calf, who my father said was born a beautiful snow-white color, had been still-born. As much as I loved Bessie and her new calf "Snow," Daddy would never let me see the calf. Many people say that animals don't have feelings, but anyone who has been around a grieving cow knows differently. Bessie searched for over a week on the farm, calling to Snow. Even though I never got to see or know Snow, my heart grieved over him and I loved him. Especially when Bessie would cry, so did I.

Years later, I eventually started to cast God's love and grievance over us in the same light. When something bad happens to us and we grieve, so does God. The love and connection with us to God is much greater than my connection to a cow. His love is immeasurable. When I am hurting, He knows about it and He mourns, too.

Prayer:

Father, thank You for loving us when we are hurting. I ask for the comfort and peace that only You can give. Restore my brokenness with new blessings. Take my loss and love it in a better way than I can. Take what I think is broken forever and turn it into a joyful blessing. In Jesus' name. Amen.

"When the going gets tough, the tough get going."

"'For my thoughts are not your thoughts, neither are your ways my ways,' declares the LORD." Isaiah 55:8

Our family cat enjoys climbing trees. He makes the most forlorn "meow" asking for someone to help him down. My husband puts his ladder up every time and rescues him. Recently, the cat found his way up on the roof of the house. Unlike being stuck in a tree, where he has limited space to move around, the roof allowed the cat to walk around. When my husband came home from work, he placed his ladder up to the edge of the roof, but the cat was not interested in coming to him. He strutted around, sat down, and just calmly watched as we all desperately called his name trying to help him. My husband had a pole that used to try to herd the cat closer to him. "Felix" wasn't interested and threw his paw up mid-air pawing at the pole as if it were a new toy. Only later when Felix was completely exhausted and stressed did he relent and receive help.

If this storyline sounds familiar, it is because too often we, as humans, refuse the help of God. God is there in our dilemma but instead of walking straight to Him with our issue, many times we don't. Like my husband with his metal pole trying to convince the cat that there is an easier way, God gives us assurance of His promises for tomorrow. However, like Felix, we usually either ignore God or "throw paws" at the idea and fight what God wills for our life. Many times, we wait until we are desperate and exhausted to finally concede that we cannot fight the battle alone.

Prayer:

God, Help us in our moment of trials to immediately go to You, because You love us. You are waiting to carry me to safety and show me a better way, but many times I run the other direction. Forgive me. I place my problems into Your hands. Give me peace in the comfort of Your arms. In Jesus' name. Amen.

"You can't teach an old dog new tricks."

"For God so loved the world, that he gave his only begotten Son, that whosoever believeth in him should not perish, but have everlasting life." John 3:16

Once, while driving down the road in my hometown, I got behind a truck carrying a giant white dog. He looked old and tired but was enjoying the breeze. As I was headed to my destination, I began to get an overwhelming dread in my stomach that the truck was heading to the dog pound. The dog pound was near my destination, so I decided to see if the truck would turn into the pound. Sure enough, it did. When the driver got out, I asked if she was surrendering the dog and she said "yes." She was agreeable to giving him to me. While old and tired, he was tall and proud. He had seen better days but was still enjoying life. Because of his grand stature I named him, "Chiefy." While there is no way for me to know how old Chiefy was, it is obvious to many that he was at the end of his last days.

After a while, Chiefy perked up a little and was happy living with us. He lived a happy, full year before he passed away. During that time, he became a family member. I could take him to the park, let him loose, and he would come to me when I called. He also trained *me* to pet *him*. When near me, he would come and sit under my hand. He was so tall that it felt only natural to pet his head when feeling a dog under your hand. He was smart!
I am not certain of his family life before he came to us, but it is fair to say he learned many new things in his last days.

It is never too late to change your life. It is never too late to call someone and say "I'm sorry." It is never too late to talk to God. It is never too late to accept God as your Savior.

Prayer:

God, Thank You for giving us this new day and a new opportunity to know You better. I accept You as my Savior. Forgive me of my sins and come into my life. In Jesus' name. Amen.

"You will never get if you never go."

"Let us fix our eyes on Jesus, the author and perfecter of our faith, who for the joy set before him endured the cross, scorning its shame, and sat down at the right hand of the throne of God. Hebrews 12:2

Several years ago in my Sunday School class, I could see that the class instructor was having a difficult time. At one time, class membership had been 20 people, and over time, through no fault of his own, the class members had spread out into other classes across the growing congregation. It always weighed on his heart that he could never get his attendance back up to 20, so he decided to leave the church. When he left the church, I felt a bit betrayed. I could not understand why he would leave. He had been there for over 20 years. In time, my feeling of betrayal was changed into realizing that he moved because he needed a new place to thrive.

Several years later, my best friend also moved away. Again, I felt betrayed that she would leave our happy friendship for city life. We frequently saw one another and after she moved to the city, I only saw her a few times a year. Eventually, I realized that she also moved because she needed a new place to thrive.

The plans for our future do not always align with others; in fact very rarely does God want us on the exact same path that our friends are taking. When we see our loved ones "go off on a wild goose chase," it might be that God is calling them down that path and has something meaningfully in place for them.

Prayer:

God, help me keep my eyes on You alone. I pray for my friends and my enemies today that they will place You at the center point of their life; that all of the moves and decisions for their life will be inspired by Your will. Help me to listen and be a good friend to them, however far away they are. In Jesus' name. Amen.

"Fall seven times, stand up eight."

"And he arose, and rebuked the wind, and said unto the sea, 'Peace, be still.' And the wind ceased, and there was a great calm." Mark 4:39

Perhaps one of the hardest things that I have dealt with in my life was taking care of my mother during her battle with cancer. My father (who also had cancer and died at my home) was a different personality type. He always handled everything head on and with pride. My mother is more of a spicy Southern flower.

Her chemo series began the month I delivered my son. So on days that she might be full of toxins and dangerous to be around, we could not see her. In the middle of each chemo treatment, she came to my house to stay. Cancer is an awful road I don't wish on anyone. It is painful to be part of, as the patient and as the caregiver. During these awful times, it is difficult to see the people you love the most wretch in pain, give up eating, or sleep for days. I praise God that my Mother was able to overcome her cancer to live another day (perhaps it is the spiciness that helped her overcome it.)

In moments like these, as a patient or a caregiver, it is a dark place. Hope feels lost. My prayers felt void. My conversations with friends and family were lacking because of the built-up tension, stress, and fear. It feels impossible to safely process what you are being forced to endure.

In these horrible moments, God is there. Even though you may not see Him or feel Him, He is the hope and light that fills tomorrow. When you feel that you cannot endure it anymore, pray for God's strength to get you through the day and He will be your strength.

Prayer:

Heavenly Father, I pray for the person reading this that feels exhausted, alone, and needs relief. Touch them that they may find healing and restoration in Your presence. Protect and be with us, God, we humbly pray. In Jesus' name. Amen.

"Discretion is the better part of valor."

"And my God will supply every need of yours according to his riches in glory in Christ Jesus." Philippians 4:19

In one of my favorite books "Sailing Alone Around the World," Joshua Slocum sets off in 1895 to visit many different countries. On one of his ports of call, a friend gave him a bag of carpet tacks. His first impression was that he didn't have a use for carpet tacks, until his friend said "be sure you don't step on them yourself." During his encounter with some tribes off the Fiji Islands, natives tried multiple times to rob him and take over his ship. Slocum poured the bag of carpet nails across the deck each night, and it kept him secure from barefoot intruders.

The innovation we use with God's resources to stop problems from arising is always inspirational. Every time I hear of someone using an everyday item to turn a bad situation into a good one, it seems to make the world stop and watch. One of my favorite shows in the 80s, "MacGyver" was a great example of such. During our everyday problems, God gives us innovative tools to combat those problems, as well. His gift of the Bible is full of passages that give hope and light in a world that seemingly has none.

Like the carpet tacks or MacGyver's chewing gum, others around us stop and pay attention to the inspiring hope that God plants within us. If you are going through something difficult, look around for Godly tools and inspiration. Pray for His guidance and wisdom in the situation.

Prayer:

Heavenly Father, Open my eyes, ears, and heart to be mindful and hopeful in every situation. With You, I have everything I need. In Jesus' name. Amen.

"Love makes the world go around."

"By this all men will know that you are my disciples, if you love one another." John 13:35

If we were lucky enough, we have all had at least one person growing up that we knew loved us. It could have been an aunt, grandfather, or neighbor. I was fortunate to have several people that helped mold me into the person I am today. These people saw the areas that were lacking in my life and tried to fill the voids with what I needed; the biggest gift being their *time*.

As a child, with my father being sick and my mother being the "bread winner," I spent considerable hours at my mother's office. There were several office co-workers that always took time to ask me about my day. Some of them picked me up from school when my father had to go to the hospital. Others tried to give me fun jobs to do like putting up the office Christmas tree. During school, there were also some exceptional teachers that went the extra mile in letting students know they were available to them. As a young person I viewed those actions as "kindness" and "friendship," but as an adult, I realize now that "love" was the contributing factor.

How do you contribute to loving others? Do you spend your life loving others in a way that will impact their life? Jesus, although He traveled from town to town, was very intentional in spending time with people. Besides healing them, He taught them, let them know they were loved, had a hopeful future and fed them. That selflessness is revolutionary, even by today's standards.

People will carry with them the way you love them. It becomes part of who they are in life. How will you contribute?

Prayer:

God, Show me intentional ways I can devote my time to others. Help me be a listening ear when someone needs it, give them a ride, or invite them for dinner. Place me in the frontlines of the people. In Jesus' name. Amen.

"Mighty oaks from little acorns grow."

"For nothing will be impossible with God." Luke 1:37

It has always amazed me how people in ancient times were able to move giant pieces of stone across country to build their temples. The ancient Egyptians moved 2.5 ton stones across the desert sand, as did the Olmec people of Mexico, who moved 40 ton stones across mountains to sculpt the faces of their leaders. The Aztec people founded Mexico City and created their city on top of a lake in an elaborate entry system.

The South shares in the wonder of ancient engineering in moving iron and timber by use of the river ways. I heard once that when the people of (the now ghost town) Old Cahawba packed up and moved to other parts of Alabama, that several families put their homes on logs and floated them down the river to Selma. This must have been a wonder to see considering the great worth of the mansions of Old Cahawba. When the city of Clanton began growing in the 1920s, they moved homes and churches by placing logs under them.

People have ingenuity and the ability to create something magnificent which either helps or destroys mankind. Every person has this capability by using their talents. Possibilities are endless with the help of God. Don't allow insecurities or what you think is "impossible" to keep you from what God desires for your life.

Prayer:

Heavenly Father, Open my mind and heart into accepting the tasks You will for my life. Like the many before me who thought they were insignificant or not capable, anoint my head and give me the strength to see Your task complete. In Jesus' name. Amen.

"If the shoe fits, wear it."

"Whoever isolates himself seeks his own desire; he breaks out against all sound judgment." Proverbs 18:1

I love porches. I am not sure why porches are such a Southern staple of life, but they are! Every time I visited my grandmother, part of our visit included her saying, "well, let's go outside and sit on the porch a bit." It was a big porch that looked out over two blocks. You could see and wave at every person passing by; most knew her by name. Sometimes drivers would roll down the window and speak. Now that I am older, nothing has changed. I still watch and wave at all of the cars passing. I have hosted parties and teas on the porch, and many dinners. The porch also serves as my own private sanctuary–a place where I go and talk with God, surrounded by the sunrise, birds, and nature.

My love of the porch has also made me wonder where porch sitting came from. It is not likely that you will find people sitting on their porch in England or China. Do they even have porches? When I think about popular hang-out spots in ancient times where people "people watched," I imagine the popular hang-out was the water well. Just like porches, the water well was a place where you could leisurely see people and possibly socialize.

Regardless of the origin of "porch-sitting," it is safe to say that it is a way to connect with others in a friendly way. God placed the desire within people to want to be near others. Having places like the porch and water well aren't fluke occurrences, they are places we are meant to congregate and know each other better. Lives can be saved and become enriched by them. A southern porch is potentially a church at your front door.

Prayer:

God, Help me reach out to others in my community to let them know they are welcome on my porch for a cup of coffee or to pray. Help me have the right words to say to someone in need and know when to be silent and listen. In Jesus' name. Amen.

"Bad news travels fast."

"The Lord will keep you from all evil; he will keep your life. The Lord will keep your going out and your coming in from this time forth and forevermore." Psalm 121:7-8

On our beloved family farm, growing up for the most part was a great adventure. However, like all things, it had its burdens and setbacks. From time to time, my father would set fire to the fields to help give nutrients back to the soil. It was sixty acres of rolling pasture, so putting together a hosepipe longer than the length of a football field seemed unmanageable. We would spread out and work together to rake burned areas to help control the fire.

One year when I was about thirteen, I realized that I was standing in the direct wind of the fire, making it hard to breath. When I looked around to find the grassy path to exit, it seemed there wasn't one. I felt afraid and panicked trying to figure out how I would exit the burning area unscathed. I yelled to the area my dad was in and he came to my rescue, beating out a path and smothering parts of the fire with his rake.

"Why didn't you beat out some of the fire with your rake?" he asked.

I was not sure how to answer. In the moment of my despair, I was not reasoning. I felt panicked and overwhelmed.

Later in life, I have found that bad situations feel eerily similar. When something happens and I am under attack, (verbally or non-verbally), a dramatic situation feels like being trapped in fire. Even when rumors and gossip spread about our personal lives, whether it is true or untrue, it feels like wildfire spreading. It is uncomfortable and smothering. I don't want to be part of it and want to walk away, yet there I am in the middle of an undesirable situation.

In the middle of life's fires we do not have to endure it alone. God gives us the freedom to respond to bad situations with control and grace. Since God is the Alpha, Omega, The Great I Am, and Creator–decision making is up to Him. He always has the last word, even when we think the situation is hopeless and at its end.

If you are feeling despair, sickened and afraid by the lack of control in your own life, remember that God is with you–always. If you are desperately looking for resources to beat out your own fire, look for help and guidance in the Bible, praying with friends, and visiting a church. God's power is much greater than an earthly rake.

Prayer:

Dear Heavenly Father, Thank You for never abandoning me. You are the keeper of the sheep, love us, and keep me well. Save me from the wrath of earthly fires. Help me navigate safely, that I might be a testimony to the goodness of Your Kingdom. In Jesus' name. Amen.

"Better to have loved and lost than never to have loved at all."

"Wait on the LORD: be of good courage, and he shall strengthen thine heart: wait, I say, on the LORD." Psalm 27:14

While working with Hispanic missions, I enjoyed attending the annual fall picnic that their congregation held. Unlike most American parties that I had attended in my life where you arrived at a certain time and left approximately two hours later, the Hispanic congregants would show up at the pastor's home at various hours and most everyone stayed for about eight hours. My first time attending was a bit of culture shock. I felt very proud that I had made dressing for about 50 people. I had purchased about 10 cans of cranberry sauce to serve with it. I put it all out on the serving table and was shocked later to discover that they had eaten all of the cranberry sauce, but none of the dressing. They didn't know what it was!

I also enjoyed watching the sports being played. After several years of attending, I felt the need to encourage the women to form their own kickball team and possibly compete against the men. I did manage to rally a group of women together. However, we were beaten shamelessly. When it was my turn to kick the ball, I kicked my ballet-styled slipper off which was projected approximately 50 feet away. In the moment, I still felt the need to run to first base, otherwise I would be letting my lady teammates down. The person who tagged me out, also retrieved my slipper, and it is a ridiculous personal moment in sports that still makes me smile today.

However, time passes by and changes our daily life and who we see. Nothing is constant in life and God's direction for my future changed. I rarely see any of those people now, but I am so grateful for the opportunity to have once played kick ball with them and have whispers made about by mysterious "dressing" casserole.

God has numerous people He wants us to meet and a journey to fulfill during our lifetime. If we kept the settings and situation the same, we would never meet others He has set for us to know; experiences to live out and gain wisdom to share. Holding on to the past and what you have lost will only make you continuously grieve; it is essentially refusing to see the hope God has laid out in your future.

Prayer:

Dear Father, I look to You for my future. At times, I feel that I am blank slate in desperate need of direction and lack the motivation to want to move from the safe place I have known for so long. Create in me the will and give inspiration for me to see the areas in my life I want to improve and people I want to reach. Remind me what I am good at and show me new talents that You want me to explore. In Jesus' name. Amen.

"Doubt is the beginning, not the end, of wisdom."

"May the God of hope fill you with all joy and peace as you trust in him, so that you may overflow with hope by the power of the Holy Spirit." Romans 15:13

I have always tried to be "open door" to all people regardless of where they were in their spiritual walk. When someone has voiced their doubts or insults about Christianity, I try to listen to why they feel the way they do and give support in the most lovingly, Jesus-inspired way I can, while praying for the Holy Spirit to help me.

One of the largest reasons many give for being a non-believer is that they are a "person of science." I have loved science my entire life and have always felt science helped support my relationship with God. Where there is "cause and effect," there must be a cause. There must be a "cause" and reason the trees turn gorgeous colors in the fall, mountain-sized waves move across the sea, and birds migrate thousands of miles without a GPS. Even for a "person of science," there is not always a known reason for why things happen. Much of creation and life is left as a mysterious wonder to us, as humans.

Another factor of science that I have also come to realize is that where something exists, it likely has a polar opposite. Whether it is the polar ends of the world's axis or the difference between darkness and light, possibilities are endless. It is hard to put a simple cap on the definition of most anything if studied enough.

God's existence and brilliance continues to marvel us (and baffle us) at the same time because we will never be able to fully detail all who God is and does. Our uncertainties and questions about Him only add to His unlimited marvel.

Prayer:

Dear God, I pray for the unbelievers in my life that they may find the hope, peace, and beauty in so much of what surrounds them already. Help guide me in my conversations with others that I might be a missing piece to their puzzle in their relationship with You. In Jesus' name. Amen.

SEPTEMBER 4

"A fool and his money are soon parted."

"Do not be deceived: God is not mocked, for whatever one sows, that will he also reap. For the one who sows to his own flesh will from the flesh reap corruption, but the one who sows to the Spirit will from the Spirit reap eternal life." Galatians 6:7-8

I am not a gambler. My first and only gambling experience came at the age of 21 when a group of friends decided to take a quick-trip to Mississippi. I found the next 24 hours miserable as I soon learned one of our friends had a gambling addiction and was unable to leave the gambling table, even to sleep. As I placed each dollar in, I also felt a sense of desperation to keep adding money to possibly get some of the money I had lost back, but the dire outcome of my finances only worsened.

We eventually made our friends leave. They blamed us for their financial loss since they were not "able to stay until they won it back." We all sat in anger on the way back from Mississippi (which is a five-hour drive of passing nothing but Magnolias). During that weekend, I learned a good lesson. Not only was I broke, tired, and angry at friends for their lack of self-control, I was angry at myself for my lack of control. At what point does one stand up and advocate for what is excellent for one's life?

God wants us to live a happy, fruitful life. Sometimes we bring misery to our own lives by our poor choices and the way we live. The world is full of sin and misery but many times the direction that we choose to take can dictate our outcome. God calls us to be smarter and make better decisions as Christians.

Prayer:

Dear God, thank You for the love and provision you give. Free us from the worldly ploy that evil uses to lure us in that we might live free from bondage with You. In Jesus' name. Amen.

"Actions speak louder than words."

"Refrain from anger, and forsake wrath! Fret not yourself; it tends only to evil." Psalm 37:8

Perhaps one of the most difficult things for me to do is be nice to someone who has been unkind to me. When seeing them in public, I like to justify ignoring the person by saying "ignoring them is the nicest reaction I can give to someone like them," but it is not kind. We cannot be Godly, Spirit-filled people if we are unkind to others.

In what ways do we respond to a hateful, ignorant person? I will be the first to admit that political conversations in the past have made me yell at the people I love the most. Who do we despise the thought of coming into close contact with?

I am so grateful that Jesus does not despise coming into contact with anyone. He keeps His door open and His arms stretched wide to receive any of us when we need it. He is the only reason any of us can grow into becoming better people. By despising people, we are blatantly choosing to be the opposite of Jesus. It is less likely for others to know Jesus if we are not willing to show it.

Even after saying this, I know kindness and gentleness do not always come easy. There are so many people that excel at grace better than I do. In 2006, when a killer entered the Amish West Nickel Mines School and killed innocent children, they forgave the killer. He specifically targeted school aged girls to murder, yet the Amish community borrowed the power of Christ to forgive. Such actions leave me speechless as to the full power that God must hold.

Prayer:

Father, I ask for Your forgiveness in not forgiving my foes. Forgive me and forgive them. Free us both that we may fully enjoy all that You have planned for our lives. In Jesus' name. Amen.

"Walk a mile in someone's shoes before you judge them."

"Brothers and sisters, do not slander one another. Anyone who speaks against a brother or sister or judges them speaks against the law and judges it. When you judge the law, you are not keeping it, but sitting in judgment on it. There is only one Lawgiver and Judge, the one who is able to save and destroy. But you—who are you to judge."
James 4:11-12

I once bought a pair of "dream shoes." These shoes were the epitome of everything I wanted to be: attractive, professional, a "Lady Boss" by day, a smoking-hot blond by night. They were black patent with a five-inch heel. I looked great in them, and I am sure that my confidence was palpable. However, after about three hours of wearing them, my feet began to swell, causing a blister to form. I was in public, surrounded by people and the possibility of going barefoot did not seem optional. I continued to wear the shoes until I got in my car to go home.

My persistence in wearing the shoes resulted in a scar which serves as a reminder to be myself and not anyone else regardless of how "beautiful and confident" they appear. I eventually threw those heels away after realizing I am confident and beautiful in my own way.

The devil can create a long list of imperfections in our God-inspired, God-created body. God creates unique qualities in all of us. In the areas that we think are lacking and flawed, God has set something beautiful there. Sadly, sometimes the people we judge the most are ourselves.

Prayer:

God, thank You for my body and my health and the abilities You crafted in me. Help me to love myself and love everyone in the beautiful way You created them. In Jesus' name. Amen.

"An eye for an eye makes the whole world blind." - Mahatma Gandhi

"Why do you look at the speck in your brother's eye, but fail to notice the beam in your own eye? How can you say to your brother, 'Let me take the speck out of your eye,' while there is still a beam in your own eye?" Matthew 7:3-4

My late father always ate a slice of onion at the dinner table. As a child, I could not imagine a more horrible taste in my mouth than biting off a slice of onion to blend with my meal. One time he must have seen the face I made while thinking about it and asked about it. He said, "one day, your taste buds will change, and you will want to eat onion at every meal." "No way!" I thought.

Time has a funny way of changing our likes and dislikes. When I make a relish tray now, I put peppers, pickles, tomatoes and you guessed it, onions! Nothing quite goes with peas and cornbread like a slice of onion. Of course, there is not any way to describe this unique craving of cultured food without knowing it.

There are so many things to argue about in the world and we are all unique from one another. Some of the testaments from the Bible are living examples of how God uses each person differently. Sometimes we can come around to seeing the other person's viewpoint, and sometimes we can't. Where our differences seem too great, God will always be the bridge if we allow Him to be.

Prayer:

Lord, when I think others are misled, help me to continue walking the path You put me on, in spreading Your love regardless of my own viewpoints. In Jesus' name. Amen.

"As a tree bends, so shall it grow."

"Do not be conformed to this world, but be transformed by the renewal of your mind, that by testing you may discern what is the will of God, what is good and acceptable and perfect." Romans 12:2

My senior year of high school, I changed schools, and my first day at the new school left me feeling like an octopus in a tank full of fish. Some people are interested in you, while others feel intimidated and are dealing with their own self-doubt issues.

In a time that can feel like "the end of your life," it is a mere moment in time. "Growing pains" is a common expression used to describe this metamorphosis, and it might as well be called "change pains." More times than not, change hurts. It can give us anxiety and fear of the unknown. Change is inevitable and can be a positive thing. If change never happened, we would all still be in diapers, learning to crawl. We would never have made best friends, finished school, or got our first job. Obviously, there are different kinds of change. Not all of it leaves us with good memories–namely death and divorce. However, all change is part of life. The present will inevitably change too, so enjoy the good times. If you find yourself dealing with unwanted change during this season of life, trust in the Lord and look for the future. He is always with you and will give you strength when you ask.

Prayer:

Father, thank You for the new opportunities that come with each changing day. Help me connect with others and have meaningful relationships. Give me strength to get through difficult moments. In Jesus' name. Amen.

"All is well that ends well."

"Let all bitterness and wrath and anger and clamor and slander be put away from you, along with all malice. Be kind to one another, tenderhearted, forgiving one another, as God in Christ forgave you." Ephesians 4:31-32

When witnessing and trying to connect with a person on a deeper level, look for the things you enjoy most about the person. If you don't know the person that well, look for the best first-impression characteristics that unite you. When you say, "we are very different," you imply that there are qualities in someone that you find less than acceptable for your own life instead of seeing how God has chosen that person to walk their unique walk with God. Even if the person is living a noticeably different and secular life than, pointing out that they are different with a negative connotation is equivalent to building a wall between the two of you.

When we have conflict with someone, it may be possible to speak with them and leave the conversation on a positive note. It is also okay to walk away without a resolution. You are not going to be able to always make others see your viewpoint. Each person has experienced a unique history and background that has coded our personalities and opinions different from one another. Whatever the issue, always reflect God's grace and love.

Prayer:

God, help me love and communicate with others in the likeness of Christ, that my life here on earth might be a reflection of You. In Jesus' name. Amen.

"Clothes make the man."

"Therefore, brothers, by the mercies of God, I urge you to present your bodies as a living sacrifice, holy and pleasing to God; this is your spiritual worship." Romans 12:1

I have always been impressed by beautiful "Sunday's best" clothing. When I was around ten years old, my mother would take me to the "Cloth Barn" fabric store. We would spend half a day looking through the store at every dress pattern and then find the right material to go with it. It was a short-lived period in my youth. Shortly thereafter, my friends changed their style from a girl to a young lady and I followed, but I still recall it being my favorite church style during my life time.

Wearing all of the church splendor made us feel good about ourselves. Clothes and worship styles have changed over time, but the idea of making something look its best is appealing. I have frequently wondered in my life what Jesus would have thought about being fashionable on Sundays, since He was so humble and modest. However, in the Old Testament God gave instruction on how to build the temple and gave details down to the carved pomegranate ceiling. Jesus allowed His feet to be bathed in perfume. Other Biblical characters also showed attention to details.

Giving extra time and detail to our bodies is a balance. The difference is in the reason we are doing it, which is to glorify God. Your daily wardrobe is a living sacrifice to God and reflect your love and obedience to him.

Prayer:

Lord, may my actions and the way I dress my body glorify You. May I be a good representative for You in all that I say, do, and the way I present myself. In Jesus' name. Amen.

"Walk the walk."

"Therefore, go and make disciples of all nations, baptizing them in the name of the Father and of the Son and of the Holy Spirit, and teaching them to obey everything I have commanded you." Matthew 28:19-20

When people are departing from us, they frequently leave us with last words. During the September 11 attacks, many trapped in the towers called their loved ones to say their final "good-bye," "take care of the children" and "I love you." When my father passed away some of his last words to me were "be happy in life–just focus on being happy."

Giving final words to someone is not always marked by tragedy. Many people in important roles, such as presidents, leave their role with an important phrase to remember them by. From these things, we can gather that the last words of these long good-byes are frequently the most important thing that the other person wants us to know and live by.

As Jesus left this earth, His final words were, "you will be my witnesses in Jerusalem, and in all Judea and Samaria, and to the ends of the earth." (Acts 1:8) The most important thing Jesus wanted us to remember is to continue spreading His teachings, love, and the life-giving story of His resurrection! The way we devote ourselves in these acts is helping to fulfill Jesus' last words.

Prayer:

Father, thank You for the Bible, that we may know and be reminded what is important. Help me identify and connect with the lost and alone and invite them to make a connection with You. Use me, Lord. In Jesus' name. Amen.

"You have got to separate the wheat from the chaff.

"Beware of false prophets, which come to you in sheep's clothing, but inwardly they are ravening wolves." Matthew 7:15

The church I grew up in as a child and adolescent would be described by most as "strict." As a young person, I didn't always appreciate their strict takes on popular movies and opinions on which characters should be banned for "demonic characteristics." They even banned a certain troll doll that was popular while I was growing up. However, in that strict teaching I learned how to quickly identify whether something was considered "good" or "evil" within the religious community. Back then, it seemed a bit fanatical to weigh everything with that much magnitude, but as an adult, it has helped me identify people who are genuine from those that are not. The world is a mixed lot, and it is helpful to be able to judge which people or things in a group are bad and which ones are good. At every hour of the day, there is a person emailing or messaging your phone to try to scam someone. While there are many good pastors, there are many bad ones that are self-seeking that will step on their own child's head to get recognition. There are doctors that will perform unnecessary procedures for the sake of lining their pockets. In fact, "money is the root of all evil" in every profession. There are many good people in the world, but there are also many bad ones. God gives each of us the wisdom and ability to decipher truth from deception when we ask Him.

"If any of you lacks wisdom, let him ask God,
who gives generously to all without reproach, and it will
be given him." (James 1:5)

Prayer:

Dear Father God, Help me see past the tricks and greed of the world. Help me to hear Your voice along the pathway. Give me the ability to always see You in a camouflaged world. In Jesus' name. Amen.

"People pick the weirdest hills to die on."

"Because of the Lord's great love we are not consumed, for his compassions never fail. They are new every morning; great is your faithfulness. I say to myself, '"The Lord is my portion; therefore I will wait for him." Lamentations 3:22-24

Our actions and the choices we make can "make or break" us. One bad decision can determine the end of a person being considered "rational" which can take years to recover a person's reputation.

Once in the seventh grade during a CO2 model car race, I refused to share my hand warmers with other student competitors because I knew it gave me the advantage to win. Needless to say, classmates spent the next five years hating me because of it, and I learned a valuable lesson about the importance of sharing and grace (even during competitions.)

All of these "weird hills" that people "die on" are really preventable. If you have already had a dying hill moment, then there is the promise of the unwritten future on the horizon. God forgives, and His plans are waiting on you. If you have been fortunate to avoid making bad choices in life, then pray now for God's help for when difficult choices arise. Nothing can equip you better than the power and strength of the Lord. These events are seldom planned so asking for God's guidance now may seem unnecessary, but will be life changing.

Prayer:

God, thank You that tomorrow is unwritten and that I have a new opportunity to change my life. I ask for Your protection and guidance when choosing my words, actions, and footsteps. Help me. In Jesus' name. Amen

"Live like you were dying." -Tim McGraw

"And do this, understanding the present time: The hour has already come for you to wake up from your slumber, because our salvation is nearer now than when we first believed." Romans 13:11

The South is full of country music. We have set our hearts and ears in tune with country singers who sing from life experiences that we can all relate to. Whether you like country music or not, everyone can agree that country music is definitely earmarked as being regionally "Southern." In one of my favorite country music songs, Tim McGraw sings to "live like you were dying." In the song, after a terminal diagnosis, he starts living a good and meaningful life and says what he adjusted including reading the Bible, forgiving others and intentionally spending more time with friends and family members. To Christians everywhere, "Live like you were dying" should be a daily motivator in living a Christian lifestyle!

What would you do with this week if it was your last? Every day and every moment is the opportunity to change the world for the better. Would you watch another episode of your favorite show or would you make sure that your children know how Jesus can deliver them from fear and oppression during dark times? Time is precious, and while God also requires that we rest and restore ourselves, He has given us a precious ticking gift.

Prayer:

Father, help me use my time more effectively for You. Help me appreciate the joys and laughter of each day, but also to listen to those lost and hurting. Guide me and set my path, Lord. Allow me to be Your hands and feet and use my time on earth in a way that is pleasing to You. In Jesus' name. Amen.

"It takes one to know one."

"Fulfill my joy by being like-minded, having the same love, being of one accord, of one mind. Let nothing be done through selfish ambition or conceit, but in lowliness of mind let each esteem others better than himself. Let each of you look out not only for his own interests, but also for the interests of others." Philippians 2:2-4

In the late 1990s, I took a mission trip to rural Venezuela. During my stay there, most of what I experienced was foreign to me however, to my disbelief, I saw a few people that I had met before (from the southern United States!) An American couple I saw there would cross my path again while working in missions in Ecuador 20 years later.

During my time with them in Ecuador, I mainly worked with the wife. She gave me a bilingual Bible story book. As I went back to the States and thought about how I would use the book she gave, I realized that I could create a Christian children's theatre for Spanish-speaking kids in Alabama and did so.

Looking back in time, I can see how God used the Venezuela trip to form a connection in my life. It was a door for me to know the Missionary's wife, receive the storybook and create the children's theatre, which eventually helped me learn Spanish. God has used my Spanish-speaking ability on more than one occurrence since then to talk to others about the gift of forgiveness and love of Jesus Christ to reach a large immigrant population in my community.

People frequently ask, "how did you learn Spanish" and the answer is that learning the language was solely provided by God. From the time that I received the bilingual story Bible, I spoke fluent Spanish less than a year later. Whatever need you have, God can and will provide it. It will move like a miracle over your life because it is the Holy Spirit.

God provides the resources and essential people needed when He wants you to begin a new chapter in life. Perhaps God has showed you that it is time you move on to a different ministry or congregation. Finding those new connections in your life is essential to receiving the maximum teaching and blessing from the Lord.

Prayer:

Dear Heavenly Father, thank You for the overwhelming group of people You have placed in the world to love and teach us. Help me understand my place and future within the church and be mindful that the people around me can help fulfill my spiritual work for You. May we lift You high, with our actions and work together. In Jesus' name. Amen.

"There is more than one way to skin a rabbit."

"Be strong and of a good courage; be not afraid, neither be thou dismayed: for the Lord thy God is with thee whithersoever thou goest." Joshua 1:9

Sometimes when I see my husband doing something around the house, it seems he is doing it the opposite way of how I would have started the task. I think most people would say that he mostly uses the left side of the brain, while I use the right side. Knowing this about our relationship brings attention to the stories in the Bible that are seemingly backwards to me when I imagine being there during certain scenes from the Bible. After Moses left Egypt after murdering an Egyptian, as his wife, I would have begged him to not go back. It was dangerous, and I probably would have called him "crazy." Yet, God had a remarkable plan for him. Even after he made it back to Egypt, he was bold to demand everything from Pharaoh. Those are actions that, at the time, I would not have supported. God told Moses that the Hebrews would walk out of Egypt with the Egyptians' silver and gold, to which they boldly did.

There will never be a constant group or individual in your life that always agrees with the direction you are taking. Knowing God's direction is essential to fulfilling our purpose on Earth. The true test of character is when you keep doing what God has instructed you to do even without the support of your friends and family. Prayer:

God, may I always go to where You call me without falter and without listening to the opinions of people around me. May I always boldly walk with You. In Jesus' name. Amen.

"A bushel and a peck and a ring around the neck."

"Thoughtless words cut like a sword. But the tongue of wise people brings healing." Proverbs 12:18

"A bushel and a peck and a ring around the neck"- This loving expression meaning a kiss and hug is popular for grandmothers to share with small children. They are simple words of love that are sweet and quickly received by babies. Even though no one in my family ever said this phrase, I always loved hearing my friends' parents say it. The world would be a much kinder place if it was used more often.

During my life, I have said too many things out of hate that I regretted later. One of the main examples that comes to mind was an English teacher that was new to my high school. One day, when she corrected me, I made a joke about her flamboyant clothes and dresses. She heard me and said something quick-witted, but I knew that it hurt her. In truth, I really admired her and the freedom she carried in being herself. She was always affirming, positive, and had a jovial personality. Over twenty years later, I still regret those words. I wish I would have told her, "I love you a bushel and a peck." Affirming her positivity would have only made her teaching experience better for future students. Instead, I chose to put ugly words into an ugly world instead of spreading God's light and making the world a better place.

P.S. If you are reading this Ms. Walker, I love you a bushel and a peck and am grateful to have met you!

Prayer:

God, help me choose my words carefully and be slow to speak in anger. Give me more opportunities to give "bushel and peck" love affirmations. Open my eyes to those that feel lost and broken, and especially need to hear it. In Jesus' name. Amen.

"Let bygones be bygones."

"From him the whole body, joined and held together by every supporting ligament, grows and builds itself up in love, as each part does its work". Ephesians 4:16

Honey bees are such a perfect example of how to truly live in unison and live a Christian life. They all live under the same roof, yet they are so different. You never hear of a discontent honey bee upset because one bee is a worker bee and the other is a drone bee. They all work together to create the sweet honey that the world enjoys.

Sometimes, we, as individuals, feel too small to change the world. How could one person make such an impact on Earth? The honey bee never lets that way of thinking interrupt their work. Even though they are a thousand times smaller than a person, they set out into the world every day to complete their mission. Together with the other caste of bees, they work together to make their kingdom greater. In doing so, they also make the world better by pollinating, which is essential to nature.

Honey bees working together is the ideal relationship that Christians should model. "Working together" does not have to mean physically building something. It means that your daily conversation and actions collaborate and create something positive for God. Collaboration changes the community, world and magnifies the Kingdom of God.

Prayer:

God, forgive me for not always looking for the best qualities in my Christian brothers and sisters. Help each of us identify our unique gifts and ways that we can work together to create something beautiful to glorify You. In Jesus' name. Amen.

"Live like there's no tomorrow."

"Never let the fire in your heart go out. Keep it alive. Serve the Lord. When you hope, be joyful. When you suffer, be patient. When you pray, be faithful. Share with God's people who are in need. Welcome others into your homes." Romans 12:11-13

When people get a bad prognosis at the doctor's office, they frequently change their lifestyle immediately. Sometimes they sell all of their belongings, grab a backpack, and head to the places their heart has called them for years. Some get in touch with loved ones and letting them know how much they are loved.

Being told you have limited time sets a serious tone for how to spend the remainder of your time and helps identify what is most important. Most choose to "live like there's no tomorrow" and embrace all of the experiences the day offers. Too frequently, when we experience something hurtful, we stop for too long to focus on that one occurrence when life has more to offer.

We are all going to eventually die. So, there is truth in living like there is no tomorrow. Our life is more fruitful when we give it a Christian direction: loving people, forgiving people, helping those in need, telling people how God has changed your life, thanking God for the ways He has changed you and actively pursuing a life without sin minute to minute. God compels us to live our best life and our "kitchen timer" has been set.

Prayer:

Jesus, come into my heart. Forgive me of my sins. Holy Spirit, move me to share my life with others through love, forgiveness, and expressing the freedom that comes by knowing You. Help me embrace this day as one of my last and use it to the fullest to glorify You. In Jesus' name. Amen.

"Never reveal a man's wage and woman's age."

"Do not let any unwholesome talk come out of your mouths, but only what is helpful for building others up according to their needs, that it may benefit those who listen." Ephesians 4:29

Years ago, my sister and I were raking leaves in my grandmother's yard. There was literally a mountain-sized pile, and we got into a disagreement of if we should bag the leaves or not. Bagging would have required 40+ industrial-sized garbage bags, and I was not a proponent of that option. While the entire task was pretty insignificant, it led to a huge verbal argument in the yard, which led to both of us sharing hurtful feelings that we had bundled up for 20 years.

Sometimes the other person you are with has a mouth "as big as Texas" and you can feel your blood starting to slowly boil. Do you smile and walk away or do you confront them?

"When you are so astonished you don't know what to say, it is best to not say anything until you can say it with a gentle soft tongue." (Proverbs 15:1)

Everyone can relate to a time where quick responses and the need to be right, turned into an uglier situation. It's okay to stop the argument. It's okay to stop responding. If the other person has the last word, it's okay! I think about all of the time I have wasted arguing with people, and it's okay to be the person that stops feeding the fire. Use that time to get to know the person better, what their dreams are, what is important to them, what bothers them and how you can pray for them.

Prayer:

God, Quiet my heart when I feel myself about to boil over. Help me listen more closely to the other person. Help me connect with them instead of looking for opportunities to tear them down. In Jesus' name, Amen.

"Oil and water do not mix."

"How good and pleasant it is when God's people live together in unity!" Psalm 133:1

My mother used to keep a little glass box on her desk of blue ocean waves that you could watch float from side to side. The liquids, made of oil and water, were practically impossible to shake together. I am sure that the solution was meant to create a peaceful feeling and lower blood pressure, but as a child, I shook that thing to death trying to get the two liquids to merge. However, that is not always the case for oil and water. I find when baking a delicious cake that oil and water work together wonderfully and keep the cake moist. The key difference in unity is adding in the other ingredients like flour, sugar, and eggs.

People can be very comparable to oil and water. I know a few people that I wouldn't dream of inviting to the same party, and yet, God saw to it to place them together in the same environment. Even though some people go together like oil and water, they can merge together just like that cake. The key ingredient is not flour, but God.

It does take more effort for the two people to find the same common ground and come together, but the result is more delicious than cake.

Prayer:

Dear Heavenly Father, help me look for the key Godly ingredients in bringing people together. Help us look for unity. In Jesus' name. Amen.

"If you are looking for the devil, he will find you."

"Above all else, guard your heart, for it is the wellspring of life." Proverbs 4:23

Growing up, my parents were strict about which T.V. programs were acceptable to watch, as well as music. Even though it seemed crazy to me at the time, now that I have a son, I realize evil is always lurking in the world. Family network TV shows frequently curse or have violence. Horror and scary movies have creatures that can only be seen in hell, and yet it has become the social norm to show these things to the world.

With all of these things, it is no wonder that people have nightmares, are afflicted with panic attacks, and have depression. What you feed your mind through TV, music, or on your smart phone determines who you are. If you are pouring the devil into your soul, he will find you.

If you need a book, you go to the library. If you need medical care, you go to the doctor. It is only right that when we need spiritual care, we go to church. If you find yourself affected by these evils, be proactive in cleaning your life from them. Every day is a new opportunity to start afresh.

Prayer:

Dear God, help us say no to media that hurts us. It is an unpopular idea to turn off the TV in the middle of a show or song. Help my friends and family see that is the only way to preserve our sanctity. I pray for those in the entertainment industries, that they will be compelled to start a new, clean revolution of programming for the world. May we as Christians, stand together against it. In Jesus' name. Amen.

"I haven't seen him in a coon's age!"

"While Peter was still speaking these words, the Holy Spirit fell upon all those who were listening to the message. All the circumcised believers who came with Peter were amazed, because the gift of the Holy Spirit had been poured out on the Gentiles also. For they were hearing them speaking with tongues and exalting God." Acts 10:44-46

A true telling of a Southerner is using words like "I woulda swunney," which means "I would have sworn." Another favorite is "Gah!" which means, "Wow! I can't believe it!" I'm not sure where these words came from, but they have been filling the mouths of my 'kin for a "coon's age." Considering these contributions to language, it brings to mind that God is a God of numerous languages. He was able to speak ancient Egyptian Coptic to Moses, Greek to Saul, Aramaic to Jesus, and continues to speak directly to our hearts in multiple languages.

A few times in my life, I have heard a multi-lingual congregation pray aloud. Somehow the chaotic sound of all the languages and prayers transform into a lovely symphony that is more felt than it is heard. It is the embodiment of the Holy Spirit that has broken down barriers and is unfolding because of the people's invitation. Words are important, but not nearly as important as the heart of the person praying to God. Whatever you are afraid of in public speaking, such as saying the wrong thing or not communicating effectively, your prayer to God is felt more than it is heard. He has the power to change what the audience hears. The love and passion behind your prayer is more important.

Prayer:

Holy Spirit, You are welcome here. We long to feel Your presence. May we pray with resilient strength, knowing You are stronger than our fears. In Jesus' name. Amen.

"Talk is cheap."

"Do not let any unwholesome talk come out of your mouths, but only what is helpful for building others up according to their needs, that it may benefit those who listen. And do not grieve the Holy Spirit of God, with whom you were sealed for the day of redemption. Get rid of all bitterness, rage and anger, brawling and slander, along with every form of malice. Be kind and compassionate to one another, forgiving each other, just as in Christ God forgave you." Ephesians 4:29-32

One of my favorite games growing up was "Gossip." I loved to line up and whisper the secret phrase, mouth to ear. It was always fun to hear how the ending phrase had changed and was completely different. "Gummy worms and chocolate milk are my favorite during snack time" somehow always changed into "The cafeteria is always cold in the mornings." It is such a fun childhood game, but in adulthood, gossip can destroy lives.

A popular and favorite Christian phrase of mine says, "live a life so clean, that when others hear bad things about you, they will know it is not true." That's a living truth! If you choose to always be kind and honest with people, look them in the eye, and do what you tell people you will do– you cannot put a price on how valuable that is. If you sometimes get drunk, get a little crazy on the weekend, yell and curse at people, then they might be a little afraid of you. If they hear something bad about you, they will be more likely to believe it.

Prayer:

Father God, we know we cannot live on the wild, sinful side and still be credible. We want to live in Your light and do right by You. May others know who we are by our faithfulness to You. In Jesus' name. Amen.

"The best defense is a good offense."

"In the same way, the tongue is a small thing that makes grand speeches. But a tiny spark can set a great forest on fire." James 3:5

It is inevitable in life that someone will come for you and verbally attack you. Whether it is on the 5th grade playground or in your marital relationship ... being attacked is part of life.

Social media has daily threads of people bashing one another. The devil is a very real thing and delights in these occurrences. Nothing is more delicious to evil than to hear people tearing down others that are different from them.

In Biblical times, even without social media, people were stoned if they were scrutinized by the public. People were constantly getting together to purge someone to death. When Jesus showed up to save the adulterous woman, he asked us all to examine our own life and the sins we make against God.

What would happen if we replaced our words of opposition for each other with words of love and affirmation; glorifying and affirming God and the kingdom of Heaven? The devil would find a new place to hang out (at least for a while!) As humans, we primitively think the best way to get our point across is to shout it, demand it, and insist it be the only way, but God calls us to something more holy. It is what separates us from beasts. We can speak eloquently, and use the art of speech to shed light on love and kindness. It is what separates Christians from those living in the world's darkness.

Prayer:

Be gone, devil! In Jesus' name! All honor, power, and glory belongs to God! Amen.

"Make new friends but keep the old one. One is silver and the other's gold."

"Love one another with brotherly affection. Outdo one another in showing honor." Romans 12:10

A few of my longtime "old friends", Chevonne and Susanne, have been around since the trials of my youth. Growing up is not always a pretty time. Susanne has watched me cry my eyes out when I lost my grandmother, then my uncle, then a mutual friend. From day one, Chevonne has always encouraged me to be myself and helped me see the beauty in myself and others. After knowing me 25+ years, they both know my background, the reason I tick, and my aspirations.

A friend, no matter how long you have known them, is precious. When a friend wants to talk, you lend an ear. When they need something, you try to assist. You love them and you make sure they know that.

One of the oldest, goldest friends who has loved and admired you for decades, (sometimes from afar) is Jesus Christ! He knows your background. He has watched you cry. He knows what makes you tick and like all friends, will always be there to lend His ear and love you. Make new friends, but keep the old one. One is silver and the other's gold.

Prayer:

Jesus, thank You for always being there. May I dig deeper in new meaningful ways of discovering who You are. In Jesus' name. Amen.

"A little makeup and paint will make a woman what she ain't."

"You are worthy, O Lord, To receive glory and honor and power; For You created all things, And by Your will they exist and were created." Revelation 4:11

Sometimes the world gives us things and we are not sure exactly what we are looking at. There are a multitude of occurrences that just cannot be explained. The first time I ever experienced this was on vacation. I had been driving several hours and noticed a mirage of water ahead on the pavement. I had noticed water puddle mirages on roadways since I was a little girl, but this time was different. Beside the roadway were pine trees, and in the water puddle mirages, I could see the pine trees reflecting off the mirage water. How I could see a reflection off a mirage still baffles me! When speaking with a scientist friend I learned that this phenomenon is actually called a Fata Morgana.

Our God is a big Creator and omnipotent. Things we experience and see are not always going to be easily explained to us. We might never know the reasons some things happen. Some things are out of our control. However, it makes me feel good that such an almighty Creator, who gives attention to small details such as mirage water puddles has given my life that much detail as well. Trust in Him.

Prayer:

Dear Creator, You are marvelous! Thank You for the wonders that we come to know and the other wonders that are light-years away; for what is seen and unseen. May we trust You and relax in the comfort of Your hands in knowing that you formed and love us. We give You thanks. In Jesus' name. Amen.

"The leopard does not change his spots."

"Jesus answered, 'I am the way and the truth and the life. No one comes to the Father except through me.'" John 14:6

Even though I am a lifelong resident of Alabama, Southern foods like "Shrimp and Grits" and "Gumbo" are completely foreign to me. Perhaps, it is because my family lives about four hours from the nearest beach but seafood has long remained an odd thing at our family table. As I have become older, I have tried to broaden my skills and learn how to cook seafood but it still remains a mystery. In my most recent recipe, I learned that "oyster sauce" is apparently not the same as "clam juice" after pouring an entire bottle into my fish soup. What resulted was a soup that tasted like ketchup and soy sauce with chunks of fish in it. It was hideous! Sometimes recipes don't have room for substitutions. Only the actual ingredient will suffice.

I also find that when someone is having a major problem in their life, there are not any substitutions that can be made to make them feel better – only God can do that. Southerners, (even though they mean well) will tell you exactly what you need to do to fix a problem. The aim is to fix the problem but more times than not, unsolicited advice comes across as "you must be stupid, so let me tell you the answer."

Life's journey can be difficult and sometimes people just need a person to listen and a shoulder to cry on. When someone has poured their heart out, it is okay to listen quietly without giving "oyster sauce" to their situation. Let them know that you are grateful they chose you to share with and ask to pray with them.

Prayer:

God, help me be an outlet to someone that needs a listening ear. May I be understanding and silent when I need to be. I pray that others might experience Your peace, through me. In Jesus' name. Amen.

"A rose by any other name would smell as sweet."
-Shakespeare

"I praise you because I am fearfully and wonderfully made; your works are wonderful, I know that full well." Psalm 139:14

When my husband and I were dating, we went to a taco stand. We love Mexican food! On their menu, they offered "churi-queso tacos." Neither of us had heard of them before and we order two, so that we could each try one. What happened afterward was a mouthwatering revolution! The next day we both remarked how delicious the tacos were and that churi-queso was so delicious, that we liked them as well as we liked each other. So we dubbed one another "Churi-queso" and "Churi-quesa" as pet love names. Several years later, we still say things like, "You are my Churi-queso, forever."

In life, you might be marred by names that you think are unfair and a past that weighs you down emotionally, physically, and spiritually. Bad things might have happened in your life and you might be dubbing yourself as "unwanted," "stupid," or "ugly." Despite whatever negative names you have called yourself , you have the ability, with God's help, to create a new future.

Even though my pet name, "Churi-queso" seems ridiculous, there is love behind it. There is also love behind the creation of you. In whatever past you come from, you came from God, the Creator, and He wants to call you "His" and love you.

Prayer:

God, May we break free of the chains from the past. Help and give us strength to overcome our past shadows and search for Your light, Your love, and our new identity in You. In Jesus' name. Amen.

"Hope deferred maketh the heart sick."

"Trust in the Lord with all your heart; do not depend on your own understanding. Seek his will in all you do, and he will show you which path to take." Proverbs 3:5-6

My mother and aunt are a real hoot together. They are close-knit sisters that laugh, travel, and cry together–sharing all life experiences! Several years ago while at my grandmother's house, my mother open the door to the attic. Like most old houses, it has one giant staircase that leads up to the second level. Mother's eyes instantly froze in fear. At the top of the stairs, she could see a pair of legs lying across the top step. She quietly backed away and went to get my aunt. When my aunt saw the legs, they decided that some unknown person had been secretly living up there and was either asleep or passed out drunk. They both quietly slipped away and called the police to have the person removed. About ten minutes later, when the police arrived, they were all surprised that the person had not moved at all. Because of the lack of body movement, the police concluded that it seemed the person might be dead upstairs and asked my mother and aunt to wait on the porch until he came back down.

About this time, I arrived to find my aunt and mother crying on the porch. When I asked them what was wrong, with tears in their eyes, they had decided that the dead body was my uncle (who left town a few weeks prior and no one had been in contact with him.) I was trying to console them, saying that "he was a good person and had lived a good life" when the policeman finally came back downstairs. "It seems that the pair of legs at the top of the staircase belongs to a life-sized Pink Panther doll." In disbelief everyone laughed in shock and relief that it wasn't my uncle!

The uncertainty of situations can make us all sick. The fear of the unknown creeps in and suddenly we have imagined the worst-case scenario. God gives us hope so during those times of uncertainty, we can cling to the best-case scenario. Most of the time, the scenario is completely out of our control anyway. Only God has full control and He will never abandon us.

Prayer:

Heavenly Father, thank You that sometimes we can turn our fears into laughter. May we be reminded that You are always with us, through thick and thin. Thank You for the gift of hope–that even in the worst-case scenario we know that in the end You win and are victorious. Through Your victory and eternal life, we shall be also. In Jesus' name. Amen.

"Dang if you do and dang if you don't."

"The LORD is close to the brokenhearted and saves those who are crushed in spirit." Psalm 34:18

Many times in life we are dealt a difficult hand of cards to play, sometimes having to choose between difficult and awful.

A friend suffering from the effects of Alzheimer's came to visit my family recently, and I had to ask them to leave for fear of their growing aggression, especially with our small child nearby. It hurt having to choose between possibly never seeing them again over the safety of my family. In the midst of our hurt and trauma, it feels isolating that no one around us can identify with our issues. As individuals, we are taught to keep our negative feelings hidden from others. Society has created a "happy face, happy life" attitude regarding everything. So when experiencing life's hurtful moments, it can be hard to share that with others, especially when they might not be able to identify.

In those broken moments when you feel your life is in pieces, it is invaluable to remember that God is always with you. Psalm 56:8 says, "You keep track of all my sorrows.-You have collected all my tears in your bottle. You have recorded each one in your book." If you feel you are facing a giant, know that God is bigger. Ask Him for help.

Prayer:

God, I need you. Areas in my life are broken and I do not know how to repair them. I can't repair them. I need you to intercede for me. Protect me and my family. Help me find comfort and refuge in Your love and Bible. In Jesus' name. Amen.

"Hope deferred maketh the heart sick." (revisited)

"May the God of hope fill you with all joy and peace as you trust in him, so that you may overflow with hope by the power of the Holy Spirit." Romans 15:13

A friend of mine recently posted on social media that her husband had pancreatic cancer and that they would be radically fighting it. Since my father passed from having pancreatic cancer, her post gave me an awful feeling as that diagnosis does not offer much time left on this earth. I prayed daily for them and his medical team. She is so humble and she always remained positive; hopeful in her own dark times.

Through a miracle from God, after a few weeks and a big surgery, his pancreatic cancer diagnosis was changed to a neuroendocrine tumor diagnosis, which is a life-giving difference.

When receiving medical diagnoses that are not favorable (or any bad news) it tends to fill us with fear. Even when we are surrounded by prayer warriors it can feel like we are being eaten alive, but God is with us. Regardless of what news or future we are facing, He is at the forefront. Deuteronomy 31:6 says, "Be strong and courageous. Do not be afraid or terrified because of them, for the LORD your God goes with you; he will never leave you nor forsake you."

"Weeping may tarry for the night, but joy comes with the morning." (Psalm 30:5)

Prayer:

God, thank You for always watching over me. Help me through my trials. Please send reminders of hope and hopeful people to get me through the day when I need You most. May my life be a testimony to Your Power. In Jesus' name. Amen.

"Your eyes are bigger than your stomach."

"Give us today our daily bread." Matthew 6:11

My grandmother passed away 25 years ago. I grew up listening to her old stories and handy tips for life. She was born in 1906 and had a slew of knowledge and experience from growing up in simpler times and during the Great Depression. She had everything she needed but was not frivolous by any means. However, at Thanksgiving she made a big spread of dishes and desserts for all of the family members. Her buffet of desserts was my favorite. She always had a pineapple cake! After eating all of her soul food, it was painful to also eat that pineapple cake but was deemed necessary by her. At the end of every Thanksgiving everyone always felt overstuffed and a little miserable because of it.

Many years later, we still put out a pineapple cake in her memory, and we still overeat on Thanksgiving. It never leaves us with a good feeling. Much like our desire to consume all the riches of the world (a big house or two, multiple cars, adult toys, etc,) the desire to have everything might be the most common and least Christian error we make.

God gives us everything we need. His provision and promises are full. He always gives us exactly what we need for today. There is never any reason to hoard His blessing.

Prayer:

God, Just as you look after the sparrow, may I be ever mindful of Your love. "Give me this day, my daily bread" and give me Your peace to not worry about other things. In Jesus' name. Amen.

"Gone water does not mill anymore."

"Now on the last day, the great day of the feast, Jesus stood and cried out, saying, "If anyone is thirsty, let him come to Me and drink. He who believes in Me, as the Scripture said, 'From his innermost being will flow rivers of living water.'" John 7:37-38

Have you ever been dehydrated?

A few years ago, my family visited some Mayan ruins in Mexico. Upon arrival, I noticed some Chinese tourists walking the grounds with umbrellas, to which I thought to myself "how strange and interesting that there is still a culture that carries around umbrellas when in the sun." I bought a bottle of water and set out to walk in the steps of the ancients. About 30 minutes into my walk, I felt like I was going to die! I had to stop my tour, go sit under a tree, and consume multiple bottles of water. I am sure I was minutes away from needing medics.

Recently, in an incredible sermon series I hear the pastor describe the Holy Spirit as being like water. When we lose just 5% of our body's water we become confused, disoriented, and make bad decisions. When we lose 10% of our body's water we can die from dehydration. Likewise, living with sin, (just 5-10 %) can also confuse us, complicate our lives, and ultimately kill us. The difference and variable in our Christian lives is the Holy Spirit. When we know that we aren't spiritually fully hydrated, we need to plunge into the Bible and prayer. We need to worship and communicate with God so that when the deadly heat of evil beats down on our lives, we can prevail.

Prayer:
"Spirit of the Living God, Fall fresh on me, Spirit of the Living God, Fall fresh on me. Melt me, mold me, fill me, use me.
Spirit of the Living God, Fall fresh on me. Amen. – Daniel Iverson (1926)

"Sleeping like a log."

"Religion that is pure and undefiled before God, the Father, is this: to visit orphans and widows in their affliction, and to keep oneself unstained from the world." James 1:27

When my husband sits down in the evening, he puts his Bluetooth ear buds in to listen to a podcast, closes his eyes, and is asleep within five minutes! Recently, our toddler has started picking up various cords and strings around the house (ribbons, vacuum-cleaner plug, shopping cart seat belts) and holding them up to his ear like ear buds, trying to determine what has sound and what doesn't. Toddlers really have an unbiased view of the world. I imagine everything from their perspective is fun and educational. I hunger to have the same sense of curiosity and fresh eyes for the things of God that my son has in figuring out the purpose of items. As adults, this is achievable, but only when we set aside of what the world has said is obtainable and instead, focus on what God says is obtainable.

What would we as adults, be like, if we were constantly looking for ways to communicate with God and live out His message? It is not possible for us to pick up electrical cords and listen for God's voice but we do have ways that we can connect with Him spiritually. When we actively pursue the people in our community that need our help and connect with them in a meaningful way, many times Jesus is also found in that union.

Prayer:

Heavenly Father, Open my eyes and heart to the ways that I can actively live out Your message and love for others. May my love for You always be fearless– willing to go where You need me. In Jesus' name. Amen.

OCTOBER 6

"Crooked as a dog's hind leg"

"When the Spirit of truth comes, he will guide you into all the truth, for he will not speak on his own authority, but whatever he hears he will speak, and he will declare to you the things that are to come." John 16:13

Have you ever known anyone that was known as "Bad News"? At times, I have come across people who only seem to lie, steal and cheat; claiming they only did so in order to survive. For me, these are the most difficult people to encounter. How do you respond when you know someone plans to steal or lie to you? God's grace is sufficient for everyone, but when people have no intentions of claiming God's grace or even asking for forgiveness, it can make us angry. I have always tried to figure out why someone may act this way. Have they never been shown love or kindness? While love and kindness are both gifts that Bad News Bear could definitely benefit from, I have found that they are better gifts when paired with truth.

John 17:17 says, "Sanctify them in the truth; your word is truth." The word "sanctify" means clean, purify, and make holy. The next time you know someone is "yanking your chain," remain calm and ask them if they know how much Jesus loves them and the prosperous plans He has for His children.

Prayer:

Father, Help me be the face of Christ when I know I am encountering the wicked. Help me remember that I, too, was once wicked, but You saved and purified me. Teach me the way to respond to Bad News Bears without hate or blame. Holy Spirit, flow through me and my mouth to know what to say as I act as a guide to those lost. In Jesus' name. Amen.

"She's madder than a wet hen!"

"Take good care of me, just as you would take care of your own eyes. Hide me in the shadow of your wings. Save me from the sinful people who attack me. Save me from my deadly enemies who are all around me." Psalm 17:8-9

Seeing people being chased by chickens has to be one of the greatest experiences of a Southern life. My family had chickens when I was a child and the first little group of baby chicks that came was the most adorable sight! From the first moment I saw them, I smiled and walked gently over to them. Without thinking, I reached my eleven-year-old hand down to pick one up, and out of nowhere, Mama Chicken came to attack my head and chase me up our long driveway. She was always suspicious of me after that. Mama chicken is always there to defend.

God's love and defense is the same but greater. He is always there for us, even when we may not be aware of His presence. His love for us never fails. When we are experiencing life's tough issues, it does not mean that He doesn't love us or has abandoned us. Sometimes in the midst of our troubles we want Him to come down to Earth and peck the head of the person trying to cause us trouble. However, it is important to remember that vengeance belongs to the Lord and that He loves the other person just as much as He does you (you are both baby chicks to Him). He is always with you and hears your prayers. If you are feeling vulnerable or angry, pray and ask for His comfort.

Prayer:

God, thank you for always watching out and loving me. I pray a prayer of protection that in moments when I am oblivious to predators and evil lurking that You will place me in a hedge of protection. In Jesus' name, Amen.

OCTOBER 8

"More than one way to skin a cat."

"There are different kinds of service, but the same Lord. There are different kinds of working, but in all of them and in everyone it is the same God at work." 1 Corinthians 12:5-6

Although many other people in my town knew her better than I did, a very petite woman named "Miss Helen" made her mark in our community in the most curious of ways. By most standards she was a very odd character. She lived to be almost 90, never learned to drive, never married or had children, was the mother of 30 cats and could be obtuse in her ways. However, she loved Jesus and everyone knew it. She had an amazing gift of connecting every person to God, regardless of their situation. One Christmas Eve, she had an elderly couple drive out to a foster family and deliver Christmas presents. On another occasion, she had a teenager drive their truck to pick up someone in a wheelchair to bring them to church. In the 1970s, she created Christian-based programming about nature and how God's love is abundant and obvious in the small details that He gave every living thing (including us!) She created classes for special needs children and adults and made lesson plans before special needs programming existed. Simply put, she had the love of Jesus in her heart and shared it with everyone in the most innovative of ways.

While many people don't consider themselves innovative or creative, we all have gifts. What kind of gifts do you have that you can use as a platform in sharing the Good News?

Prayer:

Father, stir something new in me, that I might use my favorite things and pass-times as tools to tell others about Your great love! In Jesus' name, Amen.

"Pretty as a picture."

"If any of you lacks wisdom, let him ask God, who gives generously to all without reproach, and it will be given him." James 1:5

The world loves "pretty," doesn't it? Any hour and day, you can turn on the T.V. or open a magazine and see some of the most beautiful people in the world. Especially in the South, there are at least a dozen different county beauty pageants each year. We love our big ball gowns and long hair! However, we are equally obsessed with flaws. There is always a talk show full of people with problems. If something bad happens to a celebrity, people can't read enough about it. The sinking of the Titanic happened in 1912 and here we are reading about it over 100 years later.

People sometimes feel "too broken" to live the life of a disciple, thinking that they aren't good enough but the characters in the Bible were broken. That's what helps us relate to them–sharing our negative experiences. It is invaluable to hear someone else's bad experience and how they coped with it.

People at times may also feel that they are too old to start something revolutionary in their life. If you are here breathing, God still has a purpose for you. My husband collects glass and crushes it to use as an insulated floor for an outdoor oven that he is building. Everything and everyone can be repurposed. Whatever the imperfections are that you feel are present in your life, God has a plan and wants to use you.

Prayer:

Father God, Use me and mold me. For all that I am, let me be Your hands and feet. I pray for strength to go when and where You lead me. In Jesus' name, Amen.

OCTOBER 10

"A day late and a dollar short"

"But the men marveled, saying, 'What manner of man is this, that even the winds and the sea obey him!'" Matthew 8:27

There are usually things throughout the year that I mean to do, but somehow time passes and the project never gets finished. I start the year wanting to lose weight but by winter, my belly is still there. In autumn, I want to start slowly buying Christmas presents, and the list goes on! We as humans do not always live up to the to-do list that we create. (My crafting friends especially know about this.) These are all fun things to get behind on, but life has a way of making you feel like you are getting behind on important things, too and drowning because of them. Work due dates paired with family needing quality time is one example. The cost of healthcare and the financial toll it takes on the sick is another. In these moments, life can feel hopeless, but it is vital to remember that God is so much bigger than whatever you are facing. He is the Creator and "even the winds obey Him."

During a sermon at Kingwood Church in Alabaster, Alabama, Pastor Jay West compared the Holy Spirit to oil saying, "the Holy Spirit is like oil; it sticks, it shines, it heals, it absorbs." For the issues we have in our life that we really need to change and have help with, the Holy Spirit is always in our presence waiting to be asked. Your balance and healing starts the moment that you reach to God and the Holy Spirit for help.

Prayer:

Holy Spirit, come! Today, I pray for the person reading this that can't even find the words to pray. I pray that You give them strength. May they know how much God loves them and that nothing is too big for Him to handle. Blanket them now with Your healing restoration. In Jesus' name, Amen.

"Let bygones be bygones."

"Go ye into all the world, and preach the gospel to every creature." Mark 16:15

The world has many countries where owning a Bible can cause you to be killed. Currently, billions of people in the world have never heard of Jesus leaving many people who are broken, feel lost, and dying, to live a life without hope.

As American Christians, we let our privileged lifestyles get in the way of sharing God's Gospel. If you have been alive long enough to remember a world before COVID-19, you have witnessed the entire world throw mud in each other's eyes. Even if you managed to escape COVID conversations, there have been many other topics regarding polarizing opinions, leaving no one unscathed.

"This Little Light of Mine" has the power to shine a light in the darkest parts of the world, but many times we use our light to shine in the eyes of other Christians and tell them every little thing that they do wrong. God call us to light the way to Him, and there are people whose lives desperately need that light.

May we, as Christians use our energy and love to light up the pathway to God.

Prayer:

God, Equip me in every way to be Your messenger. Forgive me for squandering time for the sake of my own opinion and pride. In Jesus' name. Amen.

OCTOBER 12

"Cat got your tongue?"

"My dear brothers and sisters, take note of this: Everyone should be quick to listen, slow to speak and slow to become angry." James 1:19

For the most part in every scenario, I feel confident when responding to situations and in conversation, but every now and then, like when someone dies unexpectedly or goes through something traumatizing– I have not always known what to say to their loved ones to comfort them.

Sometimes, I might not be able to relate to the issue. A friend of mine recently told me that her adult children no longer visit her. While I felt sad for her, I didn't have comforting words that could help cure her pain, so I just listened silently.

Listening might feel uncomfortable to the listener because the information they are hearing, is in fact, uncomfortable. Even though it might seem like you aren't offering any comfort to the person speaking, just voicing their issues is part of their healing process.

Not knowing what to say at times is okay; it is the way God made us. There are multiple times in the Bible where God has silenced people to send an important message. Even Jesus at times was silent (Matthew 27:14). Silence allows somethings to come to pass and pass over.

Prayer:

Lord, thank You for the gift of silence. Help me know when to speak and when to remain silent. Allow the people that come into contact with my quiet presence to receive healing from it when they need it. Let me always be a reflection of Your love in everything I say and everything that I don't say. In Jesus' name, Amen.

"Opening up a can of worms"

"Truly I say to you, whoever says to this mountain, 'Be taken up and cast into the sea,' and does not doubt in his heart, but believes that what he says is going to happen, it will be granted him." Mark 11: 23

Having a baby during the pandemic has given my family some fear-stricken moments for sure, with the threat of not having enough baby formula being at the top. What do you feed an infant when there isn't any formula for sale? I searched high and low and read countless hours on the internet about finding a local goat farmer and anything that might supplement his food. As Southerners, we have been fortunate to grow up on farms and just a mile down the road from our food source and most of us have never had to deal with hunger in modern times.

Making ends meet is an issue that is stressful. I was reminded during the baby formula shortage of The Lord's Prayer in which Jesus teaches the disciples to pray for their daily bread. I found comfort in knowing that Jesus tells us not to worry about *tomorrow's* bread, or *next week's* bread, but to request our *daily* bread; a need that has already been fulfilled by God today.

What is something that you desperately need from God? What is keeping you awake at night wondering how you will make it work? Talk to God. Ask and see that He has already provided you with everything you need today.

Prayer:

God, thank You for Your love and provision. Give me peace in knowing that I have what I need for the day. Take away my fear as I lay my troubles at Your feet and place my trust in You. Have Your way, Lord. In Jesus' name. Amen.

"Between a rock and hard place" (revisited)

"The Lord is a refuge for the oppressed, a stronghold in times of trouble." Psalm 9:9-10

One of the great Southern pass-times during fall is visiting pumpkin patches and finding your way through the corn maze. If you have ever been through a good corn maze, you know it is a joyful labyrinth of fun. Unlike hedges or concrete-wall labyrinths if you become desperately lost and cannot find your way through, you can just pass through the corn stalks to free yourself instead of becoming afraid. What a wonderful concept to just create your own exit when you need it! However, life presents with real difficult circumstances; making us feel trapped and not knowing how to get out of a bad situation.

God is always there and has the key to every door. Even if it does not feel like the circumstance can be changed to something good or that God's presence is even there– it can and He is! In such desperate times, when it would be nice to create your own corn-maze exit, and you feel like crying, cry out to God. He is there with you. He will never leave you and holds the keys to new doors. He is just waiting for you to ask.

Prayer:

Dear Father God, this prayer is for the person that feels trapped. You know their problem and their heart. Empower them to ask for Your help. Guide them through this troublesome maze to rejoice in new beginnings. In Jesus' name. Amen.

"Don't borrow trouble."

"Blessed are the peacemakers, for they will be called children of God." Matthew 5:9

So many people these days want to pick a fight about anything. It is hard enough just to physically navigate from point A to point B on the roadways much less the emotional toll that life brings with each passing day.

Last month when paying bills, I noticed that through several different accounts I was being overcharged hundreds of dollars. That can be unsettling when you don't have extra hundreds to give and needless to say, stressed me out. On top of calling companies and remaining on hold, my cell phone broke. So if I had an emergency call, I literally had to walk to the neighbor's house to dial 9-1-1.

I like the security of having a cell phone, especially with a child. Taking care of a child comes with its own unique stress. Just the other night when making dinner, I smelled a candle burning. The smell really alarmed me because there wasn't anyone to light a candle other than myself and I needed to find where the smell was coming from. Suddenly a flame appeared in my gas heater (mounted on the wall). I ran over to cut the gas line, but the flame was still going. I used my kitchen spatula to pat out the flame and could see the remnants of what was once a crayon. Any guesses of who put it there?

We have all been there. Perhaps your life is different, but stress is something that is found in every lifestyle: CEO, doctor, stay-at-home parent, construction, real estate, fast food industry, etc. Going around picking fights with other people is looking for more stress. It is like adding more crayons to my gas heater.

As much as we want to respond to drama or feel provoked, we need to manage our response, stay calm, and walk away. Jesus felt provoked several times in His life. The Bible makes a point to emphasize these stories because it speaks to His strength and character. He was tempted by the devil during His time in the wilderness. He was put on trial by the priests. The soldiers mocked him. During all of His trials, He never responded with a quick, meaningless response. He remained calm, sometimes in silence, and answered in truth–shedding light in the darkness.

Responding this way sets us apart as children of God, where the world is in desperate need of more light.

Prayer:

Heavenly Father, thank You for the amazing example You set as our guiding light. Forgive me for the times I have lashed out on others or responded just to feel satisfaction in hearing my own opinion. Holy Spirit, give me the discernment and clarity to respond to turmoil quickly as it is happening or to walk away. In Jesus' name. Amen.

"A nod is as good as a wink to a blind horse."

"Your word is a lamp to my feet and a light to my path." Psalm 119:105

One of my favorite things about best friends and couples is the ability to read each other's minds. Although they might be very different than one another, they have spent so much time together, that literally a glance and a certain look can be an entire silent conversation between the two of them.

I once lived beside an elderly couple that had been married for 50+ years. They were both very easily likable; the kind of people that didn't seem to have reservations about much of anything, but once during a social visit to their house, my parents noticed that they had subtle sign language that they would give to one another, such as resting their finger on their upper lip meant "stop talking about that." It amused my parents, and I thought it was splendid that a couple was so cohesive together.

Frequently, Christians and newcomers to Christ earnestly cry out to God and ask for guidance and direction in "what should I do? What would You have me do, Lord?" Having discernment of what God favors for your life also comes from knowing and studying Him, just like those married couples. When we spend a good amount of time with God in worship, prayer, reading scripture–we get to know Him.

Prayer:

God, thank You for Your wisdom and care over my life. Forgive me for not always pointing my compass first to You when I have unanswered questions. I will trust You to take me where I should be. Let my feet and heart be receptive and eager to Your will for my life. In Jesus' name. Amen.

"There are good ships, wood ships and ships that sail the sea, but the best ships are friendships."

"Therefore go and make disciples of all nations, baptizing them in the name of the Father and of the Son and of the Holy Spirit, and teaching them to obey everything I have commanded you. And surely I am with you always, to the very end of the age." Matthew 28:19-20

Good friendships can often last a lifetime and what a difference they make. I think about so many people in the Bible and how their friendships changed history. Could Moses have accomplished all that he did without the help of Aaron? (God anointed Aaron to be Moses' assistant because Moses had difficulty speaking (Exodus 4:10-17; 7:1). The role of friendship, played by the disciples was key in telling the story of Jesus' life: His teachings, His sacrifice, resurrection, and promise for the future. That story of hope has continued through the ages because of people's promise to God.

Imagine if your best friend called you right now and asked for a ride today at 3 p.m. Part of being a good friend is following through with your friend's needs and safety. In our role of being a friend to Jesus, He has called us to continue sharing the story of the Gospel. If we fail to show up to meet Him, we will fail in our responsibility to respond when we are needed. Not only do we leave Him hanging, but we fail in passing on hope to others.

Prayer:

God, Forgive me for the times I have failed to witness to someone. May my mouth and actions follow through in being a friend to Jesus; to share a message with others that are living in darkness, in a world without hope. In Jesus' name. Amen.

"Wet your whistle."

"Whoever drinks of the water that I will give him will never thirst again." John 4:14

Water is such a remarkable necessity for life on this planet. Recently, after an exhausting day I climbed into the shower. My body aches and pains were immediately relieved when the shower's hot water hit my neck and the top of my back. Steam is also healing. Doctors say to put babies (and adults) in a steamy bathroom if they are having breathing difficulties. We have all heard to "drink plenty of water" in order to maintain our health. Burn victims also are frequently covered in wet linens to help them retain their body's remaining water content. The benefits of water are endless!

Even before scientists would announce that the human body and planet was mainly made up of water, Jesus made reference to its importance. As a "King" most people would assume that He would have placed importance on gold or jewels, but he knew water was more precious to the world over 2,000 years ago!

With understanding the importance of water, it is clear that Jesus meant that He was life-saving when he offered water that would quench all thirst. Jesus is essential in our healing process. Whatever troubles us in life (emotionally or physically) Jesus offers an oasis, but we must be the one to ask for it.

Prayer:

Dear Lord, I give thanks that You are our refuge in the desert. I feel tired and depleted. I know that I need You in my life. Restore and give me hope. Protect and heal me. In Jesus' name. Amen.

OCTOBER 19

"Cut from the same cloth"

"There is neither Jew nor Greek, there is neither slave nor free, there is no male and female, for you are all one in Christ Jesus." Galatians 3:28

One of the areas that I would love to self-improve is sewing. Even though I can't follow a pattern or know how to make a button hole, I love T.V. shows like "Project Runway" and watching designers compete. Occasionally, contestants will select the same fabric, and it always amazes me how the exact, same fabric can be sewn into so many different looks from vintage to boutique to grunge. If contestants fail to use the fabric correctly, they are voted off the show.

Similarly, God has given us some of the same fabric to work with. Even though we might see ourselves as being very different from one another, God created all of us in His image. Some of us might present loudly, while others are quiet, but at our core, we are all made from the fabric of Jesus Christ.

When we see other's styles, we are quick to judge if they are "in or out" of our acceptability range, but only God can see people's full potential and how to use them. We should never throw other people away or discount them. When discarded people with back stories are saved, transform, and witness for the Kingdom– the whole world stops to look because it is beautiful.

Be conscience and considerate of everyone around you. Everyone has potential and is created by God.

Prayer:

Father God, thank You for creating all types of people. We trust and respect Your divine creation and will for others. May I be the best person I can be, to myself, and when loving others. In Jesus' name. Amen.

"Do not upset the apple-cart."

"But the wisdom from above is first pure, then peaceable, gentle, open to reason, full of mercy and good fruits, impartial and sincere. And a harvest of righteousness is sown in peace by those who make peace." James 3:17-18

In the small town where I live, there are two traffic lights, a grocery store and a train track that runs adjacent to the major highway. Any time a train stops it can cause havoc. I live just on the other side of the tracks, so when a train decides to take a break or there is anything wrong with the train, it can delay my schedule by 20 minutes. I remember one year there was a train derailed, and the roadway had to be rebuilt which took about a month to clean up and fix.

Our interactions with others can be much like the trains. It can be a slow process of learning someone and their behavior, how to communicate, and coexist effectively with them. However, slow the process is it is better than a derailment. When approaching someone about a sensitive issue God gives us a guide on how to communicate: "pure in heart, peaceable, gentle, open to reason, full of mercy and good fruits, impartial and sincere." If we want to be more like Jesus, this is what He asks.

It is not easy communicating with others that seemingly don't play by the rules. It certainly is not easy waiting for a mile long train going 5 mph either. God puts people in our path for a reason, for our benefit and for theirs. The next time you feel you are sitting and waiting on a train to move, pray and ask God for these wise gifts of communication.

Prayer:

Heavenly Father, thank You for each and every person. Forgive me for my anger and frustration when I encounter certain people. I ask for the precious Holy Spirit to influence the way I speak and interact with my difficult person. May every word I speak be pure, peaceful, gentle, open to reason, full of mercy, fruitful, impartial, and sincere. I ask You to bless them and help me understand them better. In Jesus' name. Amen.

OCTOBER 21

"Laugh and the world laughs with you, weep and you weep alone." –Ella Wilcox

"He is the radiance of the glory of God and the exact imprint of his nature, and he upholds the universe by the word of his power." Hebrews 1:3a

Most people know me by my welcoming smile. I rarely meet a stranger. A few years back, I went to a spiritual retreat and over the weekend received several cards and letters from friends. One of the most memorable things about those cards is how many times people compared me to "sunshine." I have since always been flattered by it as it is a wonderful thing to be compared to. I feel blessed to have a "sunny" kind of life. However, life is not sunshine for anyone, all of the time. Maybe because so many people depend on my smile and encouraging word, it can be startling and down-right scary when something does dampen or darken my mood.

In those dark moments, I don't even like to be around others to watch their reaction as they see my smile is gone. When something devastating has happened, the last thing I want to do is repeat it over and over to people–so I usually seclude myself.

While some personal alone time is healthy and okay, too much seclusion is the devil's way of eating our soul. The devil is very clever and uses what hurts us as a device to consume us. However, he only has the power to consume us if we allow it. When we call out to God in dark times, God will prevail to our advantage. During my darkest times, I have not even had the strength to formulate the words of a prayer, but just by saying the words, "God and His goodness will prevail" will give enough light and hope to scare the devil away.

Prayer:

Lord, during uncertain times help me not feel so overwhelmed. I pray for Your protection. Comfort and remind me of the hopeful promises that will come tomorrow. God, Your goodness will prevail forever. In Jesus' name. Amen.

"She keeps the home fire going."

"Jesus looked at them and said, 'With man this is impossible, but with God all things are possible.'" Matthew 19:26

Churches all across the southeast are full of people. Can you imagine if all of those people intentionally gave themselves to glorify the Kingdom of God? The South, even though it might be poor in many areas, is rich in knowledge about Jesus Christ. If we came together to worship, intentionally gave ourselves as a unit to glorify God with actions and words, and asked the Holy Spirit to use us, the results would be immeasurable.

I heard a pastor recently say, "a prayerless ministry is a dead ministry." That is true! If there is a ministry in the church that has all of the money in the world and all of the people in the world, but they are not inviting the Holy Spirit to be part of it, they might as well be a house without a porch light. Inviting God to be part of everything we do infuses our mission with power.

We use sayings like "she keeps the home fire going," but it is God who keeps us going. When we ask for His help, He creates new beginnings for us and gives sustenance to our mission.

Prayer:

Dear God, thank You for breathing life into my daily life. Holy Spirit, stir in our community a spiritual revolution; to heal hearts and minds, empower and protect young people, and tell the world about the abundant, endless love that You alone give through the gift of Jesus Christ. May we share with others how much they are loved and that You offer the opportunity to live a new life. Holy Spirit, move and compel us. In Jesus' name. Amen.

"A friend in need is a friend indeed."

"But he said to me, 'My grace is sufficient for you, for my power is made perfect in weakness.' Therefore, I will boast all the more gladly about my weaknesses, so that Christ's power may rest on me." 2 Corinthians 12:9

A few years ago, my mother and I set off on a beach trip. Not far into the trip, we had a flat tire. The spare tire was located under the car and I changed it quickly enough. However, when we were getting back on the road, the bracket that once held the spare fell and dug itself into the dirt below the car. In order to free the bracket, my poor mother had to lie on the ground and hold the bracket up; a task that she wasn't happy about but nonetheless did, and it worked! We were free to head to the beach!

There was not a way that I could have fixed that by myself. Even though it was hot and my poor mother was on the ground, we worked together and got a sweet reward!

The modern times, we are living with world hunger, disease, and wars–all serious matters that can be overwhelming. They are things that leave us feeling desperate and powerless. However, working together with other people to relieve some of the suffering that others experience is a call from God. It is one that is better done together with others and rewarding to many.

If you don't know where to begin in alleviating the hurt in the world, form a Christian circle with friends to discuss it.

Prayer:

Dear God, help me be still and feel your sense of direction and share that with others Christian friends. May we boldly and lovingly come to the rescue of others, so that others may know Your amazing grace. In Jesus' name. Amen.

"Do as I say, not as I do."

"They were looking intently into the sky as He was going, when suddenly two men dressed in white stood beside them. 'Men of Galilee,' they said, 'why do you stand here looking into the sky? This same Jesus, who has been taken from you into heaven, will come back in the same way you have seen Him go into heaven.'" Acts 1:10-11

One of the biggest job assignments that Jesus left us to fulfill is to spread the Gospel. We all program our week with sports, hobbies, and couch-surfing time but rarely does one include Gospel-sharing time.

Many of us are standing around with our faces towards Heaven asking, "what should I do, Lord? What is my destiny?" In Acts 1:11, the angels appeared and asked the disciples why they were standing around looking up towards Heaven−that there is work that needs to be done here on Earth. Jesus clearly said multiple times to "go make disciples" and "feed my sheep".

There are multiple opportunities we have every day through the people we encounter; riding bikes with others, hiking, pumping gas, carpooling. It can feel uncomfortable sometimes when sharing the Gospel. When you share it with broken people, you are going to feel some of their brokenness as their response. In Jesus' life, He touched and healed lepers. Talking with lepers was taboo, much less touching them. It could make you a social outcast. Yet, Jesus plunged in that brokenness to heal someone and give them new life.

On Sundays, with your face and arms reached up towards Heaven, are you willing to also reach out to those socially outcast in your community?

Prayer:

Holy Spirit, prepare my words and actions that I will know who and when to speak to. Set them in my pathway that I may reach out to them and tell them about Jesus. In Jesus' name. Amen.

"Laugh before breakfast, cry before supper."

"There is an appointed time for everything, and a time for every affair under the heavens." Ecclesiastes 3:1

Bad news at any time of day can be difficult to deal with. Any time I am dealing with something difficult I ask myself "do I have any control over this situation?" If the answer is "no," then I know that God removed me from making decisions in it to protect me.

A good friend of mine has Alzheimer's and she recently moved away from my hometown. Not a day goes by that I don't wonder how she is, if she has peace and if she is safe. Knowing an ill fate about someone you love hurts, is stressful, and the only thing you can do to hopefully change their fate is pray.

One of the best defenses I have found when I feel overwhelmed with bad news is to live "in the now" and really be intentional in the way I love and bless others. Bad days are certain to come for everyone, but everyone will always have good days with the bad. It is part of life. On the good days, I make sure to savor them and thank God for them.

Life is hard sometimes, and it can feel like we have navigated far from the familiar path until we are lost. No matter where we are, God is always with us. In whatever season you find yourself, God loves you and has a hopeful future.

Prayer:

Dear God, thank you for the people you have blessed my life with. I thank you for all of the spiritual gifts that you endow each person with until their last breath. May I be reminded that in the midst of autumn, when it appears everything is about to die – that spring buds and flowers are waiting to bloom, and there You are also. In Jesus' name. Amen.

"A ship in harbor is safe, but that is not what ships are built for."

"Well done, good and faithful servant! You have been faithful with a few things; I will put you in charge of many things." Matthew 25:23

Every Christian needs to feel that they are needed in order to participate in the Great Commission. If a church appears too perfect and overly organized, it can make the attenders feel that there is not any room for them to use their spiritual gifts. When there is a job that needs filling, that can be attractive for someone looking to serve. The same is true with our personal lives. To make a connection and build a relationship the other person must feel needed and that they can make a contribution.

I heard a pastor recently tell a story of his three-year-old son who asked if he could help cut the grass on the riding mower. The obvious answer to your child is "of course, you can." After his son "helped" and went back inside the house, the father had to cut the grass again and go over all of the places that his son missed. However, it is important that a child feels needed, and it grows the relationship for his son to experience it. All people are similar. God could speak and have everything done perfectly every Sunday without the need of greeters, childcare, media, and sound people, but God includes us so we can all experience it. We need to be mindful in allowing other people around us to be part of the experience and help them find and utilize their spiritual gift.

Prayer:

God, may our churches humble themselves and hunger to plug people in. Help me identify and use my God-given talents to serve those in need. We want to spread Your love and blessings around to others. In Jesus' name. Amen.

"There is many a good tune played on an old fiddle."

"John's clothes were made of camel's hair, and he had a leather belt around his waist. His food was locusts and wild honey. People went out to him from Jerusalem and all Judea and the whole region of the Jordan. Confessing their sins, they were baptized by him in the Jordan River." Matthew 3:4-6

I love to use aprons when cooking. Through the years, I have collected some pretty, vintage ones with a ruffle trim that have a small waist and flare out (a style very popular in the 1950's.) I have some made with pretty, vintage fabric and love anything with feminine detail. However, even though they fit perfectly, it seems a shame to wear something beautiful to cook in. Cooking entails cutting up raw chicken, being sprinkled in flour, and hot grease back firing onto your clothing. So, the apron that I choose to wear is a used, stained apron that one of my cousins gave to me. Likewise, my mother used to set aside "play clothes" and raised me and my sister to know when to change into play clothes for getting dirty.

Being a Christian is not always about maintaining a perfect, pretty lifestyle. For many years, I felt that the older, well-dressed "Sunday best" clothes wearers had achieved spiritual perfection, but Jesus himself was not a "Sunday best" kind of dresser. He believed in mixing with the crowds, fishing, and walking from town to town to meet people. God doesn't care where you bought your dress. He cares if your heart is functional to spreading the message of love and redemption.

Prayer:

God, help me be approachable to others. Help others know how much I love them so that they feel comfortable enough around me to share their heart and concerns. In Jesus' name. Amen.

"Fake friends are worse than open enemies."

"No one is righteous— not even one. No one is truly wise; no one is seeking God. All have turned away; all have become useless. No one does good, not a single one." Romans 3:10-12

Finding out that a friend, is not really your friend hurts pretty deeply. Whether being told on the playground that someone does not like you or having someone "stab you in the back" as an adult is heart breaking. Many people tend to think of Judas when they think of fake friends. In the Garden of Gethsemane, Jesus, being distressed and feeling alone, must have been torn beyond words by Judas' fake kiss, handing him over to people that hated him. Judas has long been hated and despised by Christians, which has cast a bad shadow over him as a person. It is our call, as Christians to love Judas. It is true that Judas committed horrible offences against Jesus and his life ended in a sad way. Nonetheless, Judas was loved by Jesus. Judas definitely had sin in his life, but don't we? Is there any of us that is without sin? Let them cast the first stone on Judas. Judas' life is not for us to judge. We sin every day, and the Bible is very clear that sin is sin. There is not a sin that God favors in comparison to another sin.

So for Judases, we should pray. For fake friends, we should pray. For our enemies, we should pray. Let us continue to speak to them in kindness and love. Let us continue to feed them from our table just as Jesus did.

Prayer:

Jesus of Love, teach us Your ways. Open our hearts to forgive those we hate. Open our arms and doors so that our enemies might know love. Clothe us with Your grace. In Jesus' name. Amen.

OCTOBER 29

"Rome wasn't built in a day."

"The earth is the Lord's and all it holds."
Psalms 24:1

One of my favorite things about living in Alabama are the beautiful natural treasures around the state. There are so many gorgeous places to see around the United States like Yosemite and Yellowstone but Alabama has places just as beautiful, which are much closer to home. Some of my favorites are Dismals Canyon, Little River Canyon, Bankhead National Forest and the white sand at our Gulf coast.

In just these few places named, it is easy to be inspired and stare at the marvel of creation. It is easy to be transported to a place of wonder when thinking about the time it took to create each place; the movement of water that formed each rock and the richness of life that lives there. I love when the Cahaba Lilies bloom each May, only for a few weeks every year, always under water and only in this part of the world.

Humans frequently get caught up in the imperfections of life. "My nose is too big." "My neck is too short." "I can't sing." But, God gave so much attention to detail with every living thing. We forget that we are masterpieces in the making. God has already made us beautiful, but when we give God permission, and ask Him to make us His masterpiece it might take time and might even hurt, but God moves mountains to make us something inspiring.

Prayer:

God, You are wonderful. Help me see the beauty in all of Your creations. Have Your way with my life and weed out what hinders Your plans. In Jesus' name. Amen.

"Half a loaf is better than no bread."

"But when you pray, go into your room, close the door and pray to your Father, who is unseen. Then your Father, who sees what is done in secret, will reward you." Matthew 6:6

Do you ever have days that feel like "nothing has gone right today" even from the time you wake up? Recently, I felt like "nothing has gone right this month!" My new phone broke, and after taking a day off to go see the manufacturer, I was told to take it to the service provider. When they sent me a new phone, I couldn't log in, and collectively these things kept me from having phone access for about two weeks. During my cell phone dilemma, I was told that I might possibly have a heart defect. So, I traveled to Birmingham, (without a cell phone), to have bubbles shot into an IV in my arm, which might sound fun but made me instantly taste and smell the medicine...a very strange uncomfortable sensation. There were also other stressors, like finances and family life, all of the things that come with life.

With all of these stress factors, I sat down to pray and realized I didn't know where to begin. It all seemed so complicated and took so much energy to explain everything that in my prayer I asked God what to pray for. In the Bible, the disciples asked Jesus for His help in knowing what to pray and he gifted them The Lord's Prayer (Matthew 6:9-13).

The prayer asks God to "give us this daily bread" that's what we are to pray for. God already knows everything going on with us, and while we can certainly list it all, it is okay to ask for just what you need to get you through the day. His grace is sufficient.... God is still God. He will sustain you and get you through no matter what the circumstance looks like.

Prayer:

Our Father, who art in heaven, hallowed be thy name; thy kingdom come; thy will be done; on earth as it is in heaven. Give us this day our daily bread. And forgive us our trespasses, as we forgive those who trespass against us. And lead us not into temptation; but deliver us from evil. For thine is the kingdom, the power and the glory, for ever and ever. Amen (The Lord's Prayer)

"There is no time like the present."

"As long as it is day, we must do the works of him who sent me. Night is coming, when no one can work." John 9:4

We all have character defects. Sometimes we allow others to get under our skin, which in turn makes us respond in a negative way. Maybe you are loud and boisterous? Or perhaps painfully shy which makes you feel nervous at parties? We all are imperfect. Understanding and acknowledging that allows room for God to help us reach our full potential.

The legacy of Jesus has lasted for thousands of years because He did something incredible. He allowed God to use Him to reach His potential. Jesus was an action-packed man that didn't sit around and wait for the world to come to Him. He went out in the world. He was a real "go-getter!" We tend to associate go-getters with great financial success, but go-getting consists of keeping a steady drive to change the present. It usually ends with success, because the person never gives up!

The Holy Spirit prompts us in identifying areas of our lives that we can change like becoming forgiving, approachable, and graceful. With prayer, God can empower and motivate us to reach new territory for His Kingdom. Your best Godly life initially starts with prayer and your willingness to become an empty canvas for God to use. The second part is becoming a Godly "go-getter" and putting into action what God wants for your life.

Prayer:

Father, Help me identify the areas of my life that can be better. Bring to my attention the areas that I need to work on and soften my heart to be willing to change. In Jesus' name. Amen.

"Thank goodness, for Heaven's sake!"

"Blessed be the God and Father of our Lord Jesus Christ! According to his great mercy, he has caused us to be born again to a living hope through the resurrection of Jesus Christ from the dead." I Peter 1:3

November seems to always kick off a month-long celebration of thanksgiving (and pumpkin pie). One of my favorite things to read every November is the "Day 1- I am thankful for.." series that many people post on social media. While it is sad that thankfulness is solely centered around 30 days out of the year, it is a great time of reflection for all of the blessings God places in our lives.

Thanksgiving and the holidays in general look very different to people. Both of my parents came from alcoholic families, so their memories and feelings about the holidays reminded them of horrific times in their childhood and gave them anxiety. With both of my parents' stress slowly starting to peak, by the time Thanksgiving finally rolled around our "family time" had usually ended in an argument and more than one Thanksgiving meal was spent around the table at a Chinese restaurant or a Waffle House (which were the only two restaurants open in the 1990s within a 50 miles radius of our house on Thanksgiving Day).

However, on the years that my grandmother was alive and able, she hosted a beautiful, classic Thanksgiving that I am grateful to have experienced. She was a friendly "sight for sore eyes" on more than one occasion.

Later in life, when I married and started my own family, I created the holiday traditions that I always wanted–a peaceful, happy environment for my family.

Holidays don't always hold happy memories for everyone, and for some, it feels like the worst time of year. The thought of "30

Days of Thanksgiving" seems unobtainable. Instead, it can create anxiety, fear and even bring back painful memories.

The great news is that as Christians we do not have to live in that perpetual state of pain. Jesus Christ created hope for those with a painful past and whatever memories exist, there is hope for redemption in creating a new future. Whatever your heart is longing for, there are ways to create it with the new life that Jesus Christ brings. That is something to be thankful for.

Prayer:

Dear Jesus, thank You for washing us clean. Take the pain I have during the holiday season and help me look for ways to make goodness out of it. Help me invest the energy I use on feeling bad on creating blessings for others and my new life; that Your hope may be part of my testimony. In Jesus' name. Amen.

"Live and let live."

"So do not worry about tomorrow; for tomorrow will care for itself. Each day has enough trouble of its own." Matthew 6:34

For several years, I volunteered in the children's ministry of my church. There was a child that attended with the best personality. He was about six years old with bright red hair, freckles and a personality bigger than Texas. He had a thick country accent and always wore cowboy boots, even in the middle of summer with his shorts.

One Sunday while I was teaching his class, a little girl announced that "Brandon has a girlfriend!" It was very disruptive and the entire class broke out in laughter, so I felt I had to address the topic. I said, "Is that so, Brandon? Do you have a girlfriend?" He smiled and responded, "No ma'am, I've got three!" His smile glowed with mischief.

Even though it has been years since I have seen him, he frequently crosses my mind. While most children are sweet and happy, Brandon was exceptional at basking in the blessing of each new day. I can't imagine very many days that go by that he doesn't look up and enjoy what God has given him.

Jesus was mindful about using His time on Earth and being in the moment of each day. Many times, people get caught up in their calendars, appointments, rushing family members from Point A to Point B, that we forget to bask in the blessing of God's gift of today. Look up and enjoy what God has given you.

Prayer:

God, thank You for today and for children that remind us of all that is important. Bless them and help us to be more like them, with the joy of anticipating each moment. In Jesus' name. Amen.

"Dressed to the nines"

"Be careful what you think, because your thoughts run your life. Don't use your mouth to tell lies; don't ever say things that are not true." Proverbs 4:23-24

Technology is so "intelligent" it can be scary. I recently learned that my cell phone is paying attention to everything I type on it. If I send my mother a text about something I bought at Target, I see Target ads for the rest of the day. It can be alarming to search for something and then be targeted for that item. From what I understand, it is computer intelligence called "cookies" that help advertisers reach us quicker.

The reason this is important to us as Christians is because your phone has the power to help or hurt you spiritually. If you are saying evil, hateful things on Wednesday, you can expect your phone to show you evil, hateful images on Thursday. However, if you are using your phone to look up scripture or for something positive, that will also reappear.

In my own experience, when I am having a difficult time in life, the last thing I need to read is something negative. It is not possible to live a life completely free of mishaps, but we can definitely be responsible for our part of our own happiness. For the other parts of our life, we have God! When we choose to give God the other part, we can trust that He will take care of us.

Prayer:

God, I love you. Thank you for being the light in the darkness. Let us be mindful with technology and to use it in a "smart," spiritual way. Speak into my life "Hope," "Love," "Clarity," "Peace," "Protection," and "Joy." In Jesus' name. Amen.

"Don't look a gift horse in the mouth."

"But in your hearts honor Christ the Lord as holy, always being prepared to make a defense to anyone who asks you for a reason for the hope that is in you; yet do it with gentleness and respect." I Peter 3:15

In light of Thanksgiving approaching, it helps me be mindful of all things to be "thankful" for. Visiting another country, especially one that is underdeveloped, will help put in perspective the abundance that we live in. Several years ago, while traveling with a mission team in South America, we passed a gated, brightly-lit community. Upon a closer look, I could see that the neighborhood was entirely made up of storage buildings (exactly like the kind we rent in the United States and park our jet skis in). The difference was that each storage unit was the room of a prostitute. It is hard to say how many existed because the community lit up the side of the valley, but it is fair to say that hundreds of storage units were there.

Unfortunately, stories like that plague every country. While the United States continues to grow and thrive, we also have testimonies of people living in destitution and lives spiraling out of control here. God gives us the opportunity to be blessed and live a life free of slavery, but He also asks us to help those around us living in it. Let us be mindful and open this Thanksgiving to reach out and pray with others living without hope.

Prayer:

God, plant in me a seed to reach out to those drowning in sin and darkness. Holy Spirit, speak through me that the saving words and hope that Jesus Christ gave will touch lives around our community and world. In Jesus' name. Amen.

"You can't squeeze blood out of a turnip."

"What do you think? If a man owns a hundred sheep, and one of them wanders away, will he not leave the ninety-nine on the hills and go to look for the one that wandered off? [13] And if he finds it, truly I tell you, he is happier about that one sheep than about the ninety-nine that did not wander off." Matthew 18:12-13

I love visiting nature centers where the animals have free reign. Recently, my family visited the parakeet center, which is about an hour from our home. In the weeks leading up to the visit, I had envisioned taking a dozen or so photos of parakeets lighting on our hands and heads as you always see them do when birdseed is available. When we got to the nature center, we purchased extra birdseed and went into the aviary. It was exciting to experience. I held out my birdseed and.... Nothing! They were not interested. Our guess is that they were already full. No matter how still or quiet we were, they didn't care.

Many times, sharing God's message with another person can be similar to the parakeet story. Some people aren't interested in hearing about God. Even though you might hold what you have up high or close to them, you feel ignored and don't get much of a positive response. Witnessing to others will ensure that you eventually come across someone who doesn't want to listen, but it is important to keep searching for others that are desperate to hear what you have to say. Jesus said to "leave the 99 sheep and search for the one" that is lost.

Prayer:

God, give me reassurance when I know I have tried my best to reach someone in Christian word and love. In Jesus' name. Amen.

"A dog is a man's best friend."

"But the Lord said to Ananias, 'Go! This man is my chosen instrument to proclaim my name to the Gentiles and their kings and to the people of Israel.'" Acts 9:15

I love to walk around my neighborhood, especially when the weather starts getting cool for fall. The leaves rustle and crackle down the street, and yards are decorated with scarecrows, hay bales and mums; it's just the perfect atmosphere to bask in while trying to get fit. I usually take my dog, Rowdy with me. However, it is Felix, the family cat who enjoys walking around the neighborhood! It is a little alarming because wherever we go, the cat will hide behind things as we make our venture. Passing cars frequently stop and ask if that is my dog *and cat.*

On the topic of "things you don't see every day," it is important to know that God loves everyone and all kinds of people. Traditional church members may feel alarmed when a "certain kind of person" becomes part of their church. As a young teenager, I briefly attended a church that had all kinds of rules, stigmas, and disassociations for people that didn't fit their mold of what a "Christian" was supposed to look like, but God calls all people and from different areas. In Acts 10:28, Peter shares God's message that we should not call other people "common" or "unclean."

Each person we encounter has a unique story, and God uses that individualism to reach others.

Prayer:

Father God, Your love is endless and abundant. Forgive us for trying to narrow Your scope of who is Yours. Thank You for the unique people and the unique ways each one blesses Your Kingdom. Help me know the ways I can support others and their relationship with You. In Jesus' name. Amen.

"Bad news is better than no news at all."

"I have seen the burden God has laid on the human race. He has made everything beautiful in its time. He has also set eternity in the human heart; yet[a] no one can fathom what God has done from beginning to end." Ecclesiastes 3:10-11

When I was about eleven, my permanent "canine" teeth were growing in, but I had not lost my baby teeth. My mother scheduled me a dentist appointment to have one pulled. All I was told about the procedure is that they would give me gas. On the day of my appointment, I waited an usually long time in the dentist office and I started becoming afraid. So afraid, that I finally escorted myself to the bathroom, took a paper towel and ripped the tooth (which wasn't loose in the least bit) out of my mouth. I then asked the secretary to call my mother and tell her that "I did it. Please pick me up."

Have you ever had to wait for the results to something you had no control over? Fear of the unknown is an awful territory to live in. The good news about the future is even if unknown – Jesus is already there. When we do not have control of a situation, we must realize that Jesus has control, and always did have. He will make everything beautiful in its time.

Prayer:

Jesus, "though I walk through the valley of the shadow of death, I will fear no evil: for thou art with me; thy rod and thy staff they comfort me. Thou preparest a table before me in the presence of mine enemies: thou anointest my head with oil; my cup runneth over. Surely goodness and mercy shall follow me all the days of my life: and I will dwell in the house of the LORD forever." (Psalm 23:4-6) In Jesus' name. Amen.

NOVEMBER 8

"Clear as mud."

"When you pray, go into your room, close the door and pray to your Father, who is unseen. Then your Father, who sees what is done in secret, will reward you." Matthew 6:6

Sometimes when I sit down to pray my concentration is broken. During a time that should be intimate with God, I can't help but think of "what is that noise?" or "what items do I need from the grocery store?" Our lives are programmed with something to do every day and every minute. It should come as no surprise that with so much scheduling, we find it difficult to sit still, be quiet and meditate with God. With a constantly busy life, how can we fully expect to concentrate on our prayer, devotion, or hear the will of God? If we don't shut ourselves off from the world and set alone time with God, we won't be able to hear Him.

I love those old game shows like "Password" or "Pictionary" where couples are timed and try to guess the hidden phrase with hints. Communicating with God can be very similar to that. We may not be able to properly communicate or understand His meaning if we do not give him enough time out of our day.

If a person is planning to become a soldier and go into battle, there are actions he or she makes to prepare like exercise, training, as well as, studying the opposition and territory. It is the same in the Christian world. As Christians, we are constantly going to battle, and we must properly put aside quiet time to pray, or we will be ill-equipped.

Prayer:

Heavenly Father, You are the peace; the quiet I need in the heat of the day. Help me to identify the noise in my life and silence it when I am in prayer. Let my ears be focused on You so that I may readily identify Your voice and will when chaos comes. In Jesus' name. Amen.

"Playing silly games will win you silly prizes."

"By faith Abraham, when called to go to a place he would later receive as his inheritance, obeyed and went, even though he did not know where he was going. And so from this one man came descendants as numerous as the stars in the sky and as countless as the sand on the seashore." Hebrews 11:8,12

If it is not evident already in this devotional, I love my home and the culture here in my town. I love the accent people use when speaking and the slow way people drive on the roads. It would be devastating to learn that I had to leave and go to a new town. What would the people be like? Is there crime there?

These questions are not unique to modern times. God asked Abraham to leave his home and venture to a new area thousands of years ago, and I am certain that anyone who starts a new chapter in a new land wonders about the risks that come with it. The key when considering any risk is asking "is this from God?" Even though God will call us to some risky tasks, it is important to discern if it is part of God's will by way of prayer, fasting, worshiping, and reading the Bible. Even though He may be asking you to leap, His requests will lead you to your inheritance.

Prayer:

Lord, I love and trust You. Whatever Your will is for my future, I will go. Help me to distinguish my will from Yours. In Jesus' name. Amen.

NOVEMBER 10

"It is better to give than to receive."

"For God so loved the world that he gave his one and only Son, that whoever believes in him shall not perish but have eternal life." John 3:16

When reflecting on my Christian life, I am so grateful for the Christian witnesses that cared about me. Even as a young person, there were people that intentionally invested their time into helping me spiritually. They cared about me and let me know that they loved me. As I have become older, I have experienced the same love, kindness, and caring through Christian people, not always even from people that I know. Once while traveling and out of town, a random woman at a restaurant stopped to pray with me and my husband when we were having car trouble (which she couldn't have known.)

In John 3:16, God cares for us so much that He gave His Son. When witnessing to others, the main action of how we choose to showcase our love must be caring for others. I am so grateful that God did not limit his scripture of those He loved. The world would look much different if the scripture read, "For God so loved everyone except the ...." God loves us all and Jesus died for all. To share that message with the world we must care about others in the same way that God loved us **and let people know that.**

I care about you regardless of your political affiliation. I care about you regardless of your past. I care about you regardless of whom you love. For God so loved the world, and so must we.

Prayer:

God, forgive me for the people I have been hateful toward. May my love for You be the same love I give to those that I have been in conflict with. I commit myself to loving others so that they may know Christians by their love. In Jesus' name. Amen.

"Keep your chin up."

"Though an army besieges me, my heart will not fear; though war break out against me, even then will I be confident... I am still confident of this: I will see the goodness of the Lord in the land of the living. Wait for the Lord; be strong and take heart and wait for the Lord." Psalm 27: 3, 13-14

I recently saw a Spanish film entitled, "Marcada a Fuego," (translated in English "Branded by Fire). It is a true story of a woman living in China and the way she and her family are tortured, suffered, and imprisoned in China for decades for believing in God. The movie brought to mind how many times in my life I have not served God fully by sharing my personal testimony to those who need it and how I need to be more vigilant.

Defending religious freedom comes at the cost of personal time away from loved ones, as well as mental, and physical anguish, and sometimes even death. Only God and those who stand for His goodness can make the difference. Amidst the pain, there is the Lord who sees and cares for us all. Psalm 27:14 says, "Wait on the Lord: be of good courage, and He shall strengthen thine heart: wait, I say, on the Lord."

Prayer:

God, I thank You today for all of our veterans, their sacrifices and the sacrifices their families make to keep order and freedom in this beautiful country. May they be blessed by the same goodness that they give to us all. Watch over those in active service. May they always feel Your presence and know You are with them as You are with us. In Jesus' name. Amen.

"I wish there was a way to know the good ole days before you left them."

"God will supply every need of yours according to his riches in glory in Christ Jesus." Philippians 4:19

Looking back in life's past, there are people we miss and places we would like to visit once more. For me, I would love to see my late father again, to hold his hand and tell him I loved him. I can recall a few occasions where we would stop at the country gas station on the way home from school. We would buy an assortment of Moon Pies, grape soda, and orange cream ice pops and devour them on the way home. Sometimes he would pull over once we got to the final country road home and let me ride in the back of his truck while he drove slowly. I loved the feeling of the wind in my hair and on my face. I would stand up to look over the cab, and he would slide the window open and say, "I need you to sit down."

Even though my dad has been gone a while now, God's blessings never end. Life is always transforming into a new chapter and those kinds of memories remind us of the blessings that are current and yet to come. My husband and I recently had our first child. My mother and aunt still plan crazy trips around the United States in their 70s and 80s. My best friend of 25 years recently had a baby. My sister got a new job that she loves and is living "the good life." Blessings are abundant and not always obvious, but they are nonetheless there. Praise God for giving us new blessings and joy!

Prayer:

Lord, I thank You for the good times. I thank You for time that has allowed me to enjoy each day since the "good ole days" and the joys yet to come. In Jesus' name. Amen.

"Nothing ventured, nothing gained."

"Therefore, stay awake, for you do not know on what day your Lord is coming. But know this, that if the master of the house had known in what part of the night the thief was coming, he would have stayed awake and would not have let his house be broken into. Therefore you also must be ready, for the Son of Man is coming at an hour you do not expect." Matthew 24:42-44

At the beginning of 2023, the results of a survey conducted by the Survey on American Life, a project of the American Enterprise Institute, concluded that a third of all church attenders had left the church since the beginning of the pandemic. (That's one in three people that are no longer in church.) Based from my own personal experience, perhaps the main reasons people left are because of social anxiety, depression, and a difference of political opinion.

What surprises me most about the post-pandemic survey is that we are actually living in desperate times and people pulled *away* from God, instead of *near* Him. Has that ever happened before? Matthew 24:6-13 says to expect these things and not be surprised by them, that they must come to past. The job that God has divinely given to us in these moments (and always has been) to carry on and continue spreading the message of Jesus Christ, His love, and the freedom of turning away from sin.

Prayer:

God, thank You for always being a beacon of hope amid destruction and despair. You are our only refuge in such depressing, anxiety-ridden, hateful times. May others know of Your freedom by the re-telling of Your love. In Jesus' name. Amen.

"There's no place like home."

"Therefore, confess your sins to one another and pray for one another, that you may be healed. The prayer of a righteous person has great power as it is working." James 5:16

This time of year, many are making plans to travel for Thanksgiving. Seeing loved ones that you have not seen in a while can be exciting, refreshing, and sometimes overwhelming. Even though families are usually all together and *gratitude to God* is a central theme across the country, checking in on each other spiritually is fairly rare. As children get older, grow up and move out, family togetherness becomes rarer and the opportunity to have meaningful prayer time together usually just spans over a few short days.

Larry Anderson, a pastor I worked for in 2010, loved to pray and taught the staff to pray with devotion and dedication for one another; something I never really felt until that point in my life. The staff would have an open prayer request time and then each person would openly pray for the person to their "right" or "left." What developed was the opportunity to see how your co-workers felt about you. Words were spoken in love and we interceded on each other's behalf asking for God's protection, vision, and healing for one another. Even though those prayers usually lasted thirty minutes, they were healing, heartfelt, and you could feel the blanket of the Holy Spirit in the room.

Prayer:

Holy Spirit, I pray for the families that are dreading "family time" together. I ask You to fill their homes and prompt them to put God at the center of their time together. May they use this time to love and lift one another up through prayer. In Jesus' name. Amen.

"Too many cooks spoil the broth."

"Jesus intervened: "Kings like to throw their weight around and people in authority like to give themselves fancy titles. It's not going to be that way with you. Let the senior among you become like the junior; let the leader act the part of the servant." Luke 22:25-26

Any cook will tell you that it is hard to share the kitchen with others. My family is a family of cooks, so we all have our own idea of how to go about things. We each have a different recipe for cooking spaghetti and even rice, so we all lose our minds when watching one another. I once knew a know-it-all "Nancy" (not her real name) who for whatever reason told me rice should be covered when cooking it. When she looked to me for reassurance, I couldn't even speak because all I could think was "not according to my husband who fries it in oil until it is golden and then adds tomatoes, salt, garlic, and water to it." It would have killed her if I responded with that, so I remained quiet.

As with endless recipes, God has seasoned our lives to be different from one another. It should come as no surprise that we are all different, as that seems to be the main source of our hatred for one another. Even during Jesus' time there was conflict, including within the disciples. They frequently had different ideas about things including who was Jesus' favorite. As Christians, we must identify our similarities first so that we can work together−namely that we love God, otherwise the "rice" never gets cooked and God's message isn't conveyed.

Prayer:

Father, help us identify our common interest as loving You. Silence our mouths when we feel bickering starting so that Your kingdom receives the glory. In Jesus' name. Amen.

"All things must pass."

"God is our refuge and strength, a very present help in trouble. Therefore, we will not fear though the earth gives way, though the mountains are moved into the heart of the sea, though its waters roar and foam, though the mountains tremble at its swelling." Psalm 46:1-3

During the 2008 Recession, I worked as a doctor's assistant in Birmingham. After waiting in traffic, it was usually a three-hour daily commute to work for a doctor that had a terrible temper. He once tore a chart in half and kicked a trash can across the room. I did not enjoy working in a highly-stressful environment with someone tyrannical. However, it was during the Recession, and even though it was oppressive, it kept the lights on. At the time, I don't think many people spoke about their stress and financial strain because of their embarrassment. Since then, I have heard multiple stories of those who lost their home and were hungry.

Even though the Recession is over, many are still going through difficult times. People we know, all around us, are struggling with something every day, maybe it is financial, maybe it is a failed relationship, or depression. Just like when people kept their problems to themselves during the Recession, many people still keep their hurts inside, and it doesn't help. We need to find people we can trust to share what we are struggling with. When someone tells us the issues they are facing we need to listen, pray with them in the moment, and remind them that God is with them and that the bad will pass.

Prayer:

God, I pray for those hurting today. You know their need. May they have peace in knowing that the suffering will end. May they feel Your strength and find comfort in knowing that a Christian friend is there to listen. In Jesus' name. Amen.

"Give credit where credit is due."

"I will exalt you, LORD, for you lifted me out of the depths and did not let my enemies gloat over me. LORD my God, I called to you for help, and you healed me. You, LORD, brought me up from the realm of the dead; you spared me from going down to the pit. Sing the praises of the LORD, you his faithful people; praise his holy name." Psalm 30:1-4

What is your favorite movie? Some of my favorites include, "The Ten Commandments" and "It's a Wonderful Life." I have watched these movies countless times, enough to memorize the dialogue, timing, and lyrics to the songs. Movie fans really show their dedication when they sing songs like, "Let It Go" and "A Whole New World" for years. Something that super fans rarely pay attention to though, are the credits (the part that rolls before or after the film showing every person and organization that made it possible.) Whether at the theatre or at my home, I rarely give attention to the names. When DVDs were created, people started giving even less attention to those details because we can fast forward to the parts we want. With modern day DVRs, there is not a need to watch commercials or anything besides your favorite show.

People's lack of gratuity and selfishness with their time also unfortunately relates to skipping prayer time with God. With mashed potatoes and cornbread staring you in the face, sometimes we "fast forward" straight into eating instead of verbalizing what a generous, thoughtful God we have. What has God "produced" for you today?

Prayer:

Dear God, thank you for the daily blessings of my life. May I always remember to put You at the center of everything. In Jesus' name. Amen.

"If a job is worth doing, it is worth doing well."

"And he directed the people to sit down on the grass. Taking the five loaves and the two fish and looking up to heaven, he gave thanks and broke the loaves. Then he gave them to the disciples, and the disciples gave them to the people." Matthew 14:19

During a Wednesday night class for children at church, our focus was on missions and other cultures. To prep for the class, I visited my Chinese friend, Cindy, to learn some Chinese customs and culture. Part of her immersion course was making Chinese dumplings, which sounds easy enough but apparently Cindy thought that I was not using the correct pinching technique when crimping the dumplings with both hands.

In my experience with missions, it is very rarely under perfect conditions. Missions take you to the edge of what you know and are comfortable with. I learned that lesson well while in Ecuador when I helped lead a VBS without supplies or having planned any lessons. In Venezuela, my mission team learned quickly about adapting to nature when the "rainy season" flooded our open-air hut and soaked our clothes in the middle of the night. Many cultures have different norms that are sometimes out of our comfort box and control. However, in all of the above circumstances, not having perfect, planned conditions allowed for us to connect better with local people.

God calls us to be prepared, innovative, and good stewards. He will provide the rest in His own time. In the meantime, we should enjoy being with others and sharing His message with them.

Prayer:

God, May I always be reminded that when we put You first, nothing else matters. In Jesus' name. Amen.

"Time is a thief."

"And do this, understanding the present time: The hour has already come for you to wake up from your slumber, because our salvation is nearer now than when we first believed." Romans 13:11

I think back to times in grade school and waiting for summer break to come. It seemed like years passed before finally finishing the school year. Once summer break came, I loved activities like playing dolls, riding bikes with the neighborhood children, and going swimming. Somehow summer also seemed like it took years for school to start back. I was always happy and relieved that I could go back to school.

Now that I am older, I find that time seems relatively shorter. While the months pass (in what feels like days), we also change as people. I am still the same person that I was when I graduated or the first time I learned to whistle, but time has also given me life experiences that make me different and change my perception. In the completion of this 365-day devotion, I have changed as a person. Changing as a person has also caused me to change some of my earlier devotions. God is always fine-tuning and changing us.

We can all look back and recall things that we should have responded to differently. We can't change the past, but the future is ours. If we are open to allowing God to use our future, we must invest time with Him now.

Prayer:

God, in times that feel like eternity or others where time doesn't seem to be long enough, remind me that You are there with me and that I can trust You. In Jesus' name. Amen.

"All thumbs and no fingers."

"Do not let any unwholesome talk come out of your mouths, but only what is helpful for building others up according to their needs, that it may benefit those who listen." Ephesians 4:29

As humans, we all are fallible. I try to be graceful and am very intentional about trying not to say hurtful things, but sometimes I "stick my big foot in my mouth" especially when I feel that I have been pushed too far. When we accept God's perfect love, it changes us, and people expect to see that change. God's love should erupt from Christians like an endless fountain, but when others see us act out of rage, they steer clear of us.

James 1:26-27 says, "If anyone considers himself religious and yet does not bridle his tongue, he deceives his heart and his religion is worthless. Pure and undefiled religion before our God and Father is this: to care for orphans and widows in their distress, and to keep oneself from being polluted by the world."

"To keep oneself from being polluted by the world" is a broad statement, but achievable when we stay close to God. It reminds me of when I was a child and went to social functions with my parents. I thought it was always more fun to run off with friends during the event, but if I chose to stay with my parents, I stayed out of trouble while still having fun. Other people sometimes lead us astray or even provoke us, but if we stay in a climate of holiness with God, we will be blessed while blessing others.

Prayer:

Dear Lord, May I keep You at the center of everything of my life and pray without ceasing. In conflict, may I look to You. In joyous times, may I look to You. In every aspect of my life, may I look to You. In Jesus' name. Amen.

"Old habits die hard."

"Perfume and incense bring joy to the heart, and the pleasantness of a friend springs from their heartfelt advice." Proverbs 27:9

Thanksgiving makes most of us remember old family recipes. As mentioned previously, my grandmother's potato salad was one of the great contenders of all recipes. Some people may not think there is much to making potato salad. It is easy to assume that there are potatoes, eggs, and mayonnaise and BAM−you have potato salad! Easy Peasy!

Much like a good recipe, good Christianity takes practice, skill and meditation. It took me years to realize all of the ingredients my grandmother was using, which included pickle juice and garlic. Likewise, living the ultimate Christian life is going to take time, mediating on how to respond in love, kindness, and gentleness. Wisdom comes from living an intentional Christian life, and it is not something that you can just whip up quickly together in a bowl. It is not something that can be faked.

It can be difficult to stop doing something you have been doing for decades. Sometimes it might seem like we have made a mistake and seemingly destroyed our "recipe." Those situations can leave us feeling at a loss to know how to proceed. Continuing to strive forward, by following what Jesus has taught us to do is how we perfect the finished project.

Prayer:

Dear God, Help me to focus on Your love and be intentional in sharing that with others. Forgive me of my sins. I look to You for guidance on which areas of my life to change. Use me for Your goodness. In Jesus' name. Amen.

"Mad as a wet hen."

"God desires all people to be saved and to come to the knowledge of the truth." I Timothy 2:4

Did you know that if an egg is not washed, it can be stored for a few weeks outside of the refrigerator? God made eggs with a protective coating on them and when eggs get wet, that coating washes off, which allows air and bacteria to enter the egg. I have heard "mad as a wet hen" my entire life, and I always thought it was mostly due to chickens just disliking being wet. Perhaps the chickens' dislike of water comes from a survival instinct to save their young from harm.

People are not built with a special protective coating on them but we are equipped with the Holy Spirit. When we call on the Holy Spirit, It can heal, restore, save, strengthen, and change the perception and outcome.

All things from God are good. Such a living miracle, should be revered, trusted, and used. If not, we are like the eggs, susceptible and waiting for trouble to entering our "shell."

In what areas of your life do you need "healing, restoring, saving, strengthened, and changed?" Call on the Holy Spirit to help.

Prayer:

Holy Spirit, I call on You to help my brokenness. I confess that I need God. Breathe healing and restoration into my life. I place my faith in You. Have Your way. In Jesus' name. Amen.

"Nothing succeeds like success."

"Commit your work to the LORD, and your plans will be established." Proverbs 16:3

When I started living closer to God there wasn't an inch of my life that the devil did not lurk in. All of my relationships had conflict for reasons that I cannot explain other than it was the discord of the devil. Multiple appliances in my home broke at the same time leaving me strapped for money and stressed. I received news of health concerns, which added to my stress. The list goes on. Only when I realized that all of my issues started around the time that I was living deeper with God did I feel the encouragement to continue "running the race."

Speaking of "running the race," I love the old Looney Tunes cartoons of Wile E. Coyote and the Road Runner. While it seems ridiculous that acts such as a painted tunnel and the anvil could ever work, there is so much truth in that relationship compared to us. Like Wile E. Coyote, the devil is constantly looking for angles to destroy us. The Bible has multiple scriptures that describe how the devil might manifest his evil ways into your life by "through deception, slander, greed, lust, harassment, disease" and the list goes on. These wicked afflictions may also be placed on your loved ones.

How we respond to all of the devil's attempts is something we always have control over. At the end of every Looney Tunes segment, the Road Runner always prevails with a cheerful smile, saying "meep, meep" and sets off for the future.

Prayer:

God, I commit my life to You and Your will. Help me get through hard times. Protect me. In Jesus' name. Amen.

"Use it or lose it."

"For this reason I remind you to fan into flame the gift of God, which is in you through the laying on of my hands. For the Spirit God gave us does not make us timid, but gives us power, love and self-discipline. So do not be ashamed of the testimony about our Lord or of me his prisoner. Rather, join with me in suffering for the gospel, by the power of God. He has saved us and called us to a holy life—not because of anything we have done but because of his own purpose and grace. This grace was given us in Christ Jesus before the beginning of time" II Timothy 1:6-9

Even though I wouldn't describe myself as an athletic person, I do try. Many years ago, while multiple soccer balls were plummeted at my head during a match on a missions trip, I told myself I would *never* play soccer again. Years later, I had a son who basically came into this world wanting to play soccer. Even our cat plays soccer, so most afternoons I can be found kicking a ball around in our yard.

Having great soccer skills, or any skills like dancing, singing or public speaking all comes from a tremendous amount of practice and devotion. While God gives us spiritual gifts, no one is born with super skills. Those skills come from practice and when we don't use them, over time we lose them. We have to practice our Christian skills as well, in praying, worship, reading, sharing God's message, helping others, and aligning our life with Christian principles. It is how we stay ready for spiritual warfare.

Prayer:

Lord, may we all feel the desire burning within us to practice our Christian skills so that in the middle of chaos and Hell itself, the Holy Spirit will pour out of us. Use me, Lord. In Jesus' name. Amen.

"The road to Hell is paved with good intentions."

"I urge you, brothers and sisters, to watch out for those who cause divisions and put obstacles in your way that are contrary to the teaching you have learned. Keep away from them." Romans 16:17

Church denominations widely vary on the topic of "the road to Hell." I have heard helpful tips to keep from going to hell regarding everything from make-up, dancing, tattoos, and biblical points of interest like being saved ("once saved always saved"), the Rapture (not all denominations believe in it) and if doing charitable works is a prerequisite to getting into Heaven. No matter which side of the line you are standing on, all of these topics are common arguments among Christians.

Can you imagine a world where all denominations stood together to make sure that people around the world knew about the love of God and that Jesus died for them? Nothing else matters in the universe other that spreading that important story that offers redemption and hope for people's lives.

When division and fighting is in the church, the devil is also there. People who are interested in learning more about God are desperately looking for peace, love, unity, light, hope and in discord, there is none. "The road to Hell" is found in every church that feels too proud with their own doctrine and would rather live in isolation than reach out into the world.

Prayer:

God, forgive me for all of the stubborn arguments that I have been part of. They have all lead to nowhere, and most importantly, did not lead to You. Give me a hunger to reach out to all people in the world. In Jesus' name. Amen.

"Good fences make good neighbors."

"If you think you know it all, you're a fool for sure; real survivors learn wisdom from others." Proverbs 28:26

For the most part, I have enjoyed my neighbors, but that has not always been the case. The most well-known "neighbor" stories in our family come from when I was younger. My father and our elderly neighbor thought they were both always "100% correct" to the point they were know-it-alls. A discussion broke out every time a leaf fell onto the property-line of who should clean it up. I remember several times my father getting upset that the neighbor had cut the grass on "our" side. One year, our pecan grove was overrun with crows, and the elderly neighbor commenced to shooting crows down on "our" side of the property, to which afterward my father hung the dead crow up in the tree as a warning to other crows and to deter any further shooting from the neighbor.

Proverbs 13:10 says, "Through insolence comes nothing but strife, But wisdom is with those who receive counsel." In this scripture the Bible tells us the only way to receive peace and wisdom is by listening to the "other" side, not "our" own.

Nearly all parts of the world are in conflict and chaos these days, and it is our fault for not listening and receiving counsel with the other people involved. We all demand "our" way, but fail to search for the wisdom and peace described by God.

Prayer:

God, forgive me for the conflicting cases in my life. May I be the first person to receive and hear from the "other" side. I ask you to bless them and help me understand them. In Jesus' name. Amen.

"Necessity is the mother of invention"

"I have seen the burden God has laid on the human race. He has made everything beautiful in its time. He has also set eternity in the human heart; yet no one can fathom what God has done from beginning to end." Ecclesiastes 3:10-11

I love historical non-fiction books. It is like speaking directly with someone who lived hundreds of years ago and offers a unique glimpse into their world. Some of my favorite books include, "Letters from a Woman Homesteader" written around 1909 and "Days on the Road: Crossing the Plains in 1865." Both of these are the true accounts of women that made the best of primitive living during pioneer days. They used recipes like "carrot jam" to give as gifts and based the direction of their bandwagon on the feedback of others they passed on the plains. How full of faith and curiosity their daily lives must have had!

Even though we may not be enduring bandwagon times, we all deal with difficult trials that we are uncertain about. It is scary to deal with the diagnosis of a disease you don't have a cure to. We all love certainty, and life does not always give it. Disease, finances, relationships; sometimes life takes a turn and makes us feel alone and in despair. During these trials our role and relationship with Jesus is life-saving. Even though we feel like a sinking ship, Jesus is there with a life-preserver. He has already won the battle for us. Whatever you are facing, you are not alone. Give your hurts to God and ask for direction.

Prayer:

God, protect and comfort my family during this season. Help me remember all of the pain and sacrifice that Your son, Jesus gave and how He fights for us every day. In Jesus' name. Amen.

"Empty vessels make the most noise."

"A truthful witness saves lives, but one who breathes out lies is deceitful." Proverbs 14:25

Shortly before I began writing this devotional, I collected, edited and printed seasonal devotionals for a church. The pastor who led the project instructed me to search for people to write devotionals; the more personal the better. While reading and editing, the ones that I remember years later, are the ones that were personal.

When we speak up about our own experiences and "vouch" for God, it helps the unbeliever to see, hear, and understand God clearer. We are the living "Google reviews" or "Reddit" for Almighty God. People are usually skeptical consumers, and the same is true for the unbeliever. Your life is a living review for God. If you say, "He washes me white as snow" but are continuing to live a sinful, toxic lifestyle, unbelievers will think that your relationship with God is not real.

If you were to leave an online review for God, what would it say? What experience have you had with Him? Has he changed your life through any personal ways or encounters? Whatever your review, it needs to be part of what you are saying and living out within your life.

Prayer:

God, Help me to explain to others how you changed my life for the better, and how You saw me through my hurtful situations and struggles. Help me communicate well to the people You place in my path. Thank You for allowing me to be part of Your ground team. In Jesus' name. Amen.

"Money makes many things, but also makes the devil dance."

"The human heart is the most deceitful of all things, and desperately wicked. Who really knows how bad it is? But I, the LORD, search all hearts and examine secret motives. I give all people their due rewards, according to what their actions deserve." Jeremiah 17:9-10

The whole world seems like it is losing its mind sometimes. I grew up hearing about places like Columbine and Oklahoma City that, for the most part, have seemed far away from me. I have always felt safe in my small-town bubble, but as time passes, evil events like those happen surprisingly too close for comfort.

In the last five years, I have witnessed small children being shot and murdered within an hour from my home. One eye witness at the local shopping mall shared their cell phone video of the shooting on social media. I will never forget seeing the victim hit the floor, and his heartbroken mother standing over him screaming.

The world is sick and hurting.

We must look inside ourselves to evaluate our intentions and motivations. Frequently, we point our fingers to others when there is conflict, but we must also examine ourselves in order to be responsible, loving Christians. We must find our own evils, because we all have them, and look to God for forgiveness.

Those reading this devotion may not feel that this lesson is applicable to them because you "don't feel evil" and "would never kill someone", but evil actions come in various forms. It might translate to your job performance, your relationships, or how you interact with co-workers daily. What about all of the times we get angry while driving and experience Road Rage? It's because we think we are always right.

What is the motivation for your actions? Are we angry? Are we hurting, desperate, or demanding respect? Why must we always be right, when God calls us to listen? These named motivations are not of God.

These feelings mean that there is a deeper-rooted issue that God can and will heal if we seek Him in prayer, worship, and devotion. Healing from these evils must start with us identifying it and addressing it. Dig deep to find out what angers you and why, and give it God.

Prayer:

Heavenly Father, I ask You to forgive me of the rage and hate I feel towards others. Take away my pride and help me explore the reasons why I feel like I do. Help me heal from this pain that I feel. When I feel anger coming, may I plunge into Your abundant love. Thank you for the opportunity to live a life free of these afflictions. Through every season, good or bad, I will sing Your glory and goodness. In Jesus' name. Amen.

"Pride goeth before a fall."

"Pride goes before destruction and haughtiness before a fall." Proverbs 16:18

Pride has many different faces. For some, it is not asking for food or financial assistance when needed. Others are proud co-workers unwilling to receive suggestions. For most of us, it can also be running into someone publicly that you have ill feelings towards and not sure how to move forward. Whatever form of pride you exhibit, Merriam-Webster says it is "too high of an opinion of one's own ability or worth."

If you are like me, you might need a minute to reflect on that definition. Is it possible that my opinion is too high on certain issues? The answer is yes, and that causes each of us grief when we exhibit pride. In 1 Peter 5:5, Jesus said, "All of you, clothe yourselves with humility toward one another, because, God opposes the proud but gives grace to the humble."

Humbling ourselves, even when we feel we are right, provides a quiet platform where we can hear someone other than our own loud, voice in our heads. When we humble ourselves, the stillness creates a new space in our life for growth and healing. Whatever the issue that was creating havoc and turmoil is weakened and new steps to resolution are more accessible.

Sometimes just the mention of pride, makes us feel too "proud" in the moment and some might even feel tense reading this devotion. If that is you, the Bible is clear that a proud disposition always ends in destruction.

Prayer:

God, help me see every person as an equal to myself. Where I demand certain things, quiet my tongue and heart that I might receive the message and blessing that You have anointed for me to hear. In Jesus' name. Amen.

DECEMBER 1

"Paint the town red."

"She wrapped him in cloths and placed him in a manger, because there was no guest room available for them." Luke 2:7

In the 1980s, I remember going with my parents one Christmas to meet my Aunt Debbie for the first time. She and her husband and three small children shared a camper. Even as a small child, I knew that we were in cramped quarters, but the thing that stood out most was the joy her family had. She and her children had decorated dozens of homemade Christmas ornaments and colored pages from a coloring book to tape on the wall. I remember her also asking me if I would like some popcorn shrimp, which was a novel idea to me as I had never heard of it before. I loved their decorations (and popcorn shrimp) because I had never been exposed to it before. My parents only put up a Christmas tree and I was not used to seeing every wall, table, door post, and porch filled with décor. The most important thing that I remember and loved was their happy family celebrating every way they could think of.

Every Christmas since 1988, I haven't seen any Christmas ornaments or decorations that are better than Aunt Debbie's. It was the simple, yet very indescribable beauty that only Christmas has: the Love of Jesus. This season let everything you see, say, touch, decorate, buy, share, and gift be made with the love of Jesus. Its worth is immeasurable and memorable through the ages.

Prayer:

Prince of Peace, help me look for new ways to worship, celebrate, and encounter You. Open my eyes to the simple and pure ways that You are present. May joy, hope, peace, and love be found this season in You. In Jesus' name. Amen.

"Hope for the best, and prepare for the worst."

"The Mighty One has done great things for me— holy is his name. His mercy extends to those who fear him, from generation to generation. He has performed mighty deeds with his arm; he has scattered those who are proud in their inmost thoughts. He has brought down rulers from their thrones but has lifted up the humble. He has filled the hungry with good things but has sent the rich away empty." Luke 1:49-53

With Christmas comes hope. Hope is a resounding message of Christianity and the birth of Jesus. However, Christmastime doesn't always feel like that for everyone. After five years of my husband and me trying to conceive a child, we were concluding that because of our older age (I was 40 years old) it wasn't likely that we would be able to have a child. Imagine my surprise when I learned the week after Thanksgiving that I was expecting. It was a Christmas surprise and gift to us all!

When Mary announced to her family and Joseph that she was expecting a baby, the Child of God, I'm certain that it wasn't initially received as "hopeful" news. It would have been a culturally damaging reputation for all of them and full of shame.

Shame is a hard burden to bear. It isolates and devours us. Fortunately, when we call on God to help us with our shame, He gives us new life, strengthens us, and helps us carry on to brighter days.

Mary gave birth in the most primitive, difficult settings and Hope was born. Hope comes in many different forms to people. It is not always a new baby. It can be a second chance at life and the opportunity to live for God. It is the opportunity to say "no" to the circumstance you have been given, and the chance for God to reset your life.

Prayer:

Glory to God in the highest Heaven, and on Earth peace to those on whom His favor rests. Amen.

"The squeaky wheel gets the grease."

"Ask, and it shall be given you; seek, and ye shall find; knock, and it shall be opened unto you." Matthew 7:7

Christmas wish lists are being made out around the world right now. Eartha Kitt in Santa Baby asked for a light blue 1954 convertible, a yacht, duplex, checks, and a ring. Gayla Peevey wants "a hippopotamus for Christmas" while some just want their "two front teeth." I remember going through my parent's Macy's Christmas catalog and folding each page that had a toy I wanted. My folded section totaled approximately 200 pages. All completely ridiculous, but my child-like mind was open to the possibility that it would come true. Even though there aren't department store catalogs anymore, Christmas lists will always be made. I imagine the number of dolls and dogs on wish lists are still innumerable. Some adults are praying for their relationship to work out and others are praying for healing and miracles.

One of the wonderful things about God is He doesn't put a cap on what or how much we can ask for. We very well may ask Him for 200 pages worth of Christmas wishes, and He may not deliver them (as any good parent wouldn't). But, He loves us and wants us to share with Him what is on our mind. He also gifts us with redemption, new life, hope, love, and peace through the holy birth of Jesus.

What is your Christmas wish? Maybe it is reunion with a loved one you left on bad terms, maybe it is a job promotion, maybe it is for your marriage or for the protection of family members going into the future. If you haven't already, ask Him.

Prayer:

God, thank You for this time of year. Thank You for the joy and gift of Your son, Jesus. At this time, Lord I ask you for __________________. Help this situation. Protect me and those I love. I lay this down at Your feet and thank You for who You are and loving me. In Jesus' name. Amen.

"If I have heard that once, I've heard it a thousand times!"

"At midnight Paul and Silas were praying and singing hymns to God, and the other prisoners were listening to them." Acts 16:25

I have met numerous people who have said, "I can't sing." If I have heard that once, I have heard it a thousand times! When I am feeling down, singing is one of the few things that has the power to lift my spirits. When we sing, we are essentially picking up the burden of those surrounding us and making their load less heavy.

Christmastime is such a difficult time for so many people. Some have substance abuse problems, some are broke, some are without family, and the list goes on. It does not feel "merry" for everyone. That's why singing all of those classic Christmas carols at Christmas is more important than ever. People need to hear joy. They need to hear hope.

One of my favorite classic carols is Nat King Cole's version of "Oh Holy Night." He sings:

"Long lay the world in sin and error pining, Till he appear'd and the soul felt its worth. A thrill of hope the weary soul rejoices For yonder breaks a new and glorious morn!"

No matter what stage or chaotic season, be someone's joyful reminder this season.

Prayer:

Lord, thank You for coming to Earth to give us joy and hope. May we put You at the forefront this season and sing out for all to hear that the Savior is born. In Jesus' Name, Amen.

"If it were a snake, it would have bit you."

"Each one of us will give an account of himself to God." Romans 14:12

One of my favorite Christmas memories is the year I went to visit my friend, Petra for Christmas. Petra and I became friends as young adults, but she returned to her native country of Czechia (formerly Czechoslovakia,) and it had been many years since we had a reunion. When I entered Prague, the country's capital, I was surprised to see a large crowd in the city center. When we got closer, I could see that there were two actors dressed as the most magnificent angel and the most horrifying devil I have ever seen! The angel and devil would surround people in the crowd and ask them if they had been good or bad this year. Most everyone responded with "very good," but all responses were quickly followed by the devil asking, "are you surrre?" as the devil seemed to recall a few times during the year each person might have misbehaved; always lurking around the person waiting for individuals to falter. Later, I learned that it was St. Nicholas Day.

Witnessing this duo made me recall my own childhood questioning, "Have you been good this year?" and song lyrics like, "He knows if you've been bad or good, so be good for goodness sake!" While these are fun activities and memories for everyone, there is a serious truth to be found. We do need to examine our own life. The devil does lurk around us and wait for us to make bad decisions. Every day is an opportunity to live a Godly life. We have the chance to make a positive difference in those around us and that means sharing God's love, living with integrity and in truth.

Prayer:

Jesus, thank You for giving us new life; that no matter what bad decisions we have made You wash us white as snow when we ask for it. Forgive me for all of the ways I have failed You. Come and fill my life. In Jesus' name. Amen.

"It is better to light a candle than curse the darkness."

"How beautiful upon the mountains are the feet of him who brings good news, who publishes peace, who brings good news of happiness, who publishes salvation, who says to Zion, 'Your God reigns.' Isaiah 52:7

As a child, I enjoyed listening to my grandmother's stories from the early 1900s. My town became incorporated in 1906 and she remembered the new businesses and homes being built. The original church is still standing and was the main source of news. Before people had cell phones, social media or television, news would be shared by ringing the bell at the church. In Czechia, a dinner bell secretly rings, which signifies that Baby Jesus has come! When all of the children and family rush into the living room to hopefully get a glance of Him, they see that He has left presents for everyone and festivities begin!

Christmas bells are emblematic of "Hearing the Good News–the Son of God has been born!" Even though we don't use bells in the same way that we once did, it is important for us to carry on that same legacy.

I feel really blessed to be surrounded by a Christian culture where almost everyone has heard about Jesus and the new life that He offers us, but many people forget that when they are going through a crisis. I have known several medical professionals that were unable to treat themselves or loved ones during an illness because it is so personal. Sometimes you can't critically think when going through something traumatic and that's why it is so important to actively listen to those we love and remind everyone of the Good News of the Savior.

Prayer:

Thank you, Father for this life-changing love. May I always share the Good News with those I encounter, that Your love may multiply. In Jesus' name. Amen.

"Home is where the heart is."

"Martha was distracted by all the preparations that had to be made. She came to him and asked, "Lord, don't you care that my sister has left me to do the work by myself? Tell her to help me!" "Martha, Martha," the Lord answered, "you are worried and upset about many things, but few things are needed—or indeed only one. Mary has chosen what is better, and it will not be taken away from her." Luke 10:40-42

Even during one of the busiest times of year, my husband and I still like to prioritize our date night together. It might only be once every two weeks, but it is important that we designate that time. Our most recent date night consisted of heading to our nearest college town, ordering pizza, and then swinging by the campus Observatory to look at the constellations. It was beautiful. The question crossed my mind, "why do we continue to have date night?" Our relationship is a done deal, right? We continue to keep it in the middle of our calendar because it means having uninterrupted time together to bond and share what's on our heart and mind. It doesn't have to be fancy, just pizza and holding hands is all we need. That dedicated time also strongly resembles Devotion Time with God. Spending time with God, bonding and sharing what's on our heart and mind is all we need. It doesn't have to be fancy cathedrals or concerts: just you and Him.

I heard someone once say that if you look at your bank statements and examine what you spend your money on, it will show you what you value most. The same is true for your time. How we spend our time helps identify who we are as people. To truly feel Christ at the center of Christmas, I need to keep time with God on my calendar, so I can have alone time with Him.

Prayer:

Oh Emmanuel, Come! Be the center of our festivities and prayer. May I place You first on the list in my life. I love You. May my actions show it. In Jesus' name. Amen.

"Don't spend it all in one place."

"At daybreak, Jesus went out to a solitary place, and the crowds were looking for Him. They came to Him and tried to keep Him from leaving. But Jesus told them, "I must preach the good news of the kingdom of God to the other towns, because that is why I was sent." Luke 4:42-43

By most accounts, by this time of month most Christians have the church decorated, have their homes decorated (some of you started before Thanksgiving, you know who you are) and all of the festivities are lined up like the cantata and Children's Christmas play. We decorate and fill our homes and church with merriment and decorations because those are the places we worship and live, and it just makes good sense to start there. However, some of the most meaningful Christmas worship that I have experienced has been outside of the church when I wasn't expecting it. On vacation, I once heard "Silent Night" being sung in the street by a man with a guitar. There wasn't anything bedazzling about it. It was just the beauty and simplicity of his song at Christmas.

Decorating, worship and merriment does not all have to happen in church. Spread it around your life. I love Christmas carolers this time of year because they sing in unexpected places. Nothing is remotely similar to experiencing a choir rushing down the halls of a nursing home to sing "Joy to the World."

Some of the saddest, loneliest places are outside of the church walls and that is where God calls us to go. He wants us to share the Good News in as many dark corners as we can.

Prayer:

Heavenly Father, Raise me up, that I may sing and proclaim Your good wonders. May a revival begin in the hearts of those lost and weary. May my love for You be an inspiration to those hurting this season. In Jesus' name. Amen.

"Into every life a little rain must fall."

"We are hard pressed on every side, but not crushed; perplexed, but not in despair; persecuted, but not abandoned; struck down, but not destroyed. We always carry around in our body the death of Jesus, so that the life of Jesus may also be revealed in our body. For we who are alive are always being given over to death for Jesus' sake, so that his life may also be revealed in our mortal body. So then, death is at work in us, but life is at work in you." II Corinthians 4:8-12

This time of year, I think about what it must have been like for Mary's family saying good-bye to her. I know her parents were concerned to see their expecting daughter ride off into the wilderness and soon thereafter hear that the king had killed all of the babies. They must have worried, and might have even assumed that Baby Jesus (or all of them) were dead as the three of them fled to Egypt afterwards. Wouldn't it have been incredible if text messaging was possible back in those days? A simple text from Mary letting her family know "we r all ok."

I have experienced a few chapters in my own life that were fear-stricken, and I wasn't sure that everything was going to be okay. Life on earth is a whole obstacle course and it can be painful. It would be wonderful if we could get a text from God that says, "u r going 2 b ok." It might be simple, but it would help in that moment. However, God does give us many passages in the Bible that assure us it will be okay. (Isaiah 41:10; Proverbs 3:5; Jeremiah 29:11-14; I Peter 5:7; Psalm 118:6-9; II Corinthians 4:15-18)

We can only see the Earthly part of the story. That's why it hurts and bothers us so much! Be strong and courageous. God will see you through.

Prayer:

Father, Help and strengthen me when I feel that all is lost and broken. In my uncertainty and hurt, let me be reminded that I only know half of the story, if that much. In Jesus' name. Amen.

"Do not cast your pearls before swine."

"Do not give dogs what is sacred; do not throw your pearls to pigs. If you do, they may trample them under their feet, and turn and tear you to pieces." Matthew 7:6

Southern hospitality can be so gracious and hospitable that it can be hard to realize when you are being taken advantage of. A good Christian typically is always forgiving, always understanding, and always giving. People with a manipulating spirit look for those kinds of people to take advantage of. Jesus warned His disciples to not waste good things on people who will not appreciate them. This proverb from Matthew 7:6 says to preach only to receptive audiences. This is an important factor for Christians to remember because Jesus also tells us to forgive people of their offences "70 times 7" times, essentially always forgiving them (Matthew 18:21-22).

So, when do we, as Christians know when to invest in a sour person, and know when to walk away?

The difference in the situation is a constant, repetitive abuse from the offender. When someone mistreats us, Jesus wants us to forgive them, but does not request that we continue to place ourselves in an abusive situation with someone that does not really care about us. To some, the gift of forgiveness (pearls) is not appreciated. We must forgive the offender, and pray for the offender that they become aware of a greater, more purposeful life, but we do not have to continue offering them our best.

Prayer:

Father, help me reach the hungry and hurting, and to know the difference of when I need to move on to new people that are hungry to hear about Jesus. In Jesus' name. Amen.

"Laughter is the best medicine."

"For where two or three are gathered in my name, I am there among them." Matthew 18:20

Several years back my mother was hospitalized for pneumonia. Each day, I made several visits to see her, and after about the fourth day, during a visit she suddenly, almost instantly, coded in front of me. It was traumatic to watch. Through excellent hands-on assistance, the medical team was able to get her back into consciousness after about a day. (It turned out that she wasn't accustomed to getting the level of oxygen that she was receiving through her nasal tube.) After mother coded, I called my sister to inform her of what had happened. She immediately drove to the hospital to be with us.

There is a phase of fear and uncertainty that follows trauma and it can happen so quickly that it leaves us in a helpless state. During that first 24 hours, the best medicine for my own soul was a cold Coke that my pastor bought me, which was a reminder to take care of myself, and also the gift of seeing my sister. The jokes we made that afternoon were comforting.

God has gifted us hope and love through friends and family to help us cope and heal through loss. They help take care of us and help us laugh which helps us heal. One of the biggest lies that we hear from the devil during difficult times is "if you share what you are going through, no one will be able to relate," and that is not true. We all have human experience and understanding, and while some may not have lived through the same experience, they have compassion to give. God is the only source of hope and light during oppression and visiting with other believers summons His presence in our life.

Prayer:

God, thank You for blessing me with other believers who care and listen during hard times. Help me and lift me up. I invite and want You to pour Your Holy Spirit and healing here. In Jesus' name. Amen.

"More is caught than taught."

"People learn from one another; just as iron sharpens iron." Proverbs 27:17

December is a month-long search of trying to find the best Christmas gifts for those we love. The greatest gift is the desire to know more about Jesus and experience the joy and freedoms that come when you have a relationship with Him. That seems like a pretty steep gift, as it is not an inanimate object that I can directly put into one's hands. In fact, passing that heritage is "more caught than taught," which means I can preach it, but Christian values are better learned by example; watching them being lived out, rather than by lectures.

We usually define "happiness" by what culture tells us "happiness" is, which is why so many people collapse when they lose their money. Many times, when finances get hard, I think there is an underlying sense of guilt, that "I cannot give my child all of the toys he wants,", and the devil uses those thoughts to make us feel worse or lure us into a debt that we cannot repay.

This Christmas may you live out loud in Christian joy, truth, and light and share that with those around you. If it is the most depressing season of your life, tell those you love, "this is a sad season for me, but I know that God has me in His hand and that tomorrow will be a new day." Not only does it teach your loved ones how to cope and live, but it also affirms that hope and joy are still alive. It verbalizes a prophetic truth and victory of God.

Prayer:

Lord, hear my prayer that those I love may watch and learn from my life lessons and that it may help their spiritual walk and journey into Your arms. In Jesus' name. Amen.

"Show me your friends, and I'll show you your future."

"Do not make friends with a hot-tempered person, do not associate with one easily angered, or you may learn their ways and get yourself ensnared." Proverbs 22:24-25

One of my favorite "I Love Lucy" episodes is the "Friends of the Friendless" in which Lucy feels that no one has remembered her birthday, so she wonders into the park and is befriended by those without friends. Their testimonies are sad and lonely. I have certainly felt like that before. Beginning a new chapter in life (like a new job), exacerbates the loneliness. I have even worked for employers when literally the entire building went outside for a smoke break except for me. Being the odd person out is usually painful and makes us consider giving in to social norms to possibly be accepted. In Lucy Ricardo's case, she joins the "Friends of the Friendless" marching band, and Lucy pounds on the Bass drum.

Seeking friendship can stretch us outside of our normal social limits. Jesus befriended the "untouchables," and those considered to be the most sinful people. However, upon entry of acceptance, He made them leave their sinful ways at the door. It is always better to stand alone, than to stand wi*th* a group of people that are pouring hate and evil into the world. God will bless us for being strong until we can find people worthy of our friendship.

Prayer:

God, thank You for instilling in me a moral background to know what is right from wrong. Help me be strong when I feel like I am faced against the world. Help me examine my friendships and weed out what is killing my moral garden. In Jesus' name. Amen.

"Strike while the iron is hot."

"In their hearts humans plan their course, but the LORD establishes their steps." Proverbs 16:9

In my older years, I have learned that I enjoy Christmas shopping a little bit earlier in the season. There is more time to look without pressure. The last time I went Black Friday shopping, it was a stressful and scary experience. There is something said for people that plan early. They usually get the best product and a good deal because they don't feel pressured.

We all have things we want and need, but for one reason or another many wait around, doing nothing, until we are disappointed with the result. A friend and I frequently talk about her interest in dating a certain guy. We go through an endless cycle of: how to approach him, what to say, what his interests are, etc. She always feels hesitancy and doesn't do anything. I get that she is scared that it won't go the way she hopes, but not planning or making moves in your life is the equivalent to not existing in the situation. No harvest or bounty will be collected because nothing was planted in the spring.

What are your dreams and plans for your life? You are still alive, so God has given you a ticket to dream, pray, create, plan and "strike." No matter what we want for our lives , it is unlikely to fall in our laps without us taking some action.

God gives us the ability to dream because He hopes we will be a good steward of our abilities. If you have a dream about something, pray about it. If you still are not sure that your plan is Godly, seek the advice of Christian mentors. Your ending result may not be what you had originally envisioned but acting while being prayerful signifies to God that you are ready for the change He has in store for your life.

Prayer:

Father, thank You for giving us aspirations and dreams! Help me know the difference in Your divine will and my own. May I be motivated instead of not using the creativity You have gifted me. In Jesus' name. Amen.

"First come, first served."

"Out of his fullness we have all received grace in place of grace already given." John 1:16

In my own dealings with "first come, first served" programming it always puts me in a bit of a panic in the moment. Recently, I made plans to go to a free tree giveaway sponsored by the Arbor Day Foundation. Living in a rural county, within a rural state like Alabama, I couldn't possibly imagine that there would be many attendees. However, to my surprise, when I pulled into the parking lot at 9 a.m. on a Tuesday it was full of cars and 100 people waiting on the tree event to begin. I felt nervous that by the time it was my turn, there wouldn't be anything left but dirt. The inner-child in me just wanted to run up ahead of everyone and grab some trees!

That desperation and eagerness is the same sensation I think many people feel when they know they need to go to the altar and pray. It seems the longer one stands idle in the pew, the bigger the risk of not being served. How wonderful and refreshing it is that God's altar is not just limited to the first two or three that beat us there. It is liberating to finally get to the altar and feel God touch us with His mercy and love. My week always goes better when I have laid my heart on the altar before God.

We all make mistakes. We all have some kind of problem in our life that is out of our control. We all need help, guidance, and forgiveness–and God is waiting to serve us.

Prayer:

God, it is in Your presence that I find joy, freedom, and a good future. Forgive all my shortcomings. May I always run to You in times of joy and in times of sorrow. Thank you, Holy Spirit for moving in my life. In Jesus' name. Amen.

"Seeing is believing."

"When they saw the star, they rejoiced exceedingly with great joy." Matthew 2:10

One of my favorite Christmas memories is putting up a giant star with my father. Our family farm was on a hill. It was all open pasture land for miles around, which meant you could see quite a way in the distance. Each year, we erected a giant star made from a simple strand of white Christmas lights and hung it above our home. Thanks to modern technology, I now know that our Christmas star was visible from over a mile away. As I child, it always tickled me to see the star visible from many roads over.

Christmastime is the ideal time for Christians to share Christian joy with others. The birth of Christ "flipped a switch" in history and changed how people viewed God and His anger. Jesus sacrificing His life for ours equates to unmeasurable love. John 15:13 says, "Greater love has no one than this: to lay down one's life for one's friends." It is that great love that changes people from "lost" to "found," "blind" to "seeing." That love swells a person's heart and changes them from cold to being a forgiving person. It is a revolutionary concept that never came before Christ.

This Christmas, let your light shine, so that all might see and know God. Your light might be noticed from farther away than you thought possible.

Prayer:

Oh Emmanuel, Come into our hearts! I pray for the person that is living without You; lost, broken, and afraid. Holy Spirit, move, that the lost might have hope in You this Christmas. In Jesus' name. Amen.

"If you cannot live longer, live deeper."

"But the fruit of the Spirit is love, joy, peace, forbearance, kindness, goodness, faithfulness, gentleness and self-control. Against such things there is no law." Galatians 5:22-23

Perhaps one of the most difficult parts of Christmas is missing a certain person that you once spent the holidays with. Time has a way of changing our lives, our circumstances, and the people we associate with. Each of us has "missing someone for the holidays" in common, although we tend to think that we are alone in that feeling. Each of us remembers a time when Christmases were magical and spent with our grandparents, parents, spouse, best friend, or children. For one reason or another, time has taken some of them away, and we tend to compare our modern-day Christmas to "the good ole days."

Everyone who has lost a loved one has painful memories associated with it. The beautiful, unchangeable thing that we can be glad for is that God gifted and blessed us in that every person we have loved, lost, and miss held a piece of God with them. Their characteristics, friendship, love, humor, kindness, and goodness (that made up our loved one) is the embodiment of God and those things will live forever. They are eternal.

I am reminded of those that have passed when the Fruits of the Spirit are emphasized. Galatians 5:23 says, "against such things there is no law" and with that assurance we are reminded that the good parts of our loved ones will live eternally, because even death cannot claim its victory over the Fruits of the Lord.

Prayer:

God Eternal, Your goodness is forever and I am grateful. Bless my loved ones and me during this season when I remember those that have moved on. May the goodness of their life shine on forever. May I look for ways in my own life to be an example of Your good "fruit" to others. In Jesus' name. Amen.

"When the cat is away, the mice will play."

"But the wicked are like the tossing sea, For it cannot be quiet, And its waters toss up refuse and mud. 'There is no peace,' says my God, 'for the wicked." Isaiah 57:20-21

Early one Christmas morning, I remember my sister waking me up to go see the Christmas tree and to see if any presents had come. I can still remember the beautiful multi-colored Christmas tree in the darkness of the living room. She, being older, must have known that we were supposed to wait on Mother and Daddy but in that moment encouraged me to open "just one" (as she opened one too). I remember opening it and to my delight it was a Tropical Splash Barbie that came with beautiful earrings and real perfume! Almost as soon as we had opened our gifts, she told me that we really needed to wait on Mother and Daddy and she taped our gifts back into the wrapping paper! Would our parents know? Would Santa know? Would we be in trouble? Would I get to keep Tropical Splash Barbie?

When we have made a mistake in life, it starts to surround us like a fortress of fear. What will be the consequences? How can I absolve myself from this mistake?

No matter what the mistake is, we all can find peace in knowing that God has already seen the mistake and still loves us. Whether it was an accident or intentional, big or small, God loves us and wants us to try to amend what we have done by asking to be forgiven from Him (and from whom we offended, if applicable).

Prayer:

Lord, thank You for loving us even when we make mistakes. Forgive me for the mistakes I have made. Free me from the oppression and fortress that the devil uses to entrap us. Give me courage to be true and the person You made me to be. In Jesus' name. Amen.

"That's pretty as cash."

"Ask and it will be given to you; seek and you will find; knock and the door will be opened to you." Matthew 7:7

Money truly is a wonder to look at. I like to collect paper money and coins from around the world as a hobby. Besides the art and history that surrounds each piece, money is impressively powerful. For a piece of paper, it holds the power to make people famous or destroy them, to give life when paying for surgery or even have someone murdered. Money can bring out the worst and cause greed. Be it that it may, most people's eyes light up when they see a stack of cash because they realize it holds endless possibilities. An endless possibility is a delightful idea that people have romanced about for centuries. In The Arabian Nights, Aladdin comes across a wonderful lamp that allows him to make wishes. In modern times, millions of Americans rush to buy lotto tickets each week for the chance that their fortune and future might change. While having a genie in a lamp and winning the lottery does not seem likely, there is a window of endless opportunity with God.

The Bible is full of accounts of people that need healing, life, provision, happiness, liberation, forgiveness, and acceptance, and God provides it to everyone that asks. I have witnessed that God gives to those who need Him. In nothing short of a miracle, He can bless you and change your life with something more beautiful than cash, because it is eternal.

Prayer:

God, as the Bible tells us, You are a good father and want to give us what is good. As we ask you humbly for what we need, you know our life and know what will bless us. May I trust in the way You shape my life. Anoint my head, Father and guide me in Your light. In Jesus' name. Amen.

"Early to bed, early to rise, makes a man healthy, wealthy and wise." -Ben Franklin

"Very early in the morning, while it was still dark, Jesus got up, left the house and went off to a solitary place, where he prayed." Mark 1:35

Without a doubt, it is an important time of the year to share the message of Christianity. We all have a responsibility to make sure that our family has access to understanding the precious meaning of Christ's birth.

A few years back, I caught myself feeling overwhelmed because I had signed up for too many things. I was a Kiwanis Club chairperson, sang in the church choir, taught two different Sunday School classes, had a pottery class, while working full-time and having a family. Everything on my agenda was important to me, but I lost some of the important reflection and meaning by constantly running from one place to the next.

The saying "early to bed, early to rise" is not just for the work week. It is a reminder that we all should quiet and center our hearts in a busy Christmas season, so we can see, hear, and appreciate the holy birth of Jesus and how it changed who we are and our deepest desires for who we want to become.

Prayer: ***(Silent Night)***
Silent night, holy night!
All is calm, all is bright.
Round yon Virgin, Mother and Child.
Holy infant so tender and mild,
Sleep in heavenly peace, Sleep in heavenly peace

Silent night, holy night!
Son of God love's pure light.
Radiant beams from Thy holy face
With dawn of redeeming grace,
Jesus Lord, at Thy birth, Jesus Lord, at Thy birth. Amen.

"Every picture tells a story."

"After listening to the king, they went on their way. And behold, the star that they had seen when it rose went before them until it came to rest over the place where the child was. When they saw the star, they rejoiced exceedingly with great joy. And going into the house they saw the child with Mary his mother, and they fell down and worshiped him. Then, opening their treasures, they offered him gifts, gold and frankincense and myrrh." Matthew 2:9-11

One of my favorite times of year to look up and stargaze is December. It is too cold for weenie roasts, water balloon fights, or a nap in the hammock, and because of that everyone is inside their home. Without the neighborhood kids playing in the street and all of the squirrels and birds are tucked warmly in the trees, the night air is almost always quiet and still. The moisture from the clouds crystalizes, and you can see every star, twinkling in perfection, which gives a feeling of calm and peace.

During a long, uncomfortable journey for Joseph and Mary, they would have looked up at night at the same sky with wonder in their hearts, knowing that God's miracles have endless possibilities.

Whatever you wish you could change this Christmas, whatever is physically ailing you or weighing you down, that Christmas sky is still there and twinkling; full of wonder and a history of being full of angels singing the birth announcement of Christ. God is still full of miracles with endless possibilities.

Prayer:

God, thank You for the beautiful sky that is a reminder of Your love for us. You know the needs of my heart this Christmas. Be with me. Thank You for the hope and light that Your son, Jesus, gave to the world. May I never forget just how much You love me in that gift alone. In Jesus' name. Amen.

"Life is what you make it."

"When they arrived in Bethlehem, Mary went into labor, and there she gave birth to her firstborn son. She wrapped the newborn baby in strips of cloth, and Mary and Joseph laid him in a feeding trough since there was no available space in any upper room in the village." Luke 2:6-7

It never fails that when our family comes together to celebrate Christmas, we all grate on each other's nerves. Now, I LOVE my family. I don't want to be lax in saying that. However, when we all come together and are locked inside of a house for week, it never fails that one of them is spending too much time in the bathroom, can't keep their cell phone out of their hand, doesn't make eye contact, talks about nasty politics, discredits my recipe for dressing but didn't bring anything to eat, talks too much, etc.! One year, I took the family dog and left for the afternoon just so the dog and I could get some peace!

Before Jesus's angelic birth, the gorgeous star in the sky and angels singing–it would have been an awful experience. Mary's ride on a donkey lasted for a painful five days, on a 90-mile trip. They made the journey to fill out paperwork at the request of the government. I can't imagine how miserable they must have felt, and were nearly without a roof to deliver the baby under!

Christmas is not a time for perfection. The first Christmas account truly is a good lesson that it is not meant to be perfect. All sorts of things and life events happen. However in the midst of chaos and suffering was God–whose glory shone bright in the birth of the world's Savior. May you feel His peace this Christmas season.

Prayer:

God, in our chaos may we be reminded of the miracle birth that once happened in a lowly stable with shepherds. Speak and allow us to witness the greatest love of all–Your son, Jesus. In Jesus' name. Amen.

"Enough is as good as a feast."

"My God will supply every need of yours according to his riches in glory in Christ Jesus." Philippians 4:19

On the first Christmas that my husband and I spent in our house, we were still actively working on it so all of the new electrical wiring was not complete. We also had spent every dollar we had on trying to fix the old place up. For that reason, big, flashy decorations and gifts were not a financial option. That year, I will always remember as one of my favorite Christmases. We drove out to the countryside and on the side of the road, cut a 4-foot-tall cedar tree. When we brought it back home and put it in the living room, it was the most beautiful, simple thing I have ever seen. We also did not have much furniture yet, but as a Christmas present I bought my mother a gently used reclining chair so that the three of us could comfortably enjoy Christmas together.

I remember that Christmas with heartfelt love and memories. We each brought something to share for lunch; which was small compared to some of the dinner tables I have seen. We didn't have everything, but we had more than we needed and we all knew it. Humble Christmas decorations and presents, such as these are seemingly closer to the heart compared to others because they are a reminder of the humble birth of Jesus–beautiful simplicity that radiates truth and love. However your heart may feel this Christmas, be comforted that you are surrounded by a community of love, peace and joy. Whatever your Christmas wish is, there is hope for tomorrow because Jesus Christ is born today.

Prayer:

Help us Father, remember the true meaning of Christmas and fill us with that Spirit and love. In Jesus' name. Amen.

"First things, first"

"For unto you is born this day in the city of David a Savior, who is Christ the Lord. And this will be a sign for you: you will find a baby wrapped in swaddling cloths and lying in a manger. And suddenly there was with the angel a multitude of the heavenly host praising God and saying, "Glory to God in the highest, and on earth peace among those with whom he is pleased!" Luke 2:11-14

None of Jesus' birthing details were elaborate. The Infant King was born in a barn with animals. Shepherds (who were considered lowly) were the first to welcome Him. It is inconceivable that someone so special to the world would be born under such circumstances. However, God wanted everyone on earth to know that His Son, was born within arm's reach to us all. No one is so low that they can't experience the grace of Jesus because He came from such humble settings, as humble as you and me. His birth sent out a message to the world, that Jesus is for everyone, He is obtainable and wealth is not the key to the Kingdom of Heaven. God sealed the occurrence with His blessing with an inspiring show of the Magi, the Star of Bethlehem, an entire choir of angels showing up to sing, and was anointed by the protection of Joseph's dream.

Many times, people feel that their sin is too great to be forgiven by such a "perfect God," but God's perfection was humbled in the birth of Jesus, who accepts all who love Him.

Prayer:

God, Help us to experience the pure love and wonders that the first Christmas displayed. In Jesus' name, Let us fall on our knees and adore Him, O Emmanuel! Amen.

"Christmas only comes once a year."

"I ask that you'll have the power to grasp love's width and length, height and depth, together with all believers. I ask that you'll know the love of Christ that is beyond knowledge so that you will be filled entirely with the fullness of God." Ephesians 3:18-19

For years, my husband and I wanted a child. After continuously trying, it started to hurt too much to bring up in conversation. When our friends and family shared their announcement of a new baby, we were very happy but at the same time cried together. During that stretch of time, I would daydream things like what I would name the baby, what was most important to teach him, and what were the first words I would whisper in his ears the first moment he was born.

God did eventually bless us with a baby boy, in His perfect timing. I planned to say whisper a prayer to him at his birth. However, when the moment came and the doctor held him up for us to see him, I was so overwhelmed with appreciation to God and a flood of love that I was unable to speak. (Those that know me, know that I love to talk and am never without words.) However, in that moment my mouth was closed in the deepest love and gratefulness to the Almighty God for allowing me to witness it. I imagine that is the love that Mary and Joseph felt on Christmas morning that can be a part of every household in the world today that invites it into their living room. It is the same love that God has for you. The overwhelming love and hope that He wants to share and blanket our life with is available to us all.

Prayer:

Happy Birthday, Sweet Jesus, Savior of us all, fill me and my life with your Living Spirit that I might feel new life and the abundance of love in which You give. In Jesus' name. Amen.

"Hope springs eternal."

"Hope does not disappoint us, because God's love has been poured out into our hearts through the Holy Spirit, who has been given to us." Romans 5:5

Christmas presents have been opened, and sometimes (hopefully, not often) gift recipients are disappointed with their present. Maybe the gift was not the right size or color. Maybe some of you were hoping for an engagement ring. Maybe some were just hoping to see more of family that didn't come to visit. Maybe your family got everything they asked for but now you are in financial debt for a while and that stress factor is weighing over your head. Even though we are still in Christmas season, many things still continue to disappointment us.

It is not possible for us to have control and dominion over everything in life. What we do have control over is how we respond to such issues. More importantly, how would Jesus respond? Jesus most assuredly would have responded with a humble heart in love and thanksgiving from the act of gift giving. During His earthly ministry, things did not always go the way Jesus wanted. Many opposed Him, but He just moved on to new people that He could share His teachings and love with. Each day presents new aspects that can cause us disappointment and despair, but God is always with us and He brings hope eternal.

Prayer:

Father, thank You for gifting us with hope and new opportunity each day. Help us during disappointing times, see our blessing. May your Spirit rest on me, that instead of despair and frustration. May I exemplify gratitude and humility. In Jesus' name. Amen.

"Respect is not given, it is earned."

"Honor all people, love the brotherhood, fear God, honor the king." I Peter 2:17

We have all felt disrespected at some point in our lives. In my own Southern experience, I have felt disrespected many times when speaking to a man and being called "darling."

Once in the early 1990s, it was rumored in my small town that a man with AIDS was working at a local fast-food chain. The whole town stopped eating there, and for a while, they even closed. How must it feel for an entire town to condemn you?

Something familiar to practically every town is the way divorce splits communities. A local high-profile divorce that went on for over a decade had nearly every member of our community pick a side and those that didn't pick sides went on the stand as witnesses. How must it feel for the children and those involved?

Being disrespected leaves us all feeling hurt and angry. Whether your experience was due to age, race, sex, or someone disrespecting your professional expertise, it hurts.

Our worldly culture would have you believe "respect is earned", but love and respect is not a tricky, complicated thing. Jesus simplified it. It is meant for everyone.

Romans 12:10 says, "Love one another with brotherly affection. Outdo one another in showing honor."

Respect, love, and honor are at the forefront of our Christian heritage and allow us to know people in a deeper, more meaningful way (the way Jesus did). At the same time we are expecting respect from others, we need to freely give respect to others, even those that we don't think deserve it. Maybe you are not treating all of your co-workers as equals, maybe you are a supervisor that makes unprofessional remarks to your employees, maybe you take friends and family for granted and they don't feel seen or heard; all of these things build up anger and loneliness and is part of the devil's plan to further divide us.

In what areas of your life do you have room for improvement when respecting others?

What are ways you can build a stronger, more respectful relationship with those people?

Prayer:

Father God, only Your love can save us. Thank you for showing us that Your love and respect never ends for all people. Help me to examine my own life and how I treat others. May people see me as a friend and confidant that I may learn from them, as well as, sharing the Good News of Your forgiving grace. In Jesus' name. Amen.

"They that sow the wind shall reap the whirlwind."

"Israel cries out to me, 'Our God, we acknowledge you!' But Israel has rejected what is good; an enemy will pursue him. They set up kings without my consent; they choose princes without my approval. With their silver and gold they make idols for themselves to their own destruction. For they sow the wind, and they shall reap the whirlwind. The stalk has no head; it will produce no flour." Hosea 8:2-4,7a

One of the worst things we can do as Christians is sit back and criticize others. My daddy used to say, "When you have an issue with how something is done, don't complain about it unless you can offer a solution."

It is all-too-common of a notion that everything is broken. I must have heard a million complaints in my life of what is wrong with the church and our country. We, as Christians (and patriots), have stopped putting God at the center of our daily life. That is what's wrong with it! "They shall reap the whirlwind. The stalk has no head; it will produce no flour," is a warning to change the way we live, how we lead our families, and what we find acceptable as a culture. It is a warning against complacency. It is a call to repent and then make it right in the eyes of God.

If our church and country are going to be blessed by God, we must anoint our country as a "Godly nation" and seek God in everything we do. We need to collectively pray and ask God to intervene and let His will be done.

Prayer:

God, forgive us that we do not put You first in everything. Set a fire in us all to be the hands and feet of a new Christian movement in our nation. In Jesus' name I pray. Amen.

"That doesn't make a lick of sense."

"You will seek me and find me, when you seek me with all your heart." Jeremiah 29:13

Christmas decorations will soon be packed away and stored in attics across America. Family life is returning to the "pre-holiday norm," and that leaves us waiting for the New Year and what is to come.

For many non-believers, their life is a whirlwind, and they don't know what to expect in the future. Doubting God's existence while going through difficulties makes the weight of the world heavier. At one of the most difficult times in my life, I needed God and asked him for help. A loved one had just died. I was at a crossroads in my career. We were in an economic downturn, and I felt the weight of everything tearing me down.

When I prayed and asked God to help me, I asked for His presence to be evident in my life and as plain as day, He said, "then go to church." I had not attended for some time, and it made sense that I would find the presence of God at a church, so I went to one with an open mind. Just like someone you are dating and eager to know, I really invested time into forming a relationship with God to find the healing and answers I needed.

Since that prayer and making a commitment to a relationship with God, I was baptized for the first time. I learned a new language and shared God's message to other cultures, spent many years working at a church, found my husband at the church, and was healed from oppression.

Oppression is all that the secular world is made up of. The only relief that we have from toxicity is through Jesus Christ.

Unfortunately, I do not have the evidence that the world requires to claim that God is real, but if you knew me before my commitment and know me now, you know I am changed now and have an abundance of joy and peace. I see truths for truths and have discernment. One of the greatest victories is I have hope for the future!

The life and resurrection of Jesus Christ has to be real because no one would have made it up and expected people to believe it. However, for believers we know He lives!

<u>Prayer: *(He Lives)*</u>

"I serve a risen Savior, He's in the world today
I know that He is living, whatever men may say
I see His hand of mercy, I hear His voice of cheer
And just the time I need Him, He's always near

He lives, He lives, Christ Jesus lives today
He walks with me and talks with me
Along life's narrow way
He lives, He lives, Salvation to impart
You ask me how I know He lives?
He lives within my heart!"

"All is well that ends well."

"Death is swallowed up in victory." I Corinthians 15:54

One of my favorite scriptures, "Death is swallowed up in victory" always gives me encouragement for what is to come. The book of Revelation can be overwhelming, but the most important take away is that Jesus defeats the devil in the end, and we will be judged on our life.

Revelation 21:4 says, "He will wipe away every tear from their eyes, and death shall be no more, neither shall there be mourning, nor crying, nor pain anymore, for the former things have passed away."

Whatever it is that has hurt you (or is hurting you): disease, divorce, death, not being able to reach someone emotionally, failed pregnancies, just substitute the word "death" for the word that has caused you pain. (For example, disease is swallowed up in victory.) Even though those painful things are different than the word "death," they all have the same root as being something that hurts us and makes us grieve; something that the Devil uses to crush our spirit. They all carry a portion of death.

There is literally nothing that can defeat the victory that is to come from Christ, and that is worth celebrating now.

Prayer:

O Lord of Hope, help us see that we don't have control over any of these worldly problems and issues. You care and love us and watch us all, and one day You will make all things right. For that, we sing Your Victory today! In Jesus' name. Amen.

"History repeats itself."

"In your hearts revere Christ as Lord. Always be prepared to give an answer to everyone who asks you to give the reason for the hope that you have. But do this with gentleness and respect." 1 Peter 3:15

Every New Year's Eve, I formulate new resolutions to try to live by. Almost always one resolution is to become healthier, and I make a plan to try to jumpstart my success. That plan might consist of cutting out sweet tea, except on Sundays; going for walks on Monday, Wednesday and Friday; and adding more vegetables to every meal. Without a plan, history is destined to repeat itself.

The end of this devotion signifies that a new year begins. There are so many areas of life in which each of us need improvement, healing and prayer.

As a new Christian or old, it is too easy to get comfortable on the church pews. The new year means that we will come into contact with new people, and at any moment of the day, someone may ask us for our reason for being a Believer. Could you give your testimony and reason within two minutes? We live in a fast-paced society, and two minutes may be all the time that they give you. Christian New Year resolutions always should include sharing your testimony. The Bible says, "always be prepared to give the reason," and so that planning needs to start now.

Prayer:

Holy Spirit, work within my life. Open my eyes to what areas I should share of my personal experience when meeting someone. Speak through me that something I say may touch their life. May this new year bless me and bless others, leading us all to know God on a new level. In Jesus' name. Amen.

PRAYER REQUESTS

www.ingramcontent.com/pod-product-compliance
Lightning Source LLC
Chambersburg PA
CBHW020429130626
46549CB00001B/56

* 9 7 9 8 2 1 8 2 5 5 4 5 9 *